Collins

BTEC FIRST

Health & Social Care

Level 2

Mark Walsh

Published by Collins Education
An imprint of HarperCollins Publishers
77-85 Fulham Palace Road
Hammersmith
London
W6 8JB

Browse the complete Collins Education catalogue at
www.collinseducation.com

© HarperCollins Publishers Limited 2010
10 9 8 7 6 5 4 3 2

ISBN 978 0 00 734265 5

Mark Walsh asserts the moral right to be identified as the author of this work.

British Library Cataloguing in Publication Data.
A Catalogue record for this publication is available from the British Library.

Commissioned by Emma Woolf
Project managed and edited by Jo Kemp
Design and typesetting by Thomson Digital
Text design by Nigel Jordan
Cover design by Angela English
Artwork by Stella Macdonald and Jerry Fowler
Index by Christine Boylan
Picture research by Geoff Holdsworth/Pictureresearch.co.uk
Printed and bound by LEGO S.p.A., Lavis (Trento)

Contents

Photographic acknowledgements

Photos.com (2); Photos.com (3); iStockphoto (5t/Loretta Hostettler); iStockphoto (5b/Paul Pantazescu); Rex Features (7/Burger/Phanie); iStockphoto (8/ericsphotography); Rex Features (9/Andy Lauwers); iStockphoto (10/Sebastien Bergeron); ampetronic.com (12); iStockphoto (14/James Peragine); iStockphoto (16/Rasmus Rasmussen); iStockphoto (22/Aldo Murillo); iStockphoto (26/Lisa F. Young); iStockphoto (28/asiseeit); iStockphoto (29/Dean Mitchell); Alamy (30t/SHOUT); iStockphoto (30b/Nancy Louie); iStockphoto (32/Jaimie Duplass/PhotoEuphoria); Alamy (33/Mike Goldwater); iStockphoto (36/Richard Foreman); iStockphoto (37/Ekaterina Monakhova); iStockphoto (39/Dmitry Naumov); iStockphoto (40/Sean Locke); iStockphoto (44/1joe); Photos.com (46); iStockphoto (48/Carmen Martínez Banús); iStockphoto (49/Ekaterina Monakhova); iStockphoto (50/Chris Schmidt); iStockphoto (51/jamstock); iStockphoto (52/Olga Lyubkina); iStockphoto (53/David Marchal); iStockphoto (54t/Josef Muellek); iStockphoto (54b/Cat London); iStockphoto (56/Jorge Delgado); iStockphoto (58t/Christopher Pattberg); iStockphoto (58b/Jodi Jacobson); iStockphoto (60/Jeremy Swinborne); iStockphoto (61/alexander mychko); Photos.com (64); iStockphoto (66/Chris Schmidt); iStockphoto (69/Jason Orender); iStockphoto (74/Jerry Koch); Alamy (82/Adam James); iStockphoto (83/Dr. Heinz Linke); iStockphoto (84/Jeremy Voisey); iStockphoto (85/Andre Blais); Rex Features (86/Shout); Photos.com (88); iStockphoto (89/Nicholas Sutcliffe); Alamy (90/Photofusion Picture Library); iStockphoto (92/pixonaut); iStockphoto (93/DNY59); iStockphoto (98/Lisa F. Young); iStockphoto (103/David H. Lewis); Alamy (104/Sally and Richard Greenhill); iStockphoto (106/DWlabsInc); iStockphoto (108/Radu Razvan); iStockphoto (114/Aldo Murillo); iStockphoto (115/Rebecca Ellis); iStockphoto (120/Andrew Taylor); Rex Features (121); Rex Features (122); iStockphoto (124/Karen Moller); iStockphoto (125/yungshu chao); iStockphoto (127/Tova Teitelbaum); iStockphoto (128/syagci); iStockphoto (129/Nilesh Bhange); Rex Features (131/Jonathan Hordle); iStockphoto (132/morganl); Rex Features (133/Sipa Press); Rex Features (135/Sipa Press); Alamy (136t/Stock Connection Blue); iStockphoto (136b/Chris Schmidt); iStockphoto (138/Pamela Moore); iStockphoto (139/Miroslav Ferkuniak); Alamy (141/Janine Wiedel Photolibrary); iStockphoto (146/Max Delson Martins Santos); iStockphoto (148/Sebastian Kaulitzki); iStockphoto (156l/VikramRaghuvanshi); iStockphoto (156r/Natalya Ivaniadze); Photos.com (158t); Photos.com (158b); iStockphoto (160/Catherine Yeulet); iStockphoto (161t/Thomas Lammeyer); iStockphoto (161b/Ivan Ivanov); Alamy (163/BSIP SA); iStockphoto (164/Sean Locke); iStockphoto (166/syagci); Alamy (167/Nucleus Medical Art, Inc.); iStockphoto (169/Tyler Stalman); Alamy (170/By Ian Miles-Flashpoint Pictures); iStockphoto (172/S.P. Rayner); iStockphoto (173/Lisa F. Young); iStockphoto (175/Ana Abejon); iStockphoto (180/Ann Marie Kurtz); iStockphoto (181/Brian McEntire); iStockphoto (182/webphotographeer); iStockphoto (183/Claudia Dewald); iStockphoto (184/SteveStone); iStockphoto (185/AVAVA); iStockphoto (186/William Britten); iStockphoto (187/Joe Gough); iStockphoto (188t/druvo); iStockphoto (188b/Jacob Wackerhausen); iStockphoto (190/RonTech2000); iStockphoto (191/Chris Schmidt); iStockphoto (192t/adrian beesley); iStockphoto (192b/Aldo Murillo); iStockphoto (193/Brian Toro); iStockphoto (196/zhang bo); iStockphoto (197/Jill Lang); iStockphoto (198/David Asch); iStockphoto (199/Yiannos Ioannou); iStockphoto (202/Igor Balasanov); iStockphoto (204/Sean Locke); iStockphoto (208/Jaimie D. Travis); iStockphoto (209/DIGIcal); iStockphoto (210/Frances Twitty); Graham Woodall (214); iStockphoto (215/Claude Dagenais); Alamy (216/Paula Solloway); Alamy (217/mark downey); iStockphoto (218t/Trista Weibell); iStockphoto (218b/suemack); Karen Seymour (220, 222); Jim Dyson (223); iStockphoto (224/Sean Locke); Graham Woodall (226); Karen Seymour (227); iStockphoto (228t/Dr. Heinz Linke); Rex Features (228b/Jussi Nukari); Graham Woodall (230); iStockphoto (231/Monika Adamczyk); iStockphoto (232/Chris Schmidt); Karen Seymour (234); Graham Woodall (235); iStockphoto (236/Kim Gunkel); iStockphoto (242/Andresr); iStockphoto (243/ruben paz); Alamy (244/David Hoffman Photo Library); iStockphoto (246/emre ogan); Alamy (248t/Adrian Sherratt); iStockphoto (248b/David Joyner); Alamy (249/VIEW Pictures Ltd); iStockphoto (250/Silvia Jansen); iStockphoto (252/Terry Wilson); iStockphoto (253/Zsolt Nyulaszi); Alamy (254/Alex Segre); iStockphoto (256t/Don Bayley); Alamy (256b/Medical-on-Line); iStockphoto (258/Carmen Martínez Banús); iStockphoto (259/Kevin Eaves); iStockphoto (262/Vicki Reid); iStockphoto (264/iofoto); Alamy (265/SHOUT); Alamy (266/Bubbles Photolibrary); Karen Seymour (267); Alamy (268/Medical-on-Line); iStockphoto (270/Silvia Jansen); iStockphoto (272/Richard Goerg); Alamy (273/Adrian Sherratt); iStockphoto (275/Chris Schmidt); iStockphoto (280t/Rob Belknap); iStockphoto (280b/Jason Lugo); Rex Features (284/Paul Grover); iStockphoto (286/Catherine Yeulet); iStockphoto (287/Gansovsky Vladislav); iStockphoto (288/lorraine kourafas); iStockphoto (289/Lisa F. Young); iStockphoto (290/Noam Armonn); Alamy (291/Asia Images Group Pte Ltd); Alamy (292/Stock Connection Distribution); Alamy (294/Mike Goldwater); iStockphoto (296/Rob Friedman); Alamy (297/Charles O. Cecil); Alamy (298/Mike Stone); iStockphoto (299/draschwartz); iStockphoto (302/Aldo Murillo); iStockphoto (306t/Joe Gough); Alamy (306b/Photofusion Picture Library).

Introduction

This aim of this book is to help you develop the knowledge and understanding you will need to complete your BTEC First in Health and Social Care course. The BTEC First award you achieve at the end of your course will have one of the following titles, depending on how many credits you obtain overall:

▶ Edexcel BTEC Level 2 Diploma in Health and Social Care   (15 credits)
▶ Edexcel BTEC Level 2 Extended Certificate in Health and Social Care   (30 credits)
▶ Edexcel BTEC Level 2 Certificate in Health and Social Care   (60 credits)

Your tutor will create a learning programme that gives you opportunities to explore a wide range of health and social care topics and obtain the credits you need for the qualification you wish to obtain. It is helpful to find out at the start of your course which BTEC First qualification you are aiming to achieve and which units you will be studying.

Each chapter in this book covers one BTEC First Health and Social Care unit. The chapters provide you with opportunities to develop the knowledge and understanding you will need to successfully complete assignments and cover the assessment criteria that are part of your GCSE Health and Social Care award.

Features of the book

The book closely follows the specification (syllabus) of your BTEC First Health and Social Care award. This means that all of the topics and issues referred to in the course specification are fully covered. You will find the following features in the book:

▶ **Chapter introduction** – this is a short, introductory section at the start of each chapter that tells you what the chapter is going to focus on.

▶ **Key terms** – the main ideas (concepts) and the language of health and social care are briefly explained in this feature.

▶ **Over to you!** – these are short activities that aim to get you thinking about an issue or topic. They can usually be completed on the spot without doing any more research.

▶ **Activities** – these are designed to extend your knowledge and understanding by encouraging you to find out a bit more about a topic or issue you have been learning about.

▶ **Case study** – these are short examples of situations and stories from the world of health and social care. They encourage you to apply your knowledge and understanding to realistic situations that you might face if you worked in or used health and social care services.

▶ **Topic check** – this is a list of questions about the topic you have been studying. You should try to answer as many of these as you can.

▶ **Chapter checklist** – you will find this feature at the end of each chapter in the assessment summary. It provides you with an opportunity to think about what you have been studying and to check that you have covered everything you need to. The chapter checklist also provides you with brief information on how the topics you have been studying are assessed.

Assessment

BTEC First Level 2 awards are assessed through coursework assignments. You are required to demonstrate that you have met assessment and grading criteria for each unit. The Pass, Merit and Distinction grade criteria for each unit are outlined at the start of each chapter in the book. They are then listed again at the end so that you can check that you have covered all of the criteria you need to.

I've tried to write a book that helps you to gain a good, clear understanding of a range of care topics and also gives you a taste of what to expect from a career in the health and social care sector. Taking a BTEC First Health and Social Care course enables you to think about both the theory and practice of care work. It is hoped that you'll think about taking your interest in health and social care further when you've worked through the book and completed your BTEC First award.

Good luck with your course!

Mark Walsh

1 Communication in health and social care

Unit outline

Care workers require effective communication skills in order to work with the diverse range of people they meet in health and social care settings. This unit will introduce you to:

▶ different forms of communication
▶ factors that affect communication in care settings
▶ ways of overcoming barriers to effective communication.

You will have the opportunity to observe and discuss the communication skills of others and to practise and refine your own communication skills.

Learning outcomes

1 **Know different forms of communication.**
2 **Understand barriers to effective communication.**
3 **Be able to communicate effectively.**

Grading guide

To achieve a **pass**, you must show you can:	To achieve a **merit**, you must show you can:	To achieve a **distinction**, you must show you can:
P1 Identify different forms of communication	**M1** Describe different forms of communication	
P2 Explain barriers to effective communication within a health and social care environment		
P3 Take part in an effective one-to-one interaction	**M2** Describe the barriers to effective communication in your two interactions	**D1** Assess the strengths and weaknesses of your two interactions
P4 Take part in an effective group interaction		

Forms of communication

This topic introduces you to the forms of communication used by health and social care workers and the contexts in which they are used. When you have completed this topic, you should:

■ be able to describe and explain the communication cycle

■ know about one-to-one, group, formal and informal communication in health and social care settings

■ be able to describe a range of different forms of communication used by health and social care workers.

Key terms

Decode: make sense of the information contained in a message

Empathy: understanding and entering into another person's feelings

Formal communication: official or correct forms of communication

Informal communication: doesn't stick to the formal rules of communication (e.g. a casual, relaxed conversation, written note or text message)

Makaton: a system of communication using simple hand signs, which is used by people with language and learning difficulties

Non-verbal communication: forms of communication that do not use words (e.g. body language)

Objects of reference: objects that have a particular meaning for a person (e.g. a special ring or ornament)

Symbol: an item or image that is used to represent something else

Verbal communication: forms of communication that use words (e.g. conversation)

The communication cycle

Communication is about making contact with others and being understood. It involves people sending and receiving 'messages'. We all communicate, or 'send messages', continuously. Figure 1.1 describes the communication cycle. It shows that a communication cycle occurs when:

1. A person has an idea.

2. They code their 'message' (using words or non-verbal means).

3. They send their message to someone else (e.g. by speaking).

4. A second person then receives the message (e.g. by hearing what has been said or by noticing non-verbal communication).

5. The second person **decodes** the message.

6. The message is understood.

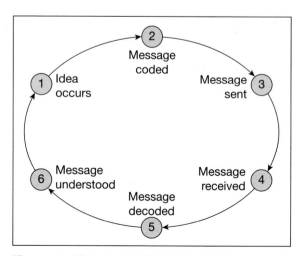

Figure 1.1 The communication cycle

Once the original message has been understood, the cycle will be repeated if the second person replies or responds. Repetitions of the communication cycle are an essential part of our relationships, and occur every time we have a conversation.

Case study

Charlie is 2 years of age. He enjoys helping his mum in the kitchen when she is making a meal. When she says, 'Can I get some fruit for you Charlie?', he puts his arms in the air, says 'me, me' and smiles at her. His mum responds by picking him up and saying, 'Okay, you take something yourself this time, Charlie'.

1. How does Charlie's mum communicate with him in this example?

2. How does Charlie communicate non-verbally with his mum in response to her question?

3. Describe how a cycle of communication occurs in this example.

Forms of communication

Care workers use different forms of communication during their working day (or night). These include the verbal communication skills of talking and listening, and various forms of non-verbal communication, such as touch, eye contact and facial expression. A care worker has to use both of these forms of communication when they:

- give or receive information about the care that is being provided for an individual
- provide emotional support to a individual or member of their family
- carry out an assessment of an individual's care needs.

Verbal communication

Verbal communication occurs when one person speaks and another person listens. Care workers need a range of verbal communication skills to:

- respond to questions
- find out about an individual's problems or needs
- contribute to team meetings
- break bad news
- provide support to others
- deal with problems and complaints.

The communication cycle demonstrates that effective verbal communication is a two-way process – speaking *and* listening must occur. Listening is much harder than speaking and there is more to this skill than just waiting for the other person to stop talking.

Over to you!

Are you a good listener? Think about what you do when you really listen to another person. Try to identify the skills and qualities needed for effective listening.

Non-verbal communication

As well as communicating through speech, people use a variety of forms of **non-verbal communication**. Some of these are referred to as body language. This is because they involve the individual using their body and appearance to communicate in some way. For example, a care worker's behaviour, appearance and attitude send 'messages' to people who receive care (as well as to colleagues) about what they think and feel. Similarly, a person's body language may tell a care worker that they are uncomfortable or experiencing pain even when they say, 'I'm okay'. Non-verbal communication is a channel of communication that is 'always on'.

Figure 1.2 Forms of non-verbal communication

Non-verbal communication	What does it involve?	Examples
Facial expression	Movements of the face that express a person's feelings	• Smiling • Frowning
Touch or contact	Physically touching or holding a person	• Holding someone's hand • Placing a hand on a person's arm or shoulder to reassure them
Gestures	Deliberate movements of the hands to express meaning	• Thumbs-up gesture to show agreement or pleasure • Shaking a fist to show anger or aggression
Proximity	The physical closeness between people during interactions	• Being physically close to someone may be reassuring and may be seen as accepting the person. • On the other hand, it might make the person feel uncomfortable and threatened. • People need less personal space when they have a close, trusting relationship.
Eye contact	Looking another person directly in the eyes	• Short or broken eye contact can express nervousness, shyness or mistrust. • Long unbroken eye contact can express interest, attraction or hostility.

Signs, symbols and objects of reference

Care organisations sometimes use signs and symbols to communicate with the people who use their premises. Signs and **symbols** are graphical ways of communicating essential information. Using images enables people who cannot speak or understand a spoken language, such as English, to communicate.

Objects of reference are items such as toys, clothes, jewellery or other everyday objects that have a special meaning for somebody. For a child, a cuddly toy may represent comfort and safety. An older person may treasure their photographs because they represent and provide memories of family, friends and relatives. Objects of reference, such as photos or toys might be used by a teacher to stimulate communication and interaction with individuals with learning disabilities.

Over to you!

When you have a chance, watch a group of people talking or socialising together. Observe the way they use their bodies to communicate. Try to work out what they are 'saying' non-verbally.

Technological aids

Technological aids, such as electronic communicators, hearing aids and videophones are designed to help disabled people who have difficulty sending or receiving 'messages' as part of the communication cycle. Many non-disabled people now also use technology in the form of mobile phones, text messaging and emails to communicate with others. Websites such as Facebook, Twitter and Bebo are also examples of technological aids that promote communication between people.

Human aids

These include people who work as:

▶ interpreters, who listen to a person speak in one language and then communicate what they have said to a second person in a different language

▶ translators, who translate what is written in one language into a second language (e.g. English to Hindi)

▶ signers, who use forms of sign language to communicate what has been said or written into a sign language, such as British Sign Language or **Makaton**.

Alternative forms of communication

People who are unable to communicate in conventional ways sometimes use alternative communication systems to send and receive messages. For example:

▶ People with visual impairments often use their sense of touch to read documents written in Braille. This uses a series of indentations made by a special stylus on one side of paper. The combinations of indentations represent letters that can be touch-read by people who understand the Braille system.

▶ People with hearing impairments or learning disabilities sometimes use lip reading and sign language to communicate. Sign language systems include finger spelling (dactylography), British Sign Language and Makaton.

▶ A range of graphical signs and symbols are also widely used in health and social care settings to warn people of health and safety hazards, provide directions and give information to people who are unable to speak or understand English.

Contexts of communication

The two main contexts in which health and social care workers use the communication cycle are one-to-one and group communication.

One-to-one communication

Care workers talk to work colleagues, to people who use care services and to their relatives on a one-to-one basis many times each day. Sometimes this involves **formal communication**, at other times it involves **informal communication**, for example when the care worker speaks to a colleague who is also a friend, or when they have got to know a patient or relative very well. Effective one-to-one communication requires:

▶ listening skills

▶ information-giving skills

▶ questioning skills.

People who use care services, and their relatives, talk to care workers about a wide variety of things that concern them. Care workers need to be able to help people talk about and express their concerns. They do this by:

▶ using open questions that give people a chance to talk at length rather than to give a one-word response (e.g. 'How are you feeling today?' is an open question)

▶ checking their understanding of what the person says to them by recapping, summarising or just asking questions like, 'Can I just check that you meant ...'

▶ using **empathy** to let the person know the care worker understands how they feel and what they think.

One-to-one communication skills are needed for basic everyday interactions in health and social care settings. They are also needed to establish and maintain supportive relationships with work colleagues and people who use care services.

Groups

People belong to a range of different groups including family, friendship and work groups. Interaction in group situations is important for social, intellectual and emotional development. Health and social care workers communicate in group situations when they participate in:

▶ report or handover meetings where individuals' needs are discussed

▶ case conferences and discharge meetings

▶ therapeutic and activity groups

▶ meetings with relatives and managers of care organisations.

The communication skills we use in group contexts are slightly different from those we use in one-to-one situations. One of the main differences is that people have to make compromises and must learn how and when to take turns at speaking and listening. Communication in groups can sometimes feel challenging, competitive and negative where a few members of the group dominate.

Activity

Role-plays provide an opportunity for you to develop and practise basic communication skills in a safe, simulated situation. With a class colleague or in a small group, role-play the following situation:

A parent approaches a nursery nurse about obtaining a place for his child at the nursery. The parent wants to know what the nursery can offer, how the child will be looked after and what the costs will be.

The nursery nurse must use verbal and non-verbal communication skills to provide appropriate information and reassurance.

However, groups can also be supportive, co-operative and productive when members respect each other, are inclusive and share information. People who are effective group members:

▶ make verbal contributions to the group

▶ listen to other group members

▶ respond positively to the group leader

▶ are open about themselves

▶ don't try to distract others or disrupt the main purpose of the group

▶ have a positive and constructive approach to other group members

▶ arrive on time and stay until the end of the group's meetings.

Assessment activity 1.1 (P1, M1)

You are working in a local day centre. The people who attend have learning disabilities. The day centre manager provides work experience opportunities for local school and college students. She believes that effective communication skills are essential to work in a care environment like the day centre. The manager has asked you to:

- Produce training materials that identify and describe forms of communication used within a health or care environment.
- Present your materials in the form of a leaflet, booklet or poster.

Topic check

1 Describe how the communication cycle works.

2 Name two main forms of communication.

3 What are the two things that people have to do during verbal communication?

4 Describe two ways that care workers might use their verbal communication skills in a care setting.

5 Identify three different examples of non-verbal communication.

6 Describe how an individual with communication problems might use technological or human aids to communicate with others.

7 Identify the two main contexts of communication in health and social care settings.

Factors affecting communication

This topic provides an introduction to a range of factors that affect communication. When you have completed this topic, you should:

- know about a range of factors that can affect an individual's ability to communicate effectively

- be able to describe ways of overcoming communication barriers.

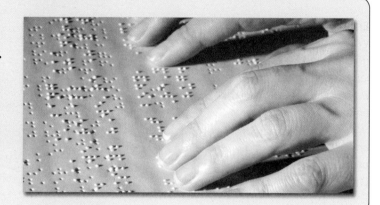

🔑 Key terms

Acronym: a word formed from the initial letters of a series of words, such as NHS (National Health Service)

Deprivation: the loss or absence of something

Dialect: a form of language spoken in a particular area

Barriers to communication

A number of factors can affect an individual's ability to communicate effectively (see Figure 1.3). These factors are sometimes known as barriers to communication because they prevent or interfere with the person's ability to send, receive or understand a 'message'.

Sensory deprivation and disability

Visual and hearing impairment can act as a barrier to effective communication. Care workers should be alert to the additional communication needs of people with sensory impairments and disabilities. Problems with sight or hearing can mean that signs can't be seen, leaflets can't be read or conversations can't be heard, for example. Conditions such as cerebral palsy, Down's syndrome and autism also

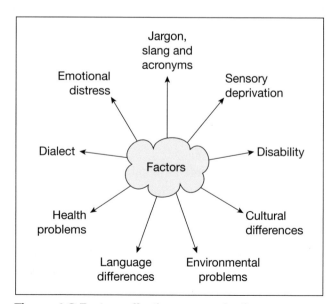

Figure 1.3 Factors affecting communication

tend to limit an individual's ability to communicate verbally and to interpret other people's non-verbal communication.

Foreign language and cultural differences

Britain is a multicultural country. Within the mix of different ethnic groups people speak a range of languages. English may be a second or even third language for some people and may not be spoken or understood at all by others. If health and social care organisations only produce and display information in English and care workers only speak English, some people will find it very difficult to find and use the care services they need.

Similarly, people from different cultural groups interpret non-verbal behaviour in different ways and may have a different sense of humour. This can lead to 'messages' being misunderstood by, or making no sense to, the person on the receiving end.

Dialect

A **dialect** is a version of a language. People who speak English using a Glaswegian dialect or a Liverpudlian dialect will pronounce the same words differently and may use some words that are local and specific to the area where they live. A person who isn't from the same area may not understand a local dialect.

Distress and emotional difficulties

Some conditions, such as having a stroke, being depressed or having other mental health problems may affect an individual's ability to communicate, because they affect the person's ability to send and receive 'messages' effectively. Similarly, when a person is angry, aggressive or upset, they may find it difficult to communicate and their own communication may be misunderstood by others.

 Over to you!

Think about the last time you were upset or unwell. How did this affect your ability to communicate? Did other people adapt the way they communicated with you or get frustrated and upset themselves?

Jargon, slang and use of acronyms

Jargon is technical language that is understood by people in a particular industry or area of work. Health and social care workers often use jargon to communicate with each other quickly. Slang is an informal type of language that is used by a particular group of people. Teenagers sometimes communicate with each other using forms of slang which their parents and teachers don't understand. **Acronyms** are the initial letters of the words in a phrase (e.g. HIV for human immunodeficiency virus). Jargon, slang and acronyms all have one thing in common – they are forms of language that only makes sense to people with specialist knowledge. A person who doesn't have this specialist knowledge won't understand a message that includes jargon, slang or acronyms.

Over to you!

Can you think of any slang terms that are used by young people in your local area? Do you think that adults or other young people from a different area would know what these terms mean?

Health issues

Illness and injuries can cause people to withdraw and feel they don't wish to see others or talk about how they are. Medication and operations may also affect an individual's ability to speak, concentrate or use non-verbal methods of communicating.

Environmental problems

A physical environment that is noisy, uncomfortable, has poor lighting or that lacks privacy reduces people's ability to communicate effectively with each other. Noisy environments affect our ability to listen and concentrate. Poor lighting can affect our ability to notice non-verbal communication and could reduce a hearing-impaired person's ability to lip read. Environments that are too hot or cold cause discomfort. Environments that lack privacy discourage people from expressing their feelings and problems.

Over to you!

What is the environment at your GP's surgery like? Is it quiet, warm and comfortable, or does it have some of the features described above that have a negative effect on communication? How could it be improved to promote better communication?

Overcoming barriers to communication

Barriers to communication can often be overcome, or are at least reduced, by making changes to the environment, by changing the way you approach the other person or by using electronic aids to overcome communication difficulties.

Adapting the environment

Making changes to the physical environment can improve the effectiveness of communication. Environmental changes might include:

▶ replacing poor lighting with brighter lighting

▶ sound-proofing rooms, reducing background noise or creating quiet areas away from noisy activity

▶ putting up multilingual posters and displaying signs clearly

▶ fitting electronic devices, such as induction loop systems to help those with hearing difficulties.

Care workers can make the best of the care environment by:

▶ making sure they can be seen clearly by the person they are communicating with

▶ facing both the light and the person at the same time

▶ making sure their mouth is visible when speaking

▶ minimising background noise

▶ using eyes, facial expressions and gestures to communicate where necessary and appropriate.

Activity

Visit the websites of the Royal National Institute for the Deaf (www.RNID.org.uk) and the Royal National Institute for the Blind (www.RNIB.org.uk). Find out about the range of services these groups provide for people who have sensory impairments. Produce a summary of the different forms of communication support that are available to people with visual or hearing impairments.

Understanding language needs and preferences

Special interest groups work on behalf of people who have sensory impairments or whose disabilities cause communication problems. These groups provide information and services that are designed to raise awareness and help people who suffer sensory **deprivation** to overcome the barriers to communication they face.

Care workers should understand the language needs and communication preferences of people with sensory impairments and disabilities that affect their communication skills. The best way to respond to situations like this is for the care worker to:

▶ use the person's preferred language (directly or through an interpreter or signer)

▶ adapt their communication strategies to the language needs and preferences of the person.

Learning a few words of another person's language or developing some basic sign language skills can really help a care worker to establish a positive relationship with the person receiving care.

Pace

Speaking clearly and slowly, and repeating and rephrasing if necessary, are strategies that can help some people to understand what is being said to them. Speaking a little more slowly can help a person with a hearing or visual impairment, a learning disability or who is confused. The speed or pace of communication may need to be slower to allow the person to understand what is being said or communicated to them. It is also important to allow time for the person to respond. This can mean tolerating silences while the person thinks and works out how to reply.

Electronic devices

A range of electronic devices exist to help people overcome the communication difficulties they face. These include text phones, telephone amplifiers and hearing loops. Electronic devices can be used both to send and receive messages. It is important to give the person using a communication device enough time to use it when you are communicating with them.

An induction loop system helps deaf people hear sounds more clearly by reducing or cutting out background noise.

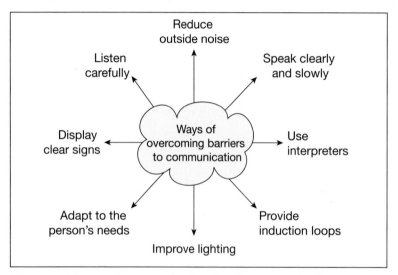

Figure 1.4 Ways of overcoming barriers to communication

Case study

Read the following scenarios. For each of them, explain briefly:

- what are the barriers to effective communication
- how these barriers could be overcome.

1. Salvo is a patient in the medical ward of a large District General Hospital. His diabetes has got worse and he has now lost his sight. Salvo finds this very distressing and tends to stay close to his bed for fear of getting lost in the ward. He is becoming worried that he will not be able to get to the toilet in time on his own.

2. Edith is 56 years old and has recently suffered a stroke. This has left her paralysed down her right-hand side and she is unable to speak. Edith cannot put her thoughts into words or understand words that are written down. She can understand some of what is said to her. You have been asked to find out what meals Edith would like to choose from next week's menu. You have been given a printed menu that patients normally fill in themselves.

Assessment activity 1.2 (P2)

The manager of the day centre who asked you to produce training materials in Topic 1.1 has decided to extend the range of training materials for work placement students. She has asked you to:

• Produce training materials that include details of a range of barriers in relation to different forms of communication, explaining ways to overcome these.

• Present your training materials in the form of a leaflet, booklet or poster.

Topic check

1 Identify two forms of sensory deprivation that affect a person's ability to communicate.

2 Describe examples of environmental problems that can reduce the effectiveness of communication.

3 Explain how care environments can be adapted to overcome the communication problems you describe.

4 What is a dialect and how can it affect communication?

5 Explain why a care worker might adjust the pace of their speech to improve the way they communicate.

6 Describe an example of an electronic device that can be used to overcome communication problems.

Getting started

This topic focuses on the skills needed for effective communication. When you have completed this topic, you should:

- know about a range of skills that can be used to make communication more effective
- be able to demonstrate effective communication skills in one-to-one and group situations.

Key terms

Empathy: putting yourself in the place of the other person and trying to appreciate how they 'see' and experience the world

Proximity: physical closeness

Communicating effectively

Effective communication in care settings helps both care workers and people who use care services to form good relationships and to work well together. People communicate most effectively when they:

- feel relaxed
- are able to **empathise** with the other person
- experience warmth and genuineness in the relationship.

Effective communication also requires the care worker to develop and use a range of skills, abilities and communication techniques (see Figure 1.5).

Active listening

A person who uses active listening pays close attention to what the other person is saying and notices the non-verbal messages they are

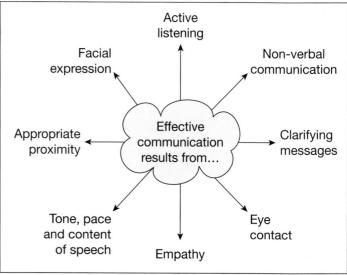

Figure 1.5 Effective communication results from...

Case study

Eileen Morgan has worked in a pre-school nursery for the last 15 years. During this time she has developed very good relationships with the children she cares for. Students who come to the nursery on work placement eventually notice that the children really like to talk to Eileen. This is partly because Eileen listens more than she talks when she is interacting with a child. Eileen is always very encouraging when a child comes to speak to her. She smiles a lot, focuses on their face, but also notices what they are doing. She says this helps her to understand what the child is feeling. She gives each child plenty of time to talk, staying quiet when the child pauses and uses sounds like 'mm', 'uh huh' and little phrases like 'I see', 'that's good' and 'tell me more' to encourage them.

1. How is Eileen using active listening skills when she interacts with children at the nursery?

2. Why does Eileen try to notice what a child is doing when they are talking to her?

3. Give an example of a minimal prompt used by Eileen to encourage children to express themselves.

communicating. People who are good at active listening also tend to be skilled at using minimal prompts. These are things like nods of the head, 'Mm' sounds and encouraging words like 'Yes, I see', or 'Go on'. Skilful use of minimal prompts encourages the person to keep speaking or to say a little more.

Use of body language and proximity

People use different forms of body language to communicate feelings and to support what they are actually saying (see Topic 1.2). Effective communicators often use the SOLER behaviours (see Figure 1.6) when they are sitting down talking to another person. These are not hard and fast rules that must always be obeyed but they do encourage more open communication.

An awareness of **proximity**, or the amount of personal space that a person requires, is also an important feature of effective communication. Sitting or standing too close to someone can make them feel uncomfortable and intimidated. Sitting too far away can make the person feel isolated and might seem unfriendly. Care workers often adjust their proximity by moving their chair or their position in response to the person's body language. It can also be a good idea to ask, 'Is it okay if I sit here?'

Face the other person **S**quarely

Adopt an **O**pen posture

Lean towards the other person

Maintain **E**ye contact

Try to be **R**elaxed while paying attention

Figure 1.6 SOLER behaviours

Activity

People communicate 'messages' to others in a variety of non-verbal ways. This activity requires you to discreetly observe people communicating non-verbally with each other.

1. Identify a public place where you can observe people communicating, e.g. a café, fast-food restaurant or station.

2. Watch for and record on a checklist (see below) examples of non-verbal behaviour.

3. Explain what the people you observed were communicating non-verbally.

Example	Description of non-verbal behaviour	What was being communicated?
Person 1		
Person 2		
Person 3		

Facial expressions and eye contact

The human face is very expressive and is an important source of non-verbal communication. A person's face usually reveals their feelings. However, sometimes people are able to disguise their true feelings and present a socially acceptable 'face'. Effective communicators are able to read and interpret other people's facial expressions and are also good at using facial expressions to convey their own emotions.

A person's eyes, and the eye contact they make, can also be a good indicator of their feelings, for example, long, unbroken eye contact can indicate either hostility or attraction. A person who makes eye contact for longer than is socially expected, and who widens their eyes, is likely to be seen as friendly, especially if they also smile. Effective communicators use eye contact to let people know they are paying attention and to establish trust and provide reassurance.

Over to you!

Can you think of an example from your own experience where a person's facial expression told a different story from their verbal message?

Activity

1. In pairs, role-play an interaction between a social worker talking to a client about her welfare benefits or a nurse talking to a patient about how she feels. Take it in turns to be the care worker and the person using care services. You should:

   - sit opposite each other in chairs of equal height
   - interact for about four minutes
   - let the care worker start and lead the conversation.

   The service user should not listen, but the care worker must try to get them to listen using verbal and non-verbal means.

   The care worker must not touch or shout at the listener.

2. After each person has played the care worker role, take it in turns to tell each other what you liked and disliked about the activity. Write a short comment on what it felt like not to be listened to and identify the main factors that inhibited the communication cycle.

3. Repeat the activity but this time the service user should do the talking and the care worker should use the SOLER behaviours to promote effective communication.

4. Take it in turns to share what you liked/disliked about this part of the activity. Write a short comment on how the SOLER behaviours affected communication between you.

Appropriate language, tone and pace

A person's choice of words, as well as the way they speak, influences the effectiveness of their communication. The pace, tone, pitch and volume of the speaker's voice are important. For example, it is never a good idea to shout, or to talk so loudly that the listener believes you are shouting. This kind of behaviour is likely to draw attention away from the verbal 'message' or content of what is being said. Mumbling, speaking too quickly, failing to complete sentences and using a hostile or aggressive tone will also impair the effectiveness of communication.

It is important to speak clearly and at a pace the other person can follow. Effective communicators also avoid using slang, jargon and acronyms, to prevent misunderstandings developing. Speaking in a measured, clear and reasonably paced manner will help listeners to hear and understand what is being said. A relaxed, encouraging and friendly tone of voice also helps the speaker to convey warmth, sincerity and appropriate respect for the listener.

Case study

Edith is 56 years old and has recently suffered a stroke. This has left her with paralysis down her right side and limited speech. She cannot put her thoughts into words or understand words that are written down. She can understand some of what is said to her. Edith has never been in hospital before and appears to be quite anxious when her husband and son are not visiting. She seems to enjoy meal times and looks at photographs of her family and pet dog quite a lot. At other times she is tearful and looks quite sad. Edith's husband has told you that his wife feels lonely and frustrated because she can't communicate with the other people around her at the moment.

1. Suggest three things you could do to help Edith to communicate more effectively with the ward staff.

2. Explain why it is important to pay attention to Edith's non-verbal communication when you are speaking to her.

3. How would you go about finding out what Edith would like to eat at dinner time, taking her communication problems into account?

Clarifying or repeating

An effective communicator may clarify or repeat aspects of what the other person has said during a conversation as a way of checking their understanding. They might, for example, repeat some of the speaker's words directly back to them to check that they have understood or to summarise a part of the person's 'message'. This is sometimes done to pick up and explore the main points or key issue the person is concerned with. Alternatively, they may say something like, 'Can I just check that you meant...' in order to clarify that their summary or understanding of a service user's conversation is correct. Doing this helps the person to avoid misunderstanding what has been said. However, it is important not to repeat or clarify too often in a conversation, as this will interrupt the speaker's flow and might make them think you are 'parroting' or repeating their points too directly.

Activity

1. In pairs, role-play a nursery nurse talking to a parent who is concerned about health and safety at her child's nursery. You should:

   • sit opposite each other in chairs of equal height

   • interact for about four minutes.

   The parent should talk about health and safety concerns at the nursery.

   The nursery nurse should listen, using SOLER behaviours and also repeating and clarifying what the parent has said every so often.

2. After each person has played the care worker role, take it in turns to tell each other what you liked and disliked about the activity.

3. Write a short comment on how repeating and clarifying affected communication between you.

The benefits of effective communication

Figure 1.7 Benefits of effective communication

For care workers	For people who use services
1. Effective communication helps carers to give and receive information that is relevant to an individual's care and wellbeing.	1. Effective communication enables a person to feel secure and respected as an individual at a time when they may be physically and emotionally vulnerable.
2. Effective communication enables care practitioners to express trust, acceptance, understanding and support.	2. Co-operation, involvement and partnership in a care relationship requires open and supportive communication.
3. Effective communication allows a care practitioner to identify and meet the individual needs of each person.	3. Effective communication empowers individuals by allowing them to express their needs, worries and wishes.
4. Effective communication enables a care practitioner to identify and support an individual's abilities and reduces dependency.	4. People who use services need to maintain their sense of identity while receiving care. This can only be achieved if they have opportunities to express themselves and to be understood by their carers.

Being sensitive to what other people are saying, thinking and feeling, showing people who use services respect, and protecting their dignity and rights, are all features of empowering care practice. To be able to do these things, care practitioners need to be sensitive to the spoken and unspoken communication of each individual they work with. They also need to be aware of how they themselves think, feel and behave in their interactions with others.

Assessment activity 1.3 (P3, P4, M2, D1)

The manager of a local day centre that provides work experience placements for students has received feedback about training and development from a number of the students. The students have said that they eventually work out what effective communication involves, but would have liked some training on this at the start of their work placement. In response, the day centre manager has asked you to:

- Produce a training DVD demonstrating good practice in one-to-one interaction.

- Produce a training DVD demonstrating good practice in group interaction.

- Write a review of the skills you demonstrate in both interactions, identifying your strengths and weaknesses.

Topic check

1 Identify three factors or qualities that make communication more effective.
2 What does active listening involve?
3 Describe ways in which body language can be used to make communication more effective.
4 Why is it important to pay attention to facial expression when communicating?
5 How should a person speak in order to make their communication effective?
6 Explain why effective communicators sometimes repeat and clarify what is said to them during conversations.

Assessment summary

The overall grade you achieve for this unit depends on how well you meet the grading criteria set out at the start of the chapter (see page 1). You must complete:

■ all of the P criteria to achieve a **pass** grade
■ all of the P and the M criteria to achieve a **merit** grade
■ all of the P, M and D criteria to achieve a **distinction** grade.

Your tutor will assess the assessment activities that you complete for this unit. The work you produce should provide evidence which demonstrates that you have achieved each of the assessment criteria. The table below identifies what you need to demonstrate to meet each of the pass, merit and distinction criteria for this unit. You should always check and self-assess your work before you submit your assignments for marking.

Remember that you MUST provide evidence for all of the P criteria to pass the unit.

Grading criteria	You need to demonstrate that you can:	Have you got the evidence?
P1	Identify different forms of communication	
M1	Describe different forms of communication	
P2	Explain barriers to effective communication within a health and social care environment	
P3	Take part in an effective one-to-one interaction	
P4	Take part in an effective group interaction	
M2	Describe the barriers to effective communication in your two interactions	
D1	Assess the strengths and weaknesses of your two interactions	

Always ask your tutor to explain any assignment tasks or assessment criteria that you don't understand fully. Being clear about the task before you begin gives you the best chance of succeeding. Good luck with your Unit 1 assessment work!

2 Individual rights in health and social care

Unit outline

The United Kingdom (UK) is a diverse society. This means that it consists of people with a variety of different backgrounds and characteristics. Health and social care workers need to have a good awareness of diversity as this has an impact on equality and rights issues and the way people expect to be treated in health and social care environments.

This unit introduces you to individual rights in the health and social care sectors. Every individual who uses care services has the right to be respected, to be treated equally and not to be discriminated against. Knowledge of the diverse nature of UK society enables care workers to understand that providing fair and equal treatment is an essential part of good care practice.

Learning outcomes

1. **Know factors that contribute to a diverse and equal society.**
2. **Understand the principles and values which underpin the support of individuals.**

Grading guide

To achieve a **pass**, you must show you can:	To achieve a **merit**, you must show you can:	To achieve a **distinction**, you must show you can:
P1 Identify factors that contribute to the equality of individuals in society		
P2 Explain the individual rights of people who use services		
P3 Explain the principles and values which underpin the support for individuals who use services	**M1** Discuss the principles and values which underpin the support for individuals who use services	**D1** Assess how the principles and values which underpin health and social care can relate to promotion of the rights of individuals

Diversity in the United Kingdom

This topic introduces you to the different ways in which the UK is a diverse country. When you have completed this topic, you should:

- understand the concept of diversity
- know about the different forms of diversity that exist in the UK.

 Key terms

Culture: the way of life, customs, traditions and beliefs of a group of people

Diversity: difference or variety

Immigration: the movement of people from one country into another

Secular: non-religious

Social class: a group of people who have similar occupations, incomes, educational backgrounds, attitudes and values

Stereotype: an oversimplified or exaggerated generalisation

Forms of diversity

The population of the UK is diverse in many ways (see Figure 2.1). This means that it consists of people with a variety of different backgrounds, characteristics and **cultures**.

Cultural diversity

The UK is a multicultural country. An individual's culture may affect:

- how they live their everyday life
- their diet, traditions and customs
- their attitudes, values and religious beliefs
- the way they behave and dress.

Cultural differences lead to different ways of life but should be equally valued and respected. Regardless of their cultural background, every person should have equal access to opportunities and resources.

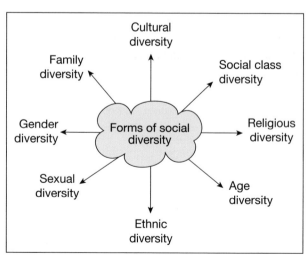

Figure 2.1 Forms of social diversity

Ethnic diversity

An ethnic group is a group of people who have a common heritage, shared customs and traditions, similar culture (e.g. language, religion and dress) and often a similar physical appearance. Because of mass **immigration**, the UK is a multi-ethnic country. Many people define their own ethnicity according to where they or their parents were born and the community they identify with. Official forms, such as the national census (carried out every 10 years) and job application forms, often ask people to define their ethnicity. They do this to obtain information on the ethnic composition of the United Kingdom and to ensure that equality of opportunity is available to everyone.

Over to you!

How many different cultural groups or communities do you know of living in your local area? How do members of these communities express and celebrate their cultural traditions and way of life?

Diverse faiths

Individuals within the UK population have a variety of religious beliefs. Christianity is the most common, but there are also significant numbers of people who are members of other faith communities, including Islam, Hinduism, Buddhism and Sikhism. There are others who don't believe in any god and don't have any religious faith, so they live **secular** lives.

Activity

How religiously diverse is your local community? Carry out some research and try to identify:

• places of worship in your local area

• the religious faith or denomination of people who attend each place of worship

• how often people go to each place of worship.

Using the information you obtain, create a table or poster that provides a summary of religious faiths in your local community.

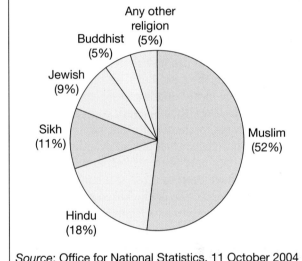

Source: Office for National Statistics, 11 October 2004

Figure 2.2 Religious diversity in the UK: the distribution of non-Christian religions, April 2001

Gender

When a person is asked to identify their 'gender', they are usually being asked to indicate whether they are male or female. This is really a question about the person's biological sex. Gender is a broader idea that refers to the social and cultural expectations that people have of males and females. Different social and cultural groups have varying ideas about how girls and women, men and boys should be brought up, treated and should behave in society. These expectations affect the way an individual develops. Some people may experience strong pressure to behave in a masculine or feminine way, whereas others may be brought up in circumstances where they are allowed to experiment with and even reject stereotypical gender roles.

Over to you!

Can you think of any gender **stereotypes**? You might want to think about the types of jobs typically thought of as 'men's work' and 'women's work', or the stereotyped roles men and women are expected to play at home.

Sexuality

Men and women can have a variety of sexual preferences. For example, a man or woman may be heterosexual, gay/lesbian, bisexual or asexual. People who are heterosexual are attracted to members of the opposite sex. Men who are gay and women who are lesbian are attracted to members of the same sex. People who are bisexual are attracted to members of both sexes. People who are asexual do not experience sexual attraction to either sex. A person's sexuality is not necessarily linked to their gender and should not be treated as 'abnormal' simply because it is not heterosexual.

Case study

Adrian and Camilla are sixth form pupils and best friends. They go out to parties and clubs together at weekends but they do also have partners. Adrian has a boyfriend who he has been seeing for 6 months. Camilla doesn't have a girlfriend at the moment but has had short relationships with older girls in the past. Both are open about their sexuality to close friends and members of their family. However, they are very concerned about other people, particularly other pupils at school, finding out about their sexual orientation. This is because they have seen how other pupils and teachers have been taunted and bullied for 'being gay'. Adrian has also been chased by a group of local teenagers on his way home from school. Camilla has recently reported two girls who have been calling her 'sick' and who sent her threatening and pornographic text messages at school.

1. How would you define Adrian and Camilla's sexuality?

2. How might a person's development be affected if they were unable to express their preferred sexuality?

3. In what ways are Adrian and Camilla being treated differently because of their sexuality?

Age and diversity

The UK population can be divided into a number of different age groupings. Health and social care organisations do this in order to plan and provide services for different groups of people. For example, a care organisation may develop services for babies and infants, children, adolescents, adults and older people. Each of these client groups is based on an age range. Care organisations have to be aware of changes in the age structure of the population in order to provide appropriate services. For example, a baby boom or an increase in the number of older people in the population will require adjustments to be made to the way services are provided.

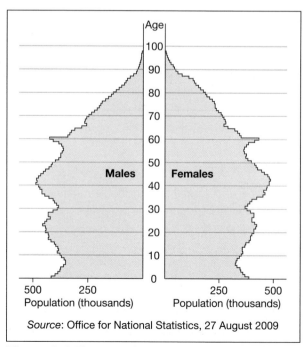

Source: Office for National Statistics, 27 August 2009

Figure 2.3 The age structure of the UK population: by gender and age, mid-2008

Diverse family structures

The structure of the family in the UK is changing. There is now a diverse range of different family structures (see Figure 2.4). An individual may live in a nuclear family, an extended family, a lone-parent family or a blended family, for example. Lone-parent families are currently the fastest growing type of family structure in the UK. A person's family is likely to play an important part in influencing their physical, intellectual, emotional and social development.

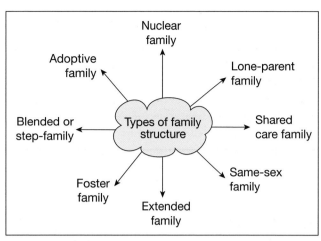

Figure 2.4 Family structures

Case study

Luke is 18 months old. His mum, Cheryl, spends most of her time with Luke, looking after him at home. Luke's dad, Simon, left to live on his own about a year ago, when his relationship with Cheryl broke down. Cheryl now has a new partner, Mike. She is planning on moving to live with Mike and his two children in a few months' time.

1. What type of family did Luke live in at the beginning of his life?

2. What type of family did Luke live in when his dad left home?

3. What type of family will Luke be living in if he and his mum move in with Mike and his children?

Activity

Look at the data table below. This provides some information on family structures in the United Kingdom. Using the data in the table, answer the questions that follow.

Dependent children in the UK by family type, 2004

Family type	Thousands	Percentages
Married couple	8,585	66
Cohabiting couple	1,421	11
Lone mother	2,829	22
Lone father	254	2
All dependent children in families	13,080	100

Source: Office for National Statistics, 7 July 2005

1. Which type of family are dependent children most likely to be living in?
2. How many (in thousands) children live in a family where parents are cohabiting?
3. What percentage of dependent children live in a lone-parent family?

Social class differences

A **social class** is a group of people who are similar in terms of their wealth, income and occupation. There are a number of different ways of identifying social classes in British society (see Unit 6 for more on this). Research into education, health and employment has shown that a person's social class has an effect on their opportunities in life. People who are born into the lower social classes tend to have fewer opportunities to attend prestigious and high-achieving schools and universities, are more likely to obtain lower-status and lower-paid work or be unemployed, and suffer higher rates of premature death than people born into the higher social classes.

Over to you!

How would your define your own social class? Do you think that social class matters in modern life?

Geography

Where a person lives can have a direct effect on their opportunities in life and on their health and wellbeing. If the quality of the physical environment is poor because of air and noise pollution, or poor housing, or because the type of area in which the person lives limits their opportunities or causes them to feel stressed, their personal development, health and wellbeing may suffer. Inequalities in wealth and income can be found in different parts of the UK, with the south of England, particularly around London, being the wealthiest area. However, there are also usually 'wealthy' and 'poor' areas within every city or large town in the country.

Over to you!

Are there some wealthier and poorer areas in the town or city where you live? If you live in the country, how do you think this affects your opportunities and health?

Biological factors

Genetics, diet and events like birth injuries and accidents in later life are biological factors that can affect an individual's development and make them different from others. For example, some people are biologically different when they are born because they inherit a condition that causes learning disabilities, such as Down's syndrome or autism, or because they acquire a learning or physical disability as a result of an accident or other traumatic life event. Disabled people are different from non-disabled people in some respects because they have a physical or intellectual impairment. Recognising a person's disability and their additional needs is an important part of treating them equally and with respect. It is important to avoid treating disabled people as 'abnormal' or as not deserving fair and equal treatment.

Case study

Kirsty is 3 years old. She lives with her mum in a high-rise flat on the edge of a large city. Kirsty's mum is very caring and spends all of her time looking after her daughter. Kirsty has a very strong attachment to her mum. However, the flat where they live is cold and damp. There is also a lot of traffic and few places to play outside in the local area, so Kirsty doesn't go out very often. Kirsty often has colds and chest infections and is underweight for her age. Kirsty's mum considers herself to be working class. She has very little money to spend on

food, heating or clothes as she is unemployed and claiming benefits. She does take Kirsty to a free playgroup, but Kirsty has never been on holiday and has few toys of her own to play with at home.

1. What kind of family does Kirsty live in?

2. How are geographical factors affecting Kirsty's health and wellbeing?

3. Explain how Kirsty's social class might have an impact on her health and development.

Topic check

1 Identify five different ways in which the United Kingdom is a diverse country.

2 Describe how people express their cultural traditions and customs.

3 Give three examples of different ethnic groups living in the UK.

4 Which is the most common religious faith in the UK?

5 Describe three different forms of family structure.

6 Explain how biological factors result in diversity and differences in the population.

Promoting equality and diversity

▶ Getting started

This topic focuses on ways of promoting equality and diversity in the health and social care sectors. When you have completed this unit you should:

- understand the concept and importance of equality
- be able to identify and discuss a range of ways in which equality and diversity are promoted within the health and social care sectors.

 Key terms

Labelling: the process of defining someone in a particular way

Legislation: written laws, also known as statutes and Acts of Parliament

Policy: a plan that is designed to achieve something

Prejudice: a strongly held negative attitude towards a particular group

Stereotyping: talking or thinking about an individual or group of people in a simplified and often negative way

Unfair discrimination: treating someone differently or unfairly

Welfare state: the term given to health, social care and education services provided by the government

Promoting equality

Each person who uses health and social care services should be treated equally and fairly. A number of laws exist in the UK that make **unfair discrimination** unlawful. These ensure that everyone has the same 'rights' of access to, for example, health, social care and early years services. Despite this, **prejudice** and unfair discrimination make it more difficult for some social groups to access care services. Challenging prejudice and discrimination and promoting equality is an important part of the work of care organisations and care practitioners.

The role of legislation

The law, in the form of **legislation**, plays an important role in giving individuals rights to equality and protecting them from unfair discrimination. There are a variety of anti-discrimination laws in the UK. Examples include:

- ▶ The Equal Pay Act (1970)
- ▶ The Sex Discrimination Act (1975)
- ▶ The Race Relations (Amendment) Act (2000)
- ▶ The Mental Health Act (2007)
- ▶ The Disability Discrimination Act (2005).

 Over to you!

Find out about the way equalities are promoted in the United Kingdom at the Equalities Commission website (www.equalityhumanrights.com).

 Activity

What rights and protections are given to individuals under each of these Acts of Parliament? Using library sources or the internet, investigate each Act and summarise your findings in the form of a table.

Health and social care organisations have a responsibility to include all of the rights that are granted to individuals by law in their equal opportunities policies. They have to ensure that the policies and procedures they develop are fair and non-discriminatory. If the rights of a care worker or a person who uses care services are breached or neglected, the organisation may be prosecuted in court.

The role of policy

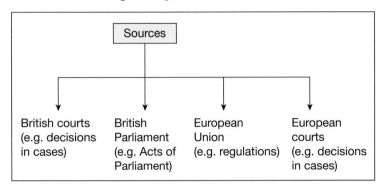

Figure 2.5 Sources of equality law

A **policy** is a plan or course of action. Governments and large organisations like the National Health Service and local authorities develop policies as ways of dealing with the health and social care problems that exist in the UK. For example, the government developed a policy to establish national minimum standards of care provision in health and social care settings in the late 1990s. This policy resulted in the Care Standards Act (2000), which established the basic standards of care provision that health and social care organisations must achieve. The aim of this policy is to ensure that everyone who uses care services receives fair and equal treatment. Care organisations are now inspected by the Care Quality Commission to check whether they meet the current national minimum standards of care.

Target setting is a second national policy that has had a big impact on the way health and social care organisations work. The aim of the target-setting policy is to ensure that people throughout the UK have a fair and equal chance of receiving the treatment and care services they require. This is done by the government setting targets for waiting times and the numbers of people who should be treated in any one year. This policy is designed to minimise waiting lists and avoid the 'postcode lottery' that can result in people receiving different standards of care provision depending on where they live.

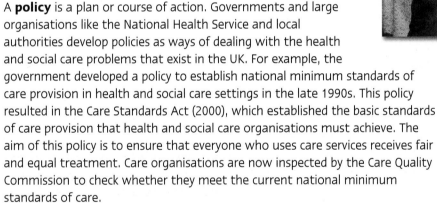

Activity

What does your local NHS Trust, Primary Care Trust or local authority say about equal opportunities for people who use their services? Use the internet to find the organisation's website and search for information on equal opportunities. Compare your findings with those of your colleagues.

The welfare state

The **welfare state** is a term given to the health, social care and education services provided free to users by the government. These services first became available in 1948. This is when the Labour government at the time founded the National Health Service (NHS). The NHS was launched to tackle widespread problems of ill health and to provide free services for everyone in the UK. Before this, health services were not available to all people. Some voluntary services existed but most people had to pay a doctor privately or join an insurance scheme if they wanted health care services. This meant that most people didn't receive good health care because they couldn't afford to pay.

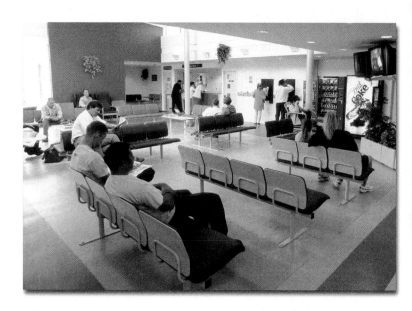

Non-discriminatory practice

Promoting equal opportunities and challenging unfair discrimination is part of the role of all care workers. Care workers often provide services for people who experience health and social problems that are triggered or made worse by unequal access to society's resources. Promoting equality in the care setting means that care workers need to address their own prejudices and tackle unfair discrimination where they see this occurring. The best way of putting equal opportunities ideas into action is through anti-discriminatory practice. This means developing ways of working that:

- recognise the needs of people from diverse backgrounds including those who come from minority religious and cultural backgrounds
- actively challenge the unfair discrimination that people have experienced
- counteract the effects that unfair discrimination has already had on people.

More information on non-discriminatory practice, **stereotyping, labelling** and prejudice can be found in Unit 6, Topic 6.3.

Activity

What does the NHS policy say about the delivery of health care services? Go to www.dh.gov.uk and find the summary of the NHS Plan. This will tell you the government's policy for providing health care services.

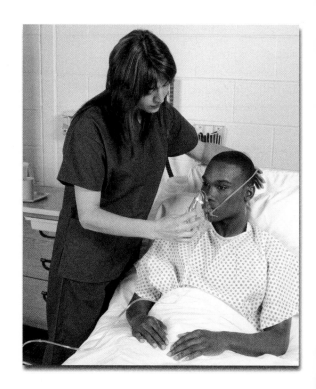

Case study

Abdullah is 32 years old. He came to the United Kingdom as a refugee and suffered a brain injury when he was attacked in the street by two men. The attack on Abdullah was treated as a hate crime because the two men shouted racial abuse before assaulting Abdullah and causing him severe head injuries. Abdullah now lives with his sister who is his main carer. He attends a day centre where he has made some friends. Abdullah has slowly had to relearn how to wash, dress and feed himself, but requires help and support to adapt to new people and changes in his routine.

He is often frightened of strangers and has to be taken to and from the day centre by his sister. Abdullah is not able to make decisions for himself or live independently at the moment.

1. What kind of prejudice led to the attack on Abdullah?
2. Identify two pieces of legislation that protect Abdullah from unfair discrimination.
3. Explain why it is important for care workers to relate to Abdullah in a non-discriminatory way.

Assessment activity 2.1 (P1)

Your local NHS Trust is holding an open day for local people. One of their priorities is to raise awareness of diversity in the area, and of the ways they are trying to ensure that they promote equality of opportunity and fair treatment for all service users. As a student of health and social care you have been approached to contribute to the open day.

• You have been asked to produce a poster which identifies factors that contribute to equality and diversity in society.
• Your poster should identify different forms of diversity in your local population and show how the rights of each potential service user are promoted and protected.

Topic check

1 Identify three different examples of legislation that promote equality by protecting people's rights.
2 Describe a government policy that is designed to promote equality in the health and social care sector.
3 What does the 'welfare state' consist of?
4 Explain how the development of the welfare state promoted better equality in the health and social care sector.
5 Explain how stereotyping and labelling people can lead to unfair discrimination.
6 Identify two things that a care worker can do to promote equality.

Principles and values

 Getting started

This topic introduces you to a range of principles and values that underpin the way care workers provide support for people who use care services. When you have completed this topic, you should:

- know about the ethical considerations that influence care practice
- understand the rights of people who use care services.

🔑 **Key terms**

Care values: a range of care values or principles that guide the work of care practitioners

Empathy: understanding and being able to appreciate another person's feelings

Empowering: giving somebody the opportunity or power to do something

Ethics: principles of right and wrong

Social justice: a principle that promotes fairness and equality for everyone in society

Ethical considerations

People who work in care settings tend see themselves as 'caring' and have a strong desire to do their best for the people who use care services. This is important because good care practice depends on the care worker being committed to:

- ▶ **social justice**
- ▶ a person-centred approach to practice
- ▶ valuing the right to life
- ▶ putting codes of conduct and policies into practice.

People who use health and social care services have the right to expect care workers to:

- ▶ treat them fairly and equally (see Topics 2.2 and 6.3)
- ▶ be honest with them
- ▶ use **empathy** as a way of understanding their problems or situation (see Topic 1.1)
- ▶ promote and protect their rights as an individual (see Topics 2.2 and 6.4).

Individuals' rights

People who use care services have a range of rights as a result of legislation and codes of practice (see Figure 2.6). These are described in detail in Topics 2.2 and 6.4. Care workers also use **care values** to promote and protect the rights and interests of people using care services.

Respect, dignity and privacy

An individual should always have privacy when personal care is being provided. For example, an individual should not be exposed to the view of others when they are being dressed, undressed, taken to the toilet or being helped to wash. Care practitioners can take simple practical precautions such as closing doors, keeping curtains drawn and not leaving individuals partially undressed where other people may walk in or see them. Knocking before entering a room and checking that it is all right to come in is also much more respectful than simply throwing the door open, carrying out tasks without asking, or sitting on a person's bed or chair without asking permission.

Showing respect for each person's dignity and privacy is a very important way of showing the person that you value them as an individual. It also shows that the care worker acknowledges the individual's rights, whatever their needs, problems or personal difficulties.

Safeguarding from danger and harm

Many people who use care services are at a vulnerable point in their life, and put a lot of trust in care workers to provide them with the protection, help and support they need. Some groups of service users, including children, older people, disabled people and people with mental health problems are vulnerable to exploitation and abuse by others. Some people who use services may also find it difficult to follow basic health and safety precautions that protect them from the dangers of everyday life, as well as abuse or exploitation by others. This can be a result of the problems they have, such as learning disabilities or memory problems, or because they are easily influenced by unscrupulous people. As a result, many people who need or who are receiving care face a greater risk of experiencing harm or a form of abuse (e.g. physical, emotional or sexual abuse).

To safeguard individuals from danger and harm, care workers should:

▶ be aware of any signs or indicators of abuse or exploitation

▶ ensure that their own health and hygiene does not pose a threat to the health and safety of others and that they manage their personal safety at work

▶ follow the infection control, moving and handling, accident and waste disposal procedures set out in their employer's health and safety policies

▶ make use of any risk assessments that have been carried out to minimise health and safety hazards

▶ respond appropriately to security risks in the workplace

▶ report health and safety and security issues to relevant people.

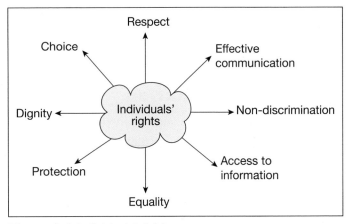

Figure 2.6 Individuals' rights

Over to you!

If you were working in a nursery with pre-school children, what could you do to safeguard them from the risks of infection?

Non-discriminatory treatment

Issues relating to discrimination and non-discriminatory practice are covered in Topics 2.2, 6.3 and 6.4.

Access to information

People who use health and social care services should be allowed access to information about themselves. The rights individuals have under the Data Protection Act 1998 are covered in Topics 2.4 and 6.4.

Promoting effective communication

Issues relating to supporting individuals to communicate using their preferred methods of communication and language are covered in Unit 1, especially Topic 1.2.

Promoting choice

Individuals receiving care need to be encouraged to make their own choices and should be enabled to make decisions on the basis of their own wishes and preferences. Ideally, care workers and service users should develop partnerships in which the service user feels equally involved. This kind of relationship is **empowering** because service users are seen as:

▶ individuals with rights and choices appropriate to their age and needs

▶ deserving of respect, regardless of their personal or social characteristics.

Care workers can also promote and support choice by:

▶ finding out what each individual's likes and dislikes are

▶ developing a unique relationship with each of the people they provide care for

▶ adapting their communication style to ensure that each individual can communicate as effectively as possible

▶ providing active support while encouraging and supporting each individual to do what they can for themselves

▶ offering individuals a choice of activities and choices regarding whether and how they participate in them

▶ giving people different options on both large- and small-scale decisions that affect them.

 Over to you!

What kinds of choices should people living in residential care be given in their day-to-day lives? Make a list of the choices you would expect to have (e.g. about food, meals, dress, personal care) if you were dependent on others to provide care and support for you.

Case study

Lianne arrived at Mrs Al Hammed's house to help her have a bath. She had never met Mrs Al Hammed before and was replacing her colleague Deirdre, who was on holiday. Mrs Al Hammed was in bed when Lianne arrived and let herself in. Mrs Al Hammed was not expecting to see a new person. Lianne thought that Mrs Al Hammed was 'a bit grumpy' and later said that she 'didn't speak to me in a polite way'. Lianne and Mrs Al Hammed were soon at odds over whether she should have a bath. Lianne had already run the bath, had chosen some clothes for Mrs Al Hammed and had collected some towels and toiletries together. She then said to Mrs Al Hammed, who was still in bed, 'you need to have a bath now'. Mrs Al Hammed said something in reply that Lianne didn't

understand. She could see that Mrs Al Hammed 'looked a bit annoyed with me'. Lianne asked Mrs Al Hammed to 'co-operate', telling her, 'I'm just doing my job'. Despite this Mrs Al Hammed remained in bed. Lianne left and reported 'the problem' to her supervisor after Mrs Al Hammed said, 'leave my house'.

1. Identify the care values that Lianne should have used in her interaction with Mrs Al Hammed.

2. How, if at all, has Lianne offered Mrs Al Hammed a choice in the way her care is provided?

3. Suggest ways in which Lianne could have promoted and supported choice in this situation.

Assessment activity 2.2 (P2, P3, M1, D1)

Identify a care setting that you know well or which you would like to investigate. This could be a setting you have been in as either a student on work placement or as a patient or service user. When you have chosen your care setting:

- Briefly describe the care setting and the services provided there.

- Explain the individual rights of people who use services in this setting.

- Discuss the principles and values that influence the practice of care workers who support people using services in this setting.

- Assess how the principles and values used by care workers in this setting promote the rights of people who use the services.

You should present your work in the form of either a short report or a magazine article for a local newspaper.

Topic check

1 Identify and briefly explain three ethical considerations that influence care practice.
2 How do users of care services expect care workers to treat them?
3 Describe two things a care worker can do to respect the dignity of a person receiving personal care.
4 What can care workers do to safeguard people who use services from danger and harm?
5 What is an empowering care relationship?
6 Explain how a care worker could promote an individual's right to choice in a care setting.

Workers' responsibilities

▶ Getting started

This topic focuses on the range of responsibilities care workers have with regard to promoting and protecting the rights of people who use care services. When you have completed this topic, you should:

- understand workers' responsibilities in relation to care provision
- be able to describe how care workers can best support individuals in care settings.

🔑 Key terms

Confidentiality: protecting the privacy of information

Disclosure: revealing or making something known

Regulatory body: an independent organisation that establishes and monitors standards of practice for a group of care workers

Care workers' responsibilities

All care workers have to work within the boundaries of the law and the codes of practice produced by their **regulatory body** and employer. For example, a registered nurse or midwife has to follow the code of practice of the Nursing and Midwifery Council (NMC), while a registered social worker has to follow the code of practice of the General Social Care Council (GSCC). Both of these organisations develop practice standards and issue guidance on how registered practitioners can meet them. A care worker who fails to meet their professional responsibilities can be reported to, and 'struck off' the register by, their regulatory body. If the person was also in breach of their contract of employment, they would lose their job too.

Care workers have a range of responsibilities which are designed to ensure that they provide safe, effective and person-centred care (see Figure 2.7).

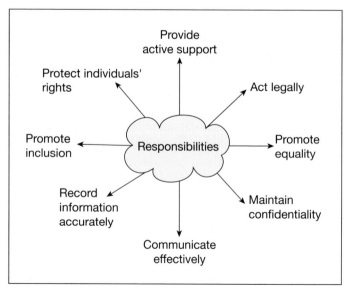

Figure 2.7 Care workers' responsibilities

Provision of active support

Care workers should provide forms of active support that enable people who use care services to communicate their needs, views and preferences. Care workers should be pro-active in the way that they look for opportunities to provide support and assistance without doing so in a way that would undermine a person's independence or reduce their self-care skills.

Use of communication skills

The importance of effective communication skills and their role in supporting diversity, inclusion and promoting equality of opportunity is outlined in Topic 1.2.

Confidentiality and privacy

Care service users must be able to trust the people who provide them with care services. If you cannot trust another person with your thoughts, feelings and dignity you are unlikely to develop a strong or deep relationship with them. The care relationship is based on trust and, particularly, on the need for care practitioners to maintain **confidentiality** whenever possible.

There are times in care work when it is important to keep confidences and information that you have about service users to yourself. For example, if a child at the nursery where you do your work placement swore at you and misbehaved one afternoon, or an elderly resident at a nursing home

refused to bathe after wetting herself, you would be breaching confidentiality to reveal these things to your friends. You should not breach confidentiality in situations where service users have a right to privacy or where their comments or behaviour do not cause harm or break the law. Where care workers gossip or talk publicly about events or issues that happen at work they are betraying the trust that service users and colleagues put in them.

Over to you!

Can you think of reasons why it is important that care workers encourage individuals to take part in meeting their own care needs?

Over to you!

How do you think you would feel if you overheard the receptionist and a doctor or nurse at your local GP practice talking openly about your health problems, where you live and what your personal circumstances are? How do you think this might affect your relationship with care workers at your GP practice?

Disclosure

Confidentiality is about sharing, transmitting and storing information about individuals in ways that are appropriate to their care needs. It is definitely not about keeping information 'secret'. This means that 'confidential' information can be shared with (disclosed to) other care team members who also need to know about and use it. Beyond this, a care practitioner must consult the service users they work with and respect their wishes about who should be informed or given access to information about them.

However, there are sometimes situations where it is necessary to disclose information about a service user that has been given in confidence. For example, where a service user requests that what they say is kept a secret, this can be overridden if:

▶ what they reveal involves them breaking the law or planning to do so

▶ they say that they intend to harm themselves or another person

▶ they reveal information that can be used to protect another person from harm.

If a service user commits an offence that could have been prevented by a care practitioner disclosing information given to them in confidence, the care practitioner could be brought to court to face charges. As a result, care practitioners should never promise service users that what they say will be absolutely confidential. They should explain that there are times when they may have to share information with their colleagues and other authorities.

 Activity

Read through the following confidentiality situations. For each scenario, explain:

• why confidentiality may be important to the client

• the dilemma facing the care worker

• whether you would break confidentiality and why.

1. Darren has an appointment with the school nurse for a BCG booster injection. He's worried about it making him ill. He says that he's just taken some ecstasy and pleads with the nurse not to tell anyone.

2. Jennifer goes to her GP for contraceptive pills. She asks her GP not to tell her parents. She is 14 years old.

3. Eileen has terminal cancer. She tells her district nurse that she's had enough of living and is going to end her own life tomorrow. She says it's her choice and asks the district nurse not to interfere.

4. Yasmin tells her new health visitor that her boyfriend is violent and is beating her. She asks the health visitor not to say anything as she is frightened of what might happen. Yasmin and her boyfriend have a 3-month-old baby.

5. Lee turns up at a hostel for the homeless. He says that he has run away from home because his father has been beating him. He asks the social worker not to contact his family. He is 16 years old.

6. A man with a stab wound arrives at the hospital casualty department. He won't give his name and asks the nurse not to phone the police. He says that he will leave if she does. He is bleeding heavily.

Dealing with tensions between rights and responsibilities

Care workers often have to deal with difficult situations where the rights of a person who uses care services clashes with the legal or professional responsibilities of the care worker. For example, a GP who is treating a person for a smoking-related illness can only advise them to give up smoking and cannot refuse to treat them if they continue to do so. Similarly, a social worker who is supporting an individual with learning disabilities who wishes to live an independent life, cannot stop the person trying independent living even where this involves some risk. They have to manage the tension between the person's rights, the risks involved and their own professional responsibilities to monitor, support and provide care for the person.

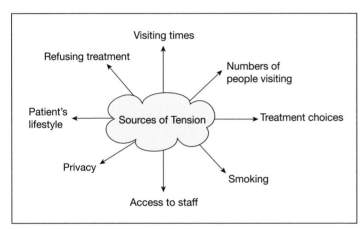

Figure 2.8 Sources of tension

 Case study

Kwame Mckenzie is a social worker in the Care of Older People team. Philip Dodds, aged 82, is one of Kwame's clients. Philip lives in the downstairs part of a terraced house on his own. He has lived in the same house for the last 52 years and is very reluctant to move. Philip has Parkinson's disease, and has difficulty moving around and meeting his own physical needs. Kerry, aged 19, is Philip's niece. She has a key to his home and comes around twice a day to help Philip get dressed and to prepare food for him. Philip and Kerry get on very well.

Kwame has recently become concerned about the way Kerry is looking after Philip. He noticed that Philip seems a little bit anxious when Kerry comes to the house. He has also noticed that Kerry is dressing Philip in the same clothes every day.

The last time Kwame came to the house, Philip complained about being hungry. He said that Kerry now collects his pension and does the shopping, but that the fridge is always empty. When Kwame asked Philip whether he would like him to speak with Kerry about the way she is looking after him and the lack of food, Philip said, 'No, you mustn't. She might get angry and go away for good.'

1. What kind of tension is there between Philip's rights and Kwame's professional responsibilities here?

2. What might be the advantages and disadvantages of Kwame speaking to Kerry about this situation?

3. What do you think Kwame should do to meet his responsibilities as a social worker?

Information management

Care workers have to accurately record, store and retrieve information about service users and the care they receive on a daily basis. They may, for example, have to take down information provided by other care workers and record it in an individual's notes or personal records. Care workers who deal with people's records also have to protect the confidentiality of the information they deal with so that others don't access the information inappropriately. Where records are kept as hard copy or manual files, they should:

▶ be kept in a locked storage cabinet

▶ only be accessed by people who are authorised to read them

▶ be filed alphabetically

▶ only be updated and changed by people who are authorised to do so. New entries should always be signed and dated.

In addition, where records are kept as electronic files:

▶ access should be password protected to ensure that only authorised people read them

▶ all records should be backed up onto disk to ensure that they are not lost or erased as a result of computer problems.

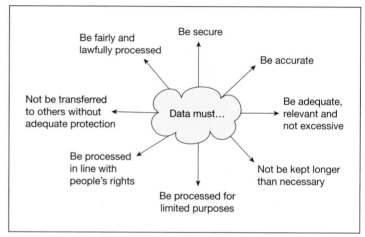

Figure 2.9 Principles of the Data Protection Act

Information about people who use care services must be managed in accordance with the Data Protection Act 1998 and the Freedom of Information Act 2000. The Data Protection Act 1998 protects the individual's right to confidentiality (paper and electronic records). An individual has the right to:

▶ know what information is held about them and to see and correct this if it is inaccurate

▶ refuse to provide information

▶ have up-to-date and accurate data held about them

▶ have data removed when it is no longer necessary for an organisation to hold it

▶ have the confidentiality of their information protected.

The Freedom of Information Act deals with access to official information held by public organisations, such as local authorities and the NHS. The Act gives members of the public the right to access information held by public authorities and requires public authorities to have a scheme that allows them to publish this information.

Case study

Andy, aged 44, woke at 10 a.m., refused breakfast but then ate a banana and yoghurt before he left the drug rehabilitation unit to go to a physiotherapy appointment. He then came back half an hour later and rested on his bed, missing two of his group sessions, until lunch time. After eating lunch alone in the dining room Andy went into the lounge and enthusiastically joined in the activities of the music group before you left at the end of your shift.

1. Which aspects of Andy's day would you write about in his records?

2. Andy has asked how his records can be 'kept confidential'. Describe what should happen to ensure that the confidentiality of his records is protected.

3. What, if anything, could you tell Andy's relatives if they phoned up and asked about his day?

Topic check

1 Identify three different responsibilities care workers have in relation to the care they provide.
2 What does 'providing active support' involve?
3 Explain the term 'confidentiality' and the reasons why care workers should take this issue seriously.
4 Identify occasions when a care worker can breach confidentiality.
5 Describe an example of a situation in which a care worker has to manage the tension between an individual's rights and their own professional responsibilities.
6 Describe good practice in terms of managing individuals' care records and other items of confidential information in a care setting.

Assessment summary

The overall grade you achieve for this unit depends on how well you meet the grading criteria set out at the start of the unit (see page 21). You must complete:

- all of the P criteria to achieve a **pass** grade
- all of the P and the M criteria to achieve a **merit** grade
- all of the P, M and D criteria to achieve a **distinction** grade.

Your tutor will assess the assessment activities that you complete for this unit. The work you produce should provide evidence which demonstrates that you have achieved each of the assessment criteria. The table below identifies what you need to demonstrate to meet each of the pass, merit and distinction criteria for this unit. You should always check and self-assess your work before you submit your assignments for marking.

Remember that you MUST provide evidence for all of the P criteria to pass the unit.

Grading criteria	You need to demonstrate that you can:	Have you got the evidence?
P1	Identify factors that contribute to the equality of individuals in society	
P2	Explain the individual rights of people who use services	
P3	Explain the principles and values which underpin the support for individuals who use services	
M1	Discuss the principles and values which underpin the support for individuals who use services	
D1	Assess how the principles and values which underpin health and social care can relate to promotion of the rights of individuals	

Always ask your tutor to explain any assignment tasks or assessment criteria that you don't understand fully. Being clear about the task before you begin gives you the best chance of succeeding. Good luck with your Unit 2 assessment work!

3 Individual needs in health and social care

Unit outline

Understanding the everyday needs of individuals is a central part of health and social care work. It is important that health and social care workers understand the everyday needs as well as the more specific, and sometimes complex, care needs of people who use care services. It is important also to appreciate some of the factors that can result in an individual's needs not being fully met, and the effects this can have on the health of individuals.

This unit introduces you to individual needs in the health and social care sectors. It looks at a range of everyday and care needs and at the risks to health and wellbeing if these needs are not met. Factors that influence this, such as physical and social factors and differences between individuals in different life stages, are explored along with the influence an individual's environment has on their health.

Learning outcomes

1 **Know the everyday needs of individuals.**
2 **Understand factors that influence the health and care needs of individuals.**
3 **Be able to plan to meet the health and wellbeing needs of an individual.**

Grading guide

To achieve a **pass**, you must show you can:	To achieve a **merit**, you must show you can:	To achieve a **distinction**, you must show you can:
P1 Outline the everyday needs of individuals		
P2 Explain factors which affect the everyday needs of individuals		
P3 Carry out an assessment of the health and wellbeing of an individual		
P4 Produce a plan for improving the health and wellbeing of an individual	**M1** Explain how the plan meets the health and wellbeing needs of the individual	**D1** Justify how the plan takes into account the individual's circumstances and preferences

Everyday human needs

This topic provides an introduction to the everyday needs of individuals. When you have completed this topic, you should:

- know that people have physical, intellectual, emotional, social and spiritual needs
- be able to describe Maslow's hierarchy of needs
- be able to identify a range of additional health and care needs.

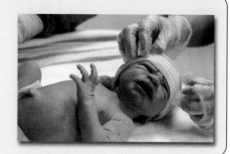

Key terms

Acute illness: short-term illness that occurs suddenly and usually ends quickly

Chronic: ongoing or long term

Emotional: related to feelings

Intellectual: related to thinking, problem-solving, memory or other mental activity

Physical: related to the body

Spiritual: related to beliefs and faith

Surgical interventions: operations

Everyday needs of individuals

Every human being has a range of physical, intellectual, emotional, social and spiritual (PIESS) needs (see Figure 3.1). A person whose PIESS needs are satisfied is likely to experience positive health, wellbeing and personal development.

Figure 3.1 Examples of PIESS needs

Type of needs	Examples of needs	
Physical needs	• Food and water • Warmth • Exercise	• Sleep and rest • Shelter • Safety, security and protection from harm, illness and injury
Intellectual needs	• Mental activities that are interesting and challenging	• Learning opportunities • New experiences and achievements
Emotional needs	• Affection, love, support and care • Relationships with others	• Self-confidence, self-esteem and a self-concept • Fulfilment and respect
Social needs	• Attachment to a trusted carer • Relationships and support from family and friends	• Group membership and acceptance by others • A sense of identity and belonging within a community
Spiritual needs	• Personal beliefs that give meaning to life	• Faith in God, religious beliefs or other spiritual ideas

A person's **physical** needs must be satisfied for them to be physically healthy. A person's **intellectual** needs are those things they require to develop their knowledge, skills and abilities. A person's **emotional** and social needs are the things they require to express feelings, develop relationships and experience wellbeing and good mental health. A person's **spiritual** needs are the things, like religious belief and worship, which make their life (and death) more meaningful.

Activity

What type of PIESS need is each of the following people meeting?

- Pupinder follows the Sikh religion, worshipping at a local temple every week.
- Yvonne goes jogging twice a week as part of her weight-loss programme.
- Tony attends a film club where he watches and talks about classic movies.
- Livingstone moved to the UK to care for his disabled brother.
- Tanya goes clubbing every Friday with her friends from work.
- Kia comforts her baby when he cries by cuddling and stroking him.

Maslow's hierarchy of needs

In 1943, Abraham Maslow (1908–1970), an American psychologist, developed a way of thinking about human needs that is very influential in care work. He suggested that a person's needs are best understood as a pyramid or hierarchy, arranged in levels of importance (see Figure 3.2).

Maslow believed that physical needs were the most important because a person must meet these to survive. He suggested that an individual will only be motivated to meet needs higher up the pyramid when they have met lower-level needs. However, according to Maslow's hierarchy of needs, an individual will be motivated to satisfy their needs at each level until they achieve 'self-actualisation', or their full potential as a person.

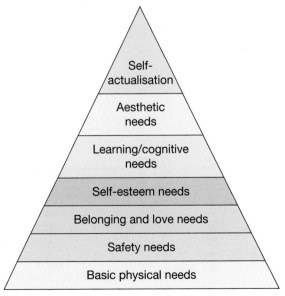

Figure 3.2 Maslow's hierarchy of needs

Over to you!

How might Maslow's hierarchy of needs help a care worker to plan and deliver care for a vulnerable person?

Case study

Imran is 2 months old. He had a normal birth. After a range of checks by the midwife and doctor at the hospital, his parents took him home the day after his birth. As a young baby, Imran is totally dependent on others for basic care and protection from harm. Imran's mum breastfeeds him several times during the day and night. She and his dad take it in turns to change his nappy, wash him and comfort him when he starts crying. Imran's parents have to make sure that he is fed properly, that he is kept warm but that he doesn't get too hot, and that he is kept clean and comfortable. Imran won't be able to meet these needs on his own until he is several years older.

1. List any other basic needs that are not mentioned in the case study that you think Imran has. (Hint: what else does he need to be a healthy baby?)

2. Identify two things that Imran's mum or dad do to meet his physical needs.

3. Which care worker usually visits a mother and baby at home shortly after the birth, to check that the baby is healthy and growing well?

Health and care needs

A person may have temporary health and care needs because they become unwell, or experience some social or developmental problems at a particular point in their life. For example, a person may require **surgical interventions** or medicines to treat a disease or condition they develop. Where the person experiences an **acute illness** or has a health problem that can be cured with treatment, their additional health and care needs will end when they recover.

A person might also develop, or be born with, a **chronic** health problem or disability that affects their basic needs and ability to function every day. Depending on the nature and severity of their problems, a person may require:

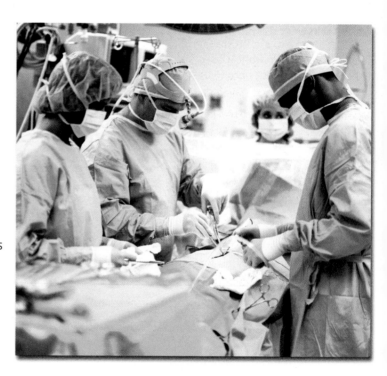

▶ personal care, such as assistance with washing, dressing and going to the toilet

▶ mobility support, such as help with walking, sitting up or turning in bed

▶ everyday living support because of difficulties with things like reading and writing, problem-solving or decision-making. For example, a child born with Down's Syndrome is likely to need lifelong health and social care support. This is because their learning difficulties are likely to limit their social and intellectual development and prevent them from developing the skills needed for independent living.

Over to you!

Have you ever had a serious illness, an operation or health problems that caused you to be confined to bed and unable to meet your personal needs? How did it feel to have to rely on other people to do this for you?

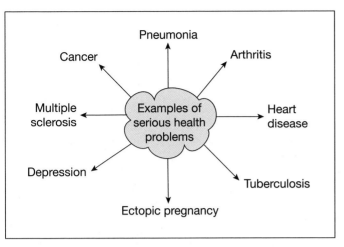

Figure 3.3 Examples of serious health problems

Assessment activity 3.1 (P1, P2)

Government agencies are considering how best to improve care services in your local area. They have decided to ask different groups of local residents about the factors that influence their health, development and wellbeing needs. You have been asked to:

- Research and discuss the range of factors which influence people's needs (socio-economic, lifestyle, physical, health) in your local area.
- Present your findings in the form of a report.

✓ Topic check

1 Identify five different types of everyday human need.
2 Briefly explain what Maslow's hierarchy of needs says about human needs.
3 Give an example of an intellectual need.
4 How can people meet their social needs?
5 Give two reasons why a person may have additional health and care needs.
6 Describe two forms of help or assistance a person may require to meet their basic physical needs if they become medically unwell or develop a physical disability.

Needs in different life stages

 ▶ Getting started

This topic focuses on the way that an individual's needs vary and change as they move through different life stages. When you have completed this topic, you should:

■ know that an individual's needs change as they grow and develop

■ understand how and why an individual's needs vary in each life stage.

 Key terms

Ageing process: both the process of growing older and the physical changes associated with this

Life stage: a period of growth and personal development

Puberty: the period of physical growth, which occurs

during adolescence, during which the body matures and becomes capable of reproduction

Stroke: a condition caused by bleeding or blockage of blood flow in the brain

Needs in different life stages

Topic 3.1 explained how all human beings have a common range of physical, intellectual, emotional, social and spiritual needs. However, the importance of these needs varies in different **life stages**. As people grow and develop, their basic everyday needs also change.

Infancy

A newborn baby is dependent on others, usually their parents, to provide them with the things they need for health, wellbeing and development. To be physically healthy and to develop normally, an infant requires a lot of practical, hands-on care from their parents and from care professionals, especially during the early weeks and months of life. A lot of the care needs of babies result from their physical dependence and vulnerability to harm. Infants become less dependent in some ways as they grow and develop into toddlers. However, a 2-year-old toddler still depends on their parents to meet most of their physical, intellectual, emotional and social needs.

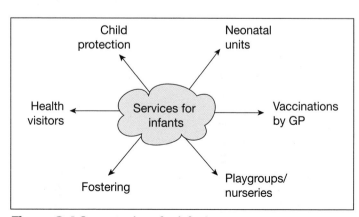

Figure 3.4 Care services for infants

Childhood

Children require less basic care from their parents than infants because they are more able to meet some of their own basic needs. For example, children learn how to feed, wash and dress themselves in early childhood. Even so, children still need a lot of help and support from parents and care practitioners to develop:

▶ self-care skills (washing, dressing, going to the toilet)

▶ physical strength and stamina (play and outdoor activities)

▶ intellectual skills (basic reading, writing and numeracy)

▶ language skills (talking, reading and writing)

▶ social skills (friendships and relationships with other children and adults)

▶ emotional control and appropriate behaviour (at home and with others).

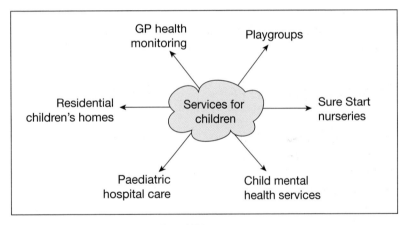

Children (and their parents) focus a great deal on meeting physical needs. Having enough to eat, going to the toilet (staying clean and dry) and getting enough exercise and sleep are common preoccupations in childhood. However, children are also aware of the need to stay safe, and spend a lot of time and energy developing friendships and learning new things. This is an example of how an individual's focus moves up Maslow's hierarchy of needs as they grow and develop.

Activity

What kind of need does making friendships meet in childhood?

Figure 3.5 Care services for children

Case study

Anna is 3-and-a-half years old. She has recently begun attending a playgroup two mornings a week. Anna's mum helps to run the playgroup. She thinks that attending playgroup is good for Anna's development. When she's at the playgroup, Anna meets and plays with up to ten other children. Anna enjoys playing with sand and water, climbing and using the trampoline. She now joins in games with other children. Her mum says that Anna has learnt how to make new friends and is much less shy than she was before she started going to playgroup.

1. Give an example of one physical, one intellectual, one emotional and one social need that a child could meet through going to playgroup.

2. What new skills or abilities might playgroup help Anna to develop?

3. Explain how play might help Anna to develop intellectual skills.

Adolescence

The needs of adolescents are different from those of children and adults. During adolescence, young people go through **puberty**. This involves major physical growth and development and emotional change (see Unit 8). Changes in diet, exercise and activity levels are needed to help adolescents meet their physical needs. During adolescence, young people often require support to help them with their rapidly changing social and emotional development. For example, young people may require:

- support to help manage relationships with parents and other adults
- opportunities to socialise, develop and express their identity
- experiences that build up confidence, self-esteem and assertiveness
- opportunities to express opinions and explore feelings
- the chance to make personal decisions about the future
- advice and guidance about relationships, sex and sexuality.

Case study

Gina is 15 years old and currently has a difficult relationship with her parents. She complains that they treat her like a child and are too strict with her. Gina believes that she is mature enough to make decisions for herself. Her parents complain that she has become 'very difficult' and that she no longer listens to what they tell her. They now insist that she doesn't go out after school during the week and won't let her stay at a friend's house at the weekend. Gina feels too angry with her parents to talk to them about any of these things at the moment.

1. What kind of social and emotional needs do adolescents like Gina have?

2. How are Gina's social and emotional needs likely to be different now from when she was a child?

3. Why do you think parents sometimes have difficult relationships with their children during adolescence?

Adulthood

Adulthood is a life stage where people are expected to be able to meet their own physical, intellectual, emotional, social and spiritual needs. However, there are always situations where people need help in meeting their needs, such as when they experience problems with their physical or mental health, or social problems due to changing circumstances. For example, adults are more likely than children and adolescents to develop health and care needs. This is because serious diseases and disorders, such as cancers and mental health problems, are more likely to occur during adulthood. Some health problems, like heart disease, respiratory disorders and arthritis, may also develop into chronic conditions during this life stage and require the person to use care services for the rest of their adult life.

Later adulthood

An individual's dietary needs, activity levels and sleep may all change because of the **ageing process**. The gradual physical decline that occurs in later adulthood may also mean that an older person is less able to meet their own needs independently. People become more vulnerable to ill health, social isolation and loneliness as they get older and require more assistance with daily living skills. An older person may develop additional health and care needs because of a condition or illness that reduces their ability to perform everyday tasks such as washing, dressing or shopping for food. On the other hand, an individual's spiritual needs may become more significant during this life stage, especially if the person has a strong religious faith.

Being physically active is a very important way of maintaining health and wellbeing in later adulthood.

Over to you!

Can you think of any care services that are targeted at older people? What needs are these services aiming to meet?

Case study

Joan Connor is 78 years of age. Until a year ago she spent most of her time looking after her house and her husband Peter, aged 80. Peter Connor had a **stroke** a year ago and has been in hospital ever since. Joan tries to visit him whenever she can but is finding life on her own very difficult. She feels that she needs help to cope with her housework and general chores like shopping, and has been lonely since her husband was admitted to hospital. Joan has also been feeling unwell recently, complaining of sore joints and a painful hip.

1. If Joan is lonely, which of her needs are not being met?

2. Describe two ways in which Joan's emotional needs could be met at this point in her life.

3. Do you think that Joan has any health and care needs?

Topic check

1 Name five different human life stages.
2 Give three examples of an infant's physical needs.
3 How do children meet their social needs during childhood?
4 Describe how a person's emotional needs can change during adolescence.
5 Explain why a person is likely to develop health and care needs at some point during adulthood.
6 Describe two ways the ageing process can have an effect on an older person's needs.

Physical and health-related factors

▶ Getting started

This topic focuses on a range of physical and health-related factors that have an important influence on an individual's health experience. When you have completed this topic, you should:

- be able to identify a range of physical factors that influence health and needs

- know how different physical factors can affect an individual's health

- know how health-related factors can affect an individual's needs.

Key terms

Disabilities: physical or mental impairments that limit some aspect of a person's ability

DNA: deoxyribonucleic acid molecules that contain the genetic instructions for human growth and development

Gender: a term given to the biological, psychological and social differences between men and women

Genes: biological segments of **DNA** that carry genetic information from one generation to the next

Pollution: contamination of natural surroundings (including air and water) by poisonous or harmful substances

Sensory impairment: damage to one of the senses, usually hearing or sight

Physical influences on health and needs

A range of physical and health-related factors influence the needs and health experience of every individual. These include:

- ▶ the **genes** we inherit from our biological parents

- ▶ any **disabilities** or **sensory impairments** we have

- ▶ the illnesses, diseases and injuries that we experience

- ▶ our sexual health

- ▶ any mental illnesses, emotional or behavioural disorders that we experience

- ▶ our age and **gender**.

Genetic inheritance

The genes that we inherit from our biological parents play a very important role in controlling our physical growth and appearance. They can also have a big impact on our health.

Genetic
inheritance

Mental
illness

Sexual
health

Accident
and injury

Factors

Disease and
illness

Age

Gender

Disability

Figure 3.6 Physical and health-related factors

Each cell in the human body contains two sets of 23 chromosomes – one set from each parent. Each chromosome can contain up to 4000 different genes. These are the 'instructions' or codes that tell our body's cells how to grow. A person's genes may also be faulty or carry defective 'instructions' that increase the risk of them developing certain genetically inherited illnesses and diseases. A person can inherit:

▶ dominant gene defects such as Huntington's disease and achondroplasia (dwarfism)

▶ recessive gene defects such as cystic fibrosis and sickle cell anaemia

▶ chromosomal abnormalities such as Down's Syndrome and Klinefelters syndrome.

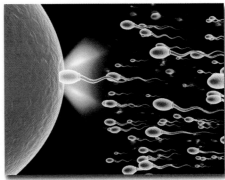

Conception happens when a man's sperm fertilises a woman's egg (ovum).

The conditions and disorders that result from gene defects and chromosomal abnormalities are rare. Other more commonly experienced health problems that have a genetic component include:

▶ eye disorders, such as glaucoma

▶ high blood pressure

▶ heart conditions

▶ high cholesterol

▶ haemophilia.

Even though a person may be genetically vulnerable to a particular disorder, lifestyle and other biological factors can limit or even prevent some genetically inherited conditions from occurring.

Activity

Use library sources or the internet to research one of the following genetically inherited conditions: phenylketonuria (PKU), Huntington's disease, cystic fibrosis, Down's syndrome, sickle cell anaemia or Friedrich's ataxia. Identify:

- what the condition is
- the main effects on the health and development needs of individuals who have the condition
- how the condition is treated.

Case study

Ajay Khan is an active, sporty 20-year-old. He avoids eating fatty food wherever he can, has never smoked and doesn't drink alcohol. Ajay is very health-conscious because he is aware of his family history of high blood pressure and heart disease. Ajay's father and grandfather both had high blood pressure and both died of heart conditions in their mid-fifties. Ajay's GP has told him he needs to be aware that there is a genetic component to these health problems and that he may be susceptible to them unless he manages his lifestyle carefully.

1. What does Ajay's GP mean when he says that there is a 'genetic component' to high blood pressure and heart disease?

2. Is Ajay bound to get heart disease like his father and grandfather?

3. What is Ajay doing that might help to reduce his genetic risk of heart disease and high blood pressure?

Disability

The term 'disabled person' is used to describe an individual who has some form of physical, mental or sensory impairment that limits their ability and causes them to have additional health and care needs.

Physical disabilities may affect people in many different ways. For example, a spinal injury may cause someone to be paralysed from the waist or neck down. In this case the person would be dependent on others for care and assistance with most aspects of daily living. A person with arthritis, however, may have difficulty walking or picking things up but would not be so dependent on others. Learning disabilities also vary in the way they affect people. Learning-disabled people have some form of intellectual impairment that limits their mental ability. Because of this, some are unable to live independently or meet their special needs without assistance. However, with help and support many people with learning disabilities do live fulfilling, healthy lives.

Sensory impairment

Human beings use their senses to see, hear, touch (feel), taste and smell. Sensory loss occurs when one or more of these senses is damaged or lost entirely. This may happen as the result of illness or an accident that damages the brain or another part of the body. Visual and hearing impairment are the most common forms of sensory loss. Children who are unable to see or hear well may have development problems and may struggle to learn unless specialist education is provided to meet their needs. Similarly, many older people who experience sensory loss as a result of ageing also require help, assistance and adapted equipment to enable them to meet their everyday needs.

Age

Ageing refers to the physical and mental changes that people experience as they grow older. Babies and older people are at the extremes of the human age span. Babies, children and adolescents gradually develop the physical, intellectual and social skills required to meet their everyday needs. Older people have to learn to cope with changes and a gradual decline in their physical abilities in later life. A person who lacks everyday living skills and abilities because they are young, or who loses some of the skills and abilities they once had as they grow old, is likely to need help and assistance in meeting their everyday needs.

Gender

A person's gender (male or female) can make a difference to their health experience. This is summed up in the phrase 'women are sicker but men die quicker'. Research shows that:

▶ Women are more likely to see a doctor and report higher rates of illness than men.

▶ Women are more likely to experience depression, especially if they are lone parents or look after children at home.

▶ Women live longer lives than men and are less likely to die prematurely as a result of accidents or other risk-related behaviours.

▶ Men are more likely to die from circulatory diseases, while the main cause of death for women is now cancer.

Infection

Infections are acute illnesses. They are causes by viruses and bacteria. Viral infections affect more than one part of the body at the same time and can be serious. Influenza ('flu) is a viral infection that can cause a person to become very unwell and require care and assistance to meet their physical and everyday needs. Bacterial infections affect specific parts of the body and result in redness, heat, swelling and pain. If a cut becomes infected with bacteria, for example, the part of the body where the cut is will become tender and painful. Infections can be transmitted by air (coughing, sneezing), water, through body fluids, by ingesting contaminated food or fluids and by physical contact. The risks of infection and cross-infection are reduced through good hygiene (e.g. hand-washing) and infection control techniques.

Injury and chronic disorder

The injuries, diseases and illnesses that an individual experiences throughout their life may have a significant impact on their health and wellbeing. This happens where the illness, disease or injury affects:

▶ the person's ability to function normally

▶ their quality of life

▶ the length of the person's life.

Chronic disorders, such as arthritis or emphysema, are ongoing and can cause the person's health and wellbeing to deteriorate slowly. Someone with a chronic disorder may gradually lose some of their everyday living skills and may have poor quality of life because of the way their condition affects them.

Mental illness and behavioural problems

Mental illness is often seen as a frightening and unusual problem to experience. However, statistics show that many people who visit their GPs with complaints about their physical health have 'hidden' mental health problems. These can be related to stress, relationship problems or substance misuse, for example. Because mental illness is stigmatised, few people are willing to admit to it. However, the anxiety, depression and behavioural problems that are part of mental illness can have a damaging effect on a person's quality of life and on their ability to meet their everyday needs.

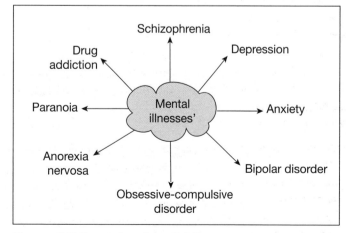

Figure 3.7 Examples of mental illnesses

Activity

Mental illness and distress are stigmatised. This means that they are seen as shameful things to experience and something many people are reluctant to admit to experiencing. There are many negative terms and ideas associated with mental illness.

1. Make a list of all the negative terms and phrases associated with mental illness (e.g. 'nutter') that you can think of.

2. Which of these terms do people use in your school, college or local area?

3. What impact do you think these terms might have on a person whom they are used against?

Case study

Finn is 6 years of age. His teachers are worried about his behaviour. Finn seems to have a lot of difficulty concentrating and doing what he is asked to do in class. He frequently starts fights with other children and has broken a classroom window. Finn's parents have recently divorced and have also been struggling to control his behaviour. Finn's mum recently reported him missing to the police when he left the house at 10 o'clock at night. The police found him riding his bike around a deserted local shopping centre. Finn has told his teacher that he is 'upset' and 'scared' sometimes and that he doesn't like being at school. He would rather stay at home or be with his dad at work.

1. What factors might explain Finn's behavioural problems?

2. How might Finn's behaviour be linked to his emotional needs?

3. What effect might Finn's behaviour have on his personal development?

Water and sanitation

Access to clean water and sanitation are basic requirements for physical health. Every year millions of people, often small children, die from infections that cause diarrhoea. The micro-organisms responsible typically spread in water contaminated by human faeces. Contamination of rivers, lakes and other sources of drinking water is less of a problem in developed countries that have sanitation systems designed to remove, process and separate sewage and industrial waste from drinking water.

Activity

Go to the Unicef website (http://www.unicef.org/wash/) and find out about the connections between ill health and water, sanitation and hygiene in less developed countries. Produce a leaflet or poster explaining the connections between unclean water, poor sanitation and ill health.

Pollution

Pollution can remain in the environment for a long time, causing health problems for whole populations for many years. Factories and cars that produce carbon-based fumes are common sources of air pollution. Often we only think about the smoke and fumes that we can see in the environment. However, other air pollutants are less visible. For example, 'acid rain' is ordinary rainwater that has become acidic because it picks up residues of sulphur and nitrogen oxides that are produced by cars, power stations and other factories, often great distances away from where the rain falls. Acid rain is thought to make respiratory problems, such as asthma, worse because it irritates surface membranes in the lungs.

Noise pollution occurs when human or machine-made sound disrupts the activity or balance of a person's everyday life. Transport systems, particularly cars, aeroplanes and trains are the main source of noise pollution. People who live in densely populated residential areas may also experience noise pollution, especially if they live near to industrial buildings. Noise pollution can lower the quality of life of those people who are exposed to it. Chronic exposure to excessive noise is linked to tinnitus (a constant ringing in the ears), increased stress levels, disturbed sleep patterns and hearing loss.

 Case study

Mr and Mrs Egbola both visit their GP on a weekly basis. They have been complaining of physical health problems, stress and sleep deprivation for the last 6 months. Their GP has told them that they both have high blood pressure, that Mr Egbola is becoming depressed and that they both need to get more sleep at night. They currently manage about 4 hours each. The reason for their lack of sleep, and the beginning of their health problems, can be traced back to the day a group of students moved in to the house next door to them. Every night the students play loud music into the early hours of the morning and regularly have noisy parties. During the day one of the students practises on his drum kit. Despite asking them to be quieter and to stop playing music late at night, the Egbolas have been unable to persuade the students to reduce the noise.

1. What impact is noise pollution having on the quality of Mr and Mrs Egbola's life?

2. Describe how the Egbolas' health is being affected by noise.

3. Write a letter to the local council's 'Noise Pollution Team', complaining about the situation and its effects on the Egbolas' health and asking for help in stopping the noise.

 Topic check

1. Identify four different physical factors that affect health and wellbeing.
2. How can genetic inheritance affect an individual's health and needs?
3. Name one inherited disorder that results from a recessive gene defect.
4. Describe how one form of disability can affect an individual's needs.
5. Give an example of an acute illness and explain how it might affect an individual's health and needs.
6. Explain the links between gender and health experience.
7. Explain how pollution and lack of sanitation can cause health problems.

▶ Getting started

This topic introduces you to examples of lifestyle factors that affect the health and needs of individuals. When you have completed this topic, you should:

- be able to identify a range of lifestyle factors that influence health and needs
- know how different lifestyle factors can affect an individual's health and needs.

Key terms

Balanced diet: a diet that contains adequate amounts of all the nutrients needed for growth and activity

Cholesterol: a fat-like substance that is made by the body and carried in the blood but which also occurs in meat, diary products and some fish

Coronary heart disease: blockage of the arteries that provide the heart with blood

Excreted: eliminated from the body

Lifestyle: a person's chosen way of life

Obesity: a condition in which a person is very overweight

Placenta: the organ that delivers oxygen and nutrients from the mother to the foetus

Self-esteem: how you feel about yourself

Lifestyle, health and needs

An individual's typical way of life, or lifestyle, involves them making choices about health-related issues like personal hygiene, diet and exercise. Lifestyle choices can have a significant impact on an individual's health and needs.

Personal hygiene

Good personal hygiene contributes to the maintenance of physical health as well as to social and emotional wellbeing. Being clean helps to keep the human body in good condition because it prevents the growth of bacteria, viruses and fungi that live on and feed off unclean skin. A person who fails to maintain good personal hygiene may develop skin conditions such as sores and rashes.

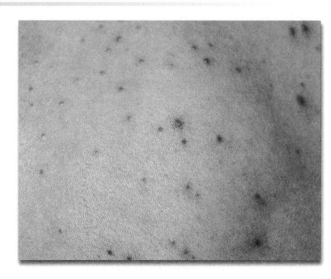

The body conditions that help bacteria and fungi to grow are:

▶ moisture from sweat

▶ warmth from body heat

▶ food from the dead cells and waste products in sweat.

The areas of the body that need most cleaning are those where sweat is **excreted** – under the arms, the groin area, the feet, the scalp and hair. Failing to take a daily bath or shower or to wash the skin and clean your teeth, results in a build-up of bacteria, dirt and odour. Personal hygiene problems may also have a negative effect on a person's relationships and social life. This is likely to lead to the person feeling rejected, isolated and having low **self-esteem**.

Diet

A healthy diet is essential for physical health and wellbeing. The amount and type of food a person requires is affected by the individual's:

▶ age

▶ gender

▶ body size

▶ height

▶ weight

▶ environment (e.g. whether they live in a cold or a warm country)

▶ level of physical activity.

A healthy, **balanced diet** is needed to meet an individual's physical needs for energy and to support their growth and development. Babies and infants, for example, need the right types of food to help them grow and develop normally, and to prevent them from developing certain illnesses. Children and adolescents also need the right types of food to promote physical growth and to supply energy for their high level of physical activity.

The links between diet, health and ill health are outlined in more detail in Unit 11.

Exercise

Exercise has a positive effect on both physical and mental health, but it is important not to do too much exercise. People are advised to find a balance between physical activity and rest in order to maintain good physical health and a sense of wellbeing. Too much exercise can lead to excessive weight loss and may result in physical damage or chronic injuries, e.g. to joints or ligaments.

The type and level of exercise that an individual can do safely will depend on their age, gender and health status. For example, moderate exercise can be safely undertaken by older and less physically mobile people, including women in the later stages of pregnancy and people with physical disabilities. Younger people who are physically fit can safely undertake more vigorous exercise. Lack of physical exercise can lead to ill health and diseases such as **coronary heart disease**, stroke and **obesity**.

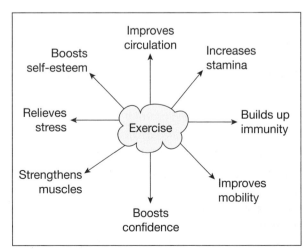

Figure 3.8 The benefits of exercise

Case study

Jack is 14 years old. He lives on a small estate on the edge of town with his parents. Jack plays a lot of computer games on his console. He's also a keen keyboard player, practising for a couple of hours each day. Jack is popular at school, partly because he is very funny. He uses his humour to defend himself when people laugh at his size. Jack is about 3 stones overweight. His parents are concerned about this, although his mum insists he does not over-eat. She believes that lack of exercise has led to his weight problem.

1. What factors might be contributing to Jack being overweight?

2. Why is Jack's weight likely to lead to health problems if he doesn't do something about it?

3. Suggest three ways Jack could increase the amount of exercise he takes each day.

Smoking

Smoking cigarettes, or tobacco in any form, has no health benefits at all. Instead, smoking directly damages an individual's physical health. This is one of the most important pieces of information that health professionals regularly give out to people. Their advice is always to stop smoking. People who don't stop smoking run a high risk of causing themselves long-term health damage and dying as a direct result of their smoking habit. The health problems associated with smoking tobacco include:

▶ coronary heart disease

▶ stroke

▶ high blood pressure

▶ bronchitis

▶ lung cancer

▶ other cancers, such as cancer of the larynx, kidney and bladder.

Smoking cigarettes is harmful to health because the smoke and harmful chemicals that are inhaled circulate deep into the body. These substances include nicotine, carbon monoxide and tar.

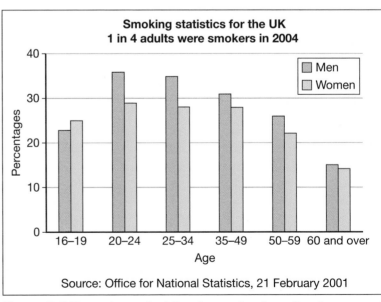

Source: Office for National Statistics, 21 February 2001

Figure 3.9 Percentage of adults who smoke cigarettes: by age and sex, 2004

Figure 3.10 Chemicals in cigarette smoke

Chemical	Effects on the body
Nicotine	• Powerful, fast acting and addictive • Absorbed into bloodstream • Increases heart rate and blood pressure • Causes changes in appetite
Tar	• Damages the cilia (small hairs) lining the lungs that help to protect them from dirt and infection • Damage to cilia results in more infections and smoker's cough • Causes mouth, throat and lung cancers when left as a deposit in the body
Carbon monoxide	• A poisonous gas • Reduces the amount of oxygen carried to a smoker's lungs and tissues • Changes in the blood can cause fat deposits to form on the walls of the arteries, hardening of the arteries and coronary heart disease

Smoking during pregnancy

When women smoke during pregnancy, the ability of the blood to carry oxygen to all parts of the body is reduced. This affects the flow of blood to the **placenta**, which feeds the foetus. Women who smoke during pregnancy have a greater risk of suffering a miscarriage. They also tend to give birth to premature or underweight babies who are more prone to respiratory infections and breathing problems. The risk of cot death among these babies is also increased.

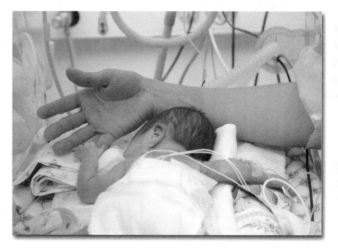

Substance misuse

Substance misuse is a general term that refers to:

▶ taking illegal drugs

▶ misusing prescribed drugs

▶ drinking too much alcohol.

Drug misuse

Legal drugs, such as paracetamol and aspirin, can be obtained from a doctor or bought over the counter at a shop or pharmacy. Drugs like these should be used for medical purposes only. If they are misused they can have damaging and even fatal effects, for example, when they are taken in excessive amounts or are taken with alcohol. Illegal drugs, such as heroin, cannabis, cocaine and ecstasy, can have very damaging effects on health. Drug misuse is now a major cause of health problems and premature death in the UK. Young people are the group most likely to risk their health through drug misuse. In addition to physical and psychological dependence, people who misuse drugs run the risk of taking an overdose which may have sudden, fatal consequences. People who are dependent on drugs often develop physical and mental health problems, and have additional health and care needs.

Alcohol misuse

Alcohol is a very popular, widely available and accepted part of social life in the United Kingdom. Some types of alcoholic drink, such as red wine, have also been shown to be good for health. This is because alcohol protects against the development of coronary heart disease. It also has an effect on the amount of **cholesterol**, or fat, carried in the bloodstream, making it less likely that the clots which cause heart disease will form. Maximum health advantage can be achieved from drinking between one and two units of alcohol a day. There is no additional overall health benefit to be gained from drinking more than two units of alcohol a day. However, there are possible negative effects from doing so.

The health risks associated with alcohol result from consuming it in large quantities, either regularly or in binges. People who frequently drink excess amounts of alcohol have an increased risk of:

▶ high blood pressure

▶ coronary heart disease

▶ liver damage and cirrhosis of the liver

▶ cancer of the mouth and throat

▶ psychological and emotional problems, including depression

▶ obesity.

Health professionals recommend safe limits of alcohol consumption. These recommended limits are based on 'pub measures'. People who drink at home, or buy alcohol from an off licence or supermarket to consume elsewhere, usually pour themselves larger measures of wines and spirits or consume stronger beer than those sold in licensed premises.

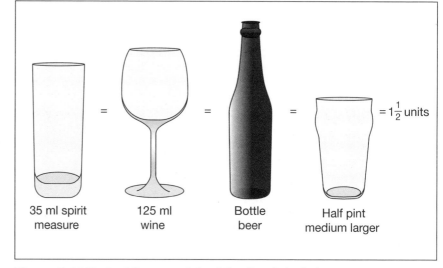

Figure 3.11 Each of these contains 1.5 units of alcohol.

Activity

Using the internet, investigate the health impact of drinking excessive amounts of alcohol. Produce a poster designed to inform 14- to 18-year-old adolescents about the links between alcohol consumption and health problems.

Stress

'Stress' is the feeling of emotional tension, worry or pressure that a person feels when they face a demanding or challenging situation. It has both psychological and physical symptoms.

Prolonged or extreme stress can lead to health problems. It can trigger mental health problems such as depression and anxiety-based illnesses. Stress is also associated with high blood pressure, heart disease and leads some people to misuse drugs and alcohol as a way of coping with their symptoms. Exercise, recreation and leisure activity are more

Case study

Jodie started drinking when she was 14 years of age. She used to drink in her local park with some older teenagers and a couple of her friends. At weekends Jodie drank a couple of bottles of cider and any vodka that was available. Jodie thought that drinking was fun and that it made her happy. She realised when she was 19 years of age that the opposite was true. Jodie found herself thinking about alcohol during work and would go to the pub for a few drinks at lunchtime. Jodie was eventually sacked from her job as a trainee hairdresser for coming to work smelling of alcohol. After making a promise to her mum and dad Jodie hasn't drunk any alcohol for 3 months. They told her about the physical effects that binge drinking and long-term alcohol abuse could have on her health.

1. Suggest some reasons why young teenagers like Jodie start drinking alcohol.

2. Identify four effects of binge drinking or long-term alcohol abuse on physical health.

3. What are the recommended limits (in units) for alcohol consumption that Jodie should stick to if she does start drinking alcohol again?

effective ways of reducing stress levels. Having supportive relationships and satisfying work also helps. Increasingly, people use sports activities to help them to relax and de-stress. Massage, talking to others about problems and feelings, thinking positively and being assertive (saying 'no' to extra work!) are all good ways of reducing stress levels.

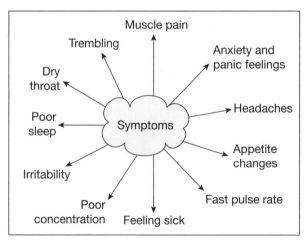

Figure 3.12 Symptoms of stress

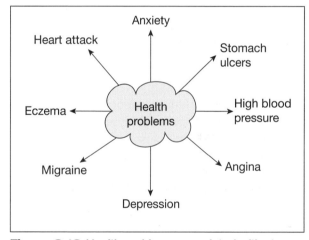

Figure 3.13 Health problems associated with stress

Case study

Neville is a 37-year-old plumber. He wants to retire as a rich, happy man when he is 50. Neville runs his own plumbing company, working between 60 and 80 hours every week. He is feeling under a lot of pressure at the moment. Neville has complained to his wife that he has had a headache for a week, feels faint at times and is having trouble sleeping. Neville will not go and see his GP as he says he is too busy. His wife is trying to persuade him to take a holiday, but he is reluctant to do so because of the amount of work he has to do.

1. What symptoms of stress does Neville have?

2. What might be causing Neville's current stress problems?

3. Explain what might happen to Neville's health and wellbeing if he continues to experience high stress levels.

4. What could Neville do to reduce his high stress levels?

Working pattern

If you want to live a healthy life, it is important to have a balance between work and non-work activity. Some people live for their work and can't think of a better way to spend their time. For many people, work is an important source of self-esteem and status. Work provides a feeling of being successful, of having a purpose and of being useful. However, even though work can be good for health and wellbeing, too much of it and a lack of rest, recreation and social activity can lead to people feeling stressed, being too tired and feeling unsupported and socially isolated.

People who have a poor work–life balance have an increased risk of experiencing high stress levels, physical and mental fatigue, poor emotional wellbeing and relationship breakdown. The high stress levels that result from a poor work–life balance can lead to a range of physical health problems from cardiovascular disease to alcohol misuse.

Sexual practices

An individual who is comfortable with and able to express their sexual orientation freely (e.g. as heterosexual, lesbian, gay or bisexual) will tend to have a better sense of self-worth, more personal confidence and higher self-esteem than a person who is ashamed of, confused or anxious about this aspect of their identity. People who do have concerns and worries about their sexual orientation may be more at risk of experiencing anxiety and depression and may lack the confidence required to form and maintain supportive and fulfilling personal relationships.

Social and community networks

Involvement in the life and activities of a local community is likely to have a positive effect on an individual's emotional and social wellbeing. Community involvement enables a person to develop a sense of belonging and identity, and also provides them with a social network in which friendships can develop and support can be found. A person who is involved with their local community will experience the mental health benefits of social inclusion. An individual who is not involved and lacks connections and support in their local community may become socially isolated and suffer poor emotional and social wellbeing as a result. Social isolation and exclusion are strongly associated with mental distress.

 Over to you!

Identify three occasions when you've felt very stressed. What were your symptoms? What caused your stress? Make a note of these points or discuss them with a colleague in your class.

 Over to you!

What kind of work–life balance do you have? How do you ensure that there is more to your life than school or college work? Are there any changes you could make to improve your work–life balance?

Case study

George (42), Helena (39) and their daughter Ruby (3) moved to live in a small village in mid-Wales 2 years ago. George had always wanted to move to the countryside so that he could grow vegetables, keep chickens and enjoy the fresh air and wide open spaces that London lacks. Helena had never been to Wales before they moved. Since arriving she has found it very hard to make friends and still feels unsettled. George, on the other hand, is now a member of the parish council, goes to the local pub quiz every week and is the main spokesperson for a group campaigning against a dual carriageway being built next to the village. George is well known and popular in the village. He is very happy living there and believes moving from London was a really good thing to do. He is aware that Helena disagrees and would like to 'go home', as she puts it.

1. How has moving from London affected George and Helena's emotional wellbeing?

2. What effect might a lack of community involvement be having on Helena?

3. Suggest some ways in which Helena and Ruby might become more involved in the life of the local community.

Topic check

1 Identify five different lifestyle factors that can affect an individual's health.

2 Describe how personal hygiene can affect a person's physical health.

3 What type of diet is needed to meet an individual's physical growth and development needs?

4 What are the main health benefits of exercise?

5 Explain how smoking, alcohol or drug misuse can have a damaging effect on an individual's health.

6 Describe the connections between stress and a person's work–life balance.

7 What effects can a person's social and community networks have on their health and wellbeing?

Socio-economic factors influencing health and needs

▶ Getting started

This topic introduces you to examples of socio-economic factors that affect the health and needs of individuals. When you have completed this topic, you should:

- be able to identify a range of socio-economic factors that influence health and needs
- know how different socio-economic factors can affect an individual's health and needs.

🔑 Key terms

Economic: money related

Income: the amount of money people receive from work, welfare benefits or other sources

Peer group: a group of people of about the same age who see themselves as belonging together in some way

Primary socialisation: the process through which children learn the 'norms' or expectations of society

Registrar-General: the government official responsible

for the registration of births, marriages and deaths in England and Wales

Secondary socialisation: involves learning skills and attitudes outside of the family, usually through education, work and friendship experiences

Social class: a group of people who are similar in terms of their wealth, income and job

Socio-economic: a combination of social and economic factors

What are socio-economic factors?

Socio-economic factors are a combination of social and economic factors that affect a person's living circumstances (see Figure 3.14).

Socio-economic factors influence an individual's personal development as well as their health experiences. There are close links between socio-economic factors and an individual's mental health and social wellbeing in particular.

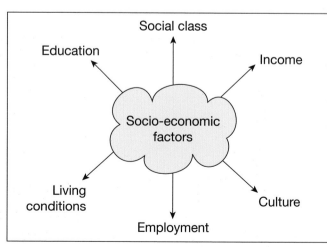

Figure 3.14 Socio-economic factors

Social class

There are a number of different ways of identifying social classes in British society. These include:

▶ A three-class scale consisting of upper, middle and working-class groups is a popular but inaccurate way of defining a person's **social class**. It is not used in official statistics or by health and social care professionals to define a person's social class.

▶ Until 2001 the **Registrar-General's** scale used the job of the head of the household a person lived in to define their social class. The scale consisted of six social classes (see Figure 3.15) and was used to compile statistics on social class.

▶ The NS-SEC (National Statistics – Socio-economic Classification) scale is now the official way of defining social class in Britain. It is based around eight classes (see Figure 3.16), with more middle-class groups than the Registrar-General's scale.

Figure 3.15 The Registrar-General's Social Class Scale

Social class	Types of occupation
Class 1 – Professional occupations	Lawyers, doctors
Class 2 – Intermediate occupations	Social workers, managers, shopkeepers
Class 3N – Skilled, non-manual occupations	Clerks, police officers, nurses
Class 3M – Skilled, manual occupations	Electricians, coal miners
Class 4 – Partly skilled occupations	Nursing assistants, farm workers, bus drivers
Class 5 – Unskilled	Porters, cleaners

Figure 3.16 The NS-SEC

Social class	Types of jobs included
Higher managerial and professional occupations	Doctors, lawyers, dentists, professors, professional engineers
Lower managerial and professional occupations	School teachers, nurses, journalists, actors, police sergeants
Intermediate occupations	Airline cabin crew, secretaries, photographers, firefighters, auxiliary nurses
Small employers and own account workers	Self-employed builders, hairdressers, fishermen, car dealers and shop owners
Lower supervisory and technical occupations	Train drivers, employed craftsmen, foremen, supervisors
Semi-routine occupations	Shop assistants, postal workers, security guards
Routine occupations	Bus drivers, waitresses, cleaners, car park attendants, refuse collectors
Never worked or long-term unemployed	Students, people not classifiable, occupations not stated

Research data shows that social class has a very strong influence on a person's life chances and health experience. The data shows that the lower a person's social class position the more likely they are to:

▶ die prematurely compared with people in higher social classes

▶ experience chronic illness than their counterparts in higher social classes.

The lifestyles, living conditions and stress levels of people in the lower social classes may partly explain their relatively poor health experiences. A lifestyle that includes a poor diet, lack of exercise and smoking, for example, is likely to lead to more health problems. Similarly, living in overcrowded, cold and damp housing and having more money worries, job insecurities and concerns about crime increase a lower-class, low-income family's risk of health problems. In contrast, more affluent families who make up the higher social classes generally have more money to spend on non-essential items such as stress-relieving holidays, gym memberships and better quality food that promote health and wellbeing.

Employment

Work and health experiences are closely linked. For example, a person's health affects their ability to get work and to keep it. People who experience poor health, especially chronic disorders or disabling conditions, often find they are unable to work. However, work can also be good for mental health and social wellbeing because it provides people with:

▶ a sense of purpose and identity ('What do you do?')

▶ self-reliance

▶ self-esteem and a sense of self-worth

▶ social relationships.

 Over to you!

What types of job do you think would be:
a) good for a person's sense of wellbeing
b) bad for health and wellbeing?
List five jobs in each category.
Compare your ideas with those of a class colleague and explain your reasons for choosing the jobs in each of your lists.

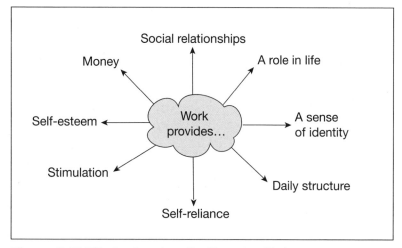

Figure 3.17 Effects of work on health and wellbeing

Employment meets a person's needs in a number of ways. For example, it provides:

▶ money to meet basic food and shelter needs

▶ intellectual stimulation and satisfaction

▶ social relationships and a sense of identity

▶ physical activity and exercise (depending on the type of work).

Some types of work can also be a risk to health and wellbeing because they are dangerous, involve long hours and cause high levels of stress as a result of demanding workloads, workplace bullying and poor working conditions.

Culture

A person's cultural background has a wide-ranging influence on their way of life and the health-related decisions they make. A person's diet, relationships, attitudes to alcohol, drug use, exercise and education are all influenced by the cultural beliefs and practices they have been exposed to while growing up. As the UK is a multicultural society in which many different ethnic groups co-exist, it is important to learn about and understand different cultures in order to appreciate the varying lifestyles of people who use health and social care services.

Living conditions

A person's housing provides them with physical shelter and protection. The quality of a person's living conditions, whether they are warm, dry, spacious and comfortable, for example, influence quality of life and may affect physical health. The place where a person lives and spends most of their time is also more than just somewhere to stay and keep warm and dry. A person's 'home' provides them with a sense of emotional wellbeing and psychological security.

Poor living conditions can have a direct effect on a person's physical health. For example, lack of adequate heating, dampness and overcrowding can lead to respiratory disorders (asthma, bronchitis), stress and mental health problems. Lack of basic amenities (e.g. a shower or bath), sharing facilities (e.g. kitchen or bathroom) between too many people, and cold or unsafe buildings make some homes unfit to live in.

Activity

Investigate the cultural beliefs, practices and lifestyle of an ethnic group other than your own. Use your findings to create a poster or leaflet about cultural influences on health, needs and wellbeing.

Lack of security, too much noise and lack of privacy can also lead to high stress levels and loss of wellbeing. Overcrowding encourages the spread of infection and infectious diseases such as tuberculosis and dysentery. Children who live in overcrowded homes are more likely to be victims of accidents. Sleeplessness and stress are also associated with overcrowding.

Case study

Courtney is 3 years old. She lives with her mum in a bedsit flat on the edge of a large city. Courtney's mum is very caring and spends all of her time looking after her daughter. The flat where they live is cold and damp. A lot of traffic passes directly in front of the flat and there are few places where Courtney can play outside in the local area. As a result, Courtney doesn't go out very often. She also gets colds and chest infections quite often and is underweight for her age. Courtney's mum has very little money to spend on food, heating or clothes as she is unemployed and claiming benefits. She has recently applied to the council for a change of flat, as she believes that her current housing conditions are harming Courtney's health and development.

1. Identify two features of the bedsit flat in the case study that may have a negative effect on health.

2. Describe two modifications to the bedsit flat that would be beneficial for Courtney's health.

Over to you!

What are good living conditions? Identify the features you feel are important in making a person's living conditions 'healthy'. Alternatively, identify the negative features that you would want to avoid if you were looking for somewhere to live. Explain, in terms of their effect on health and wellbeing, why you would try to avoid poor living conditions.

Income

The amount of money that people earn affects their lifestyle and their opportunities. People need enough money to afford the basic necessities of life, such as food, housing and clothing, which directly affect physical health. When people have paid for essential items, they can spend the rest of their **income** on things they want but which aren't essential. People with more money generally have better housing, can afford to eat better quality food and have disposable income to spend on things they want.

People who have a good income are also less likely to worry about being able to cope with everyday life. They don't experience the same stresses as people who are worried about paying their rent or feeding their children, for example. Having a good income allows people to buy luxuries such as holidays, cars, electrical goods and other desirable things.

Income has an effect on self-esteem, as money is highly valued in Western societies. People with lots of money are often seen in a positive way. Being rich and successful is seen as desirable.

Education

In the UK, most children go to school between the ages of 5 and 16 years to receive their formal education. Education meets a person's intellectual needs and promotes intellectual development because it is about learning. When education improves a person's knowledge and thinking skills it enables them to live a healthier, more productive life. Education also has a powerful effect on a person's social and emotional development. Educational experiences are part of what is known as **secondary socialisation**. This is when friends, **peer group** (people of the same age and social group) and teachers influence the attitudes, values and ways in which we behave. This builds on the **primary socialisation** that has already occurred within the family (see Unit 8 for more on this).

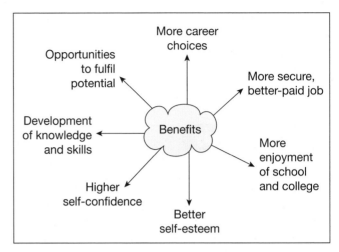

Figure 3.18 The benefits of a good education

Over to you!

1. Identify what you think are the basic necessities of life by completing this checklist.
2. Do you think that any 'basic necessities' are missing from this list? If so, what are they?
3. How much money would a person need (each week, month and year) to afford your list of basic necessities?

Figure 3.19 Basic necessities checklist

Heating	
An indoor toilet	
Satellite TV	
A damp-free home	
A washing machine	
A bath or shower	
A foreign holiday	
Beds for everyone	
A mobile phone	
Money for public transport	
Toys for children	
A warm, waterproof coat	
A refrigerator	
Access to a personal computer	
Carpets	
Three meals a day	
A bedroom for each child	
Two pairs of all weather shoes	
Party celebrations	
A roast dinner once a week	

Some people learn a lot at school, succeed at exams and see education as a positive influence on their personal development. Educational success is very good for the self-esteem and self-image of these people. However, not everybody enjoys school and not everybody succeeds. Failure and bad experiences at school can lead some people to develop a negative self-image and low self-esteem.

Case study

Ffion Roberts is 11 years old. She lives in a small village in North Wales with her parents and two younger brothers Tom, aged 8, and Geraint, aged 6. Ffion is about to finish at Wylfa Primary School and move to Glan Aber Comprehensive School in September. She knows everyone at Wylfa as all the children come from the village where she lives. Her teachers have all been at the school since she started. Ffion doesn't want to leave her primary school and admits to being scared of going to 'the big school', as she calls it. Ffion's best friend Rhian, who goes to

swimming club and church with her, will be going to a different school in September.

1. How does going to school help children like Ffion to develop social skills?

2. What type of help and support might Ffion need as she moves from primary to secondary school?

3. If you were one of Ffion's parents, what would you tell her about the likely impact of changing school on her friendship with Rhian?

Assessment activity 3.2 (P3)

Following up their initial research into the everyday needs of people in your local area, the government's health improvement agency has asked you to:

- Prepare a range of questions about health and lifestyles and create a questionnaire to assess the health and wellbeing of an individual.

- Obtain the consent (permission) of a person

(aged 16+) who is willing to complete your questionnaire.

- Carry out your questionnaire and produce a summary of the person's responses that describes:

a) positive aspects of the person's health, lifestyle and wellbeing

b) areas of the person's health, lifestyle and wellbeing that could be improved.

Topic check

1 Identify four different socio-economic factors that affect an individual's health, needs and wellbeing.

2 What effect is a person's social class likely to have on their health?

3 Name one positive and one negative effect that work can have on a person's health or wellbeing.

4 How can a person's cultural background affect their health, needs and wellbeing?

5 Describe the effect that poor living conditions can have on health and wellbeing.

6 How can education have a positive impact on health and personal development?

▶ Getting started

This topic focuses on ways of assessing an individual's health and care needs. When you have completed this topic, you should:

■ know about the main principles used to assess and plan services for people with care needs

■ understand and be able to describe the care planning cycle

■ be able to explain how health assessment information can be obtained.

🔑 Key terms

Care plan: a document that identifies how the needs of an individual will be met by care workers

Confidentiality: protection of personal information so that it is only known to those authorised to access it

Evaluate: make a judgement about

Holistic assessment: an assessment relating to the 'whole' person, which covers their PIES needs in full (see page 44)

Implementation: putting into practice or action

Individualised care: care that is planned and delivered to meet the specific needs of a particular person

Assessing needs

A full, **holistic assessment** of an individual's care needs and health status should take into account their physical, intellectual, emotional and social needs. This should also take into account any health needs arising from long-term health conditions such as asthma and diabetes. An assessment of needs should result in a written **care plan** for the individual. Care workers who assess individual's needs and health status should be aware of a number of important principles related to care planning.

Principles of care planning

Individual's who have health or care needs should be provided with **individualised care** based on a holistic assessment of their needs.

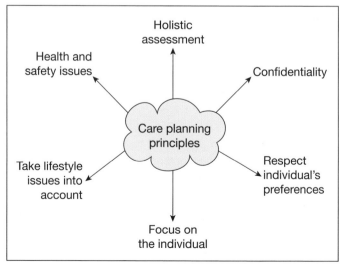

Figure 3.20 Principles of care planning

Care plans should be designed specifically to meet the individual's needs in a way that takes into account the person's wishes and preferences.

Providing individualised care involves a very different approach to practice from task-focused care work. A task-focused approach may involve making sure that everybody in a care home or hospital ward is washed, dressed and taken to the toilet before breakfast, for example. This can be impersonal, feel like 'production line' care and fails to take each individual's particular needs into account. A care worker using an individualised care approach would find out about each individual's particular needs, strengths and abilities and would then provide help and support when individuals want and need it.

Individualised care places the individual at the centre of the care planning process (see Figure 3.23). Care workers who assess individual's needs should know that they need to take a person's age and lifestyle into account when assessing their needs and planning care with them. This is because an individual's needs are closely linked to their stage of development (see Topic 3.2 for more on this) and the skills and abilities they have. Lifestyle factors, such as the person's diet, whether they exercise and whether they smoke, also affect health status and care needs. A skilled care worker should be able to use and apply the principles of planning care each time they assess an individual's needs.

Activity

In each of the following situations, identify:
- the type of care needs being addressed
- whether an individualised or task-focused approach is being used.

1. Maureen, aged 78, is woken and taken to the toilet at 6.30 a.m. because it is 'toileting time' on the ward.
2. Henry, aged 75, is asked whether he would like to choose some books to read or some music to listen to at the day centre.
3. All of the children as Snowdrop Nursery are taken to the toilet at 10.30 a.m., after the morning snack and drink.
4. The nurses on Edgar ward for older people record the date and time when each patient has a bath. They always ensure that everyone has a bath at least once every 48 hours.
5. Julia, a home care worker, always tells her client, Mr Jackson, what he has in the fridge so that he can choose the kind of meal he would like her to make for him.

Carrying out an assessment

The individual with care needs should always be at the centre of the assessment process. As a result the care worker will usually:

▶ talk and listen to the person to get information about their basic needs, wishes and preferences

▶ talk to the person's partner, relatives, other care workers who also understand the person's needs

▶ read any notes or reports about the person's previous treatment or contact with care services

▶ observe the person to identify their skills and abilities

▶ carry out basic physical and physiological tests, such as blood pressure and pulse rate, to assess aspects of their health status.

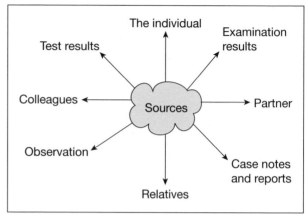

Figure 3.21 Sources of care planning information

Figure 3.22 Ways of assessing needs

Method	What does the care worker do?
Asking questions	Asks questions about lifestyle (diet, exercise, smoking, drug use, hobbies and interests), current health, social or emotional problems
Questionnaires	Helps the individual to complete questionnaires that may be about health-related matters such as the person's medical history, pain levels, current thoughts and mood or recent symptoms
Personal history	Asks questions and records information about the person's background (age, place of birth, current address, occupation, marital status) and their medical history (current and previous treatment, operations, medication)
Physical measurements	Measures and records height, weight and body mass index (BMI), for example
Physiological measurements	Measures and records peak flow, respiration rate on exertion, blood pressure and pulse rate, for example
Observations	Observes the person's abilities (mobility, dexterity, self-care skills), communication skills, physical appearance, breathing rate, behaviour, anxiety level and mood, for example

Activity

Create a care planning assessment form that could be used to collect information on an individual's medical history and current state of health and wellbeing.

• You should write a series of questions that a care worker could ask, and create a form that allows them to fill in the patient's responses.

• Your form should provide enough information for the care worker to then write a care plan for the patient.

• When you have written your form, compare the areas you have covered and the questions you ask with those of a class colleague.

Confidentiality

Whenever personal or sensitive information about an individual is being sought or shared, care workers should respect **confidentiality**. This is not the same as keeping information secret. It is about sharing and storing information about people who use care services in ways that are appropriate to the individual's care needs. Confidential information is often shared between care workers because people working as a care team need to know about and use it when providing care. However, it is not acceptable to reveal an individual's personal details or to comment freely on their care and treatment to people not directly involved in their care without first obtaining the person's permission to do so.

The care planning cycle

An assessment of needs should lead to a written care plan. Although everyone has different and particular care needs (even when they have similar health problems), the process for assessing those needs and for ensuring that the plan of care continues to meet them is the same (see Figure 3.23).

The stages of the care planning cycle are closely linked, with one leading directly on to the next, in sequence. The assessment information that the care worker obtains first is used to identify the individual's care needs. The next step is for the care worker, in partnership with the individual, to identify:

▶ the most appropriate ways of meeting the person's care needs

▶ goals or targets for the person to achieve

▶ timescales (short, medium and long term) in which to achieve the goals.

Figure 3.23 The care planning cycle

The goals or targets in the care plan must be SMART, that is:

Specific   clearly stated and focused on the person's particular needs

Measurable   there must be a measurable outcome

Achievable   realistic and possible for the individual to achieve

Relevant   appropriate to the individual's needs

Timed   achievable in a realistic period of time.

Care workers should always consult and follow individualised care plans when giving care to people. This ensures that each person receives care that is designed to meet their particular needs. Each of the goals or targets in a care plan should have a review date. When this date arrives, care workers and the person receiving the care **evaluate**:

▶ whether the goal has been achieved

▶ if the goal has not been achieved, how much progress has been made

▶ the effectiveness of the care interventions provided so far

▶ whether different forms of care need to be provided.

The individual's care plan may need to be revised and even rewritten following a review. Alternatively, once short-term goals have been achieved, the person may continue with the plan to try and achieve medium- and long-term goals.

Figure 3.24 The main stages of the care planning cycle

Stage	What happens
Assessment	The individual's abilities and needs should be assessed in a holistic way. For example, assessment should cover the person's ability to mobilise, use toilet facilities, wash, communicate, hobbies and interests and their ability to socialise with others.
Goal setting	Short-, medium- and long-term goals relating to the person's needs are set for the individual to achieve. Forms of care provision linked to the goals are also identified.
Implementation	This is the stage when care is actually provided by carrying out the activities and instructions contained in the care plan.
Review	The individual's progress in meeting their goals is assessed and the effectiveness of the different forms of care provision are evaluated on a regular basis. Short-, medium- and long-term goals are reviewed and evaluated at specific times. The person's care plan should be revised and updated following a review to ensure that their care is appropriate, in line with their preferences, and meets health and safety requirements.

Case study

Gwen Griffiths is 16 years of age. She eats a diet that is high in fat and sugar, smokes ten cigarettes a day, binge drinks cider at the weekend and is also 2 stones overweight. Gwen has recently been diagnosed with Type 2 diabetes. She now has an appointment with the practice nurse at her health centre. In a phone call, the practice nurse explained that she will ask Gwen a range of assessment questions to identify her care needs, set some health improvement targets and talk to her about ways of maintaining her health.

1. What kind of care needs do you think Gwen has?

2. How might meeting these needs improve Gwen's health?

3. Suggest a short-term, medium-term and long-term goal that could be part of Gwen's care plan.

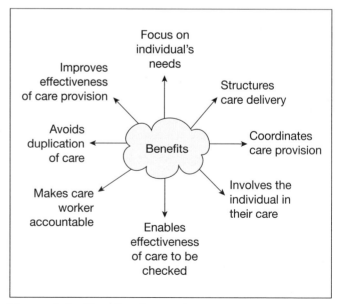

Figure 3.25 Benefits of care plans

Over to you!

Develop a simple but realistic plan for improving your own personal health and wellbeing by completing each of the following tasks:

1. Collect information about the health-related aspects of your lifestyle and record as many of your basic physical indicators of health as you can. You may want to produce a diary for the first part of this task and get some help in doing the second part.

2. Compare your personal results to those recommended for someone of your age and physical characteristics.

3. Identify those aspects of your health you need to improve and set yourself a couple of short-, medium- and long-term targets.

4. Identify ways of working towards and reaching your targets.

It is important to view health improvement as a gradual process that needs to be worked at. Sudden changes in weight, fitness or behaviour are unlikely to be maintained. If you need to develop a health improvement plan for another person, remember to take their age and physical characteristics into account when conducting the health assessment. You will also need to ensure that the person agrees with the health improvement targets and is personally motivated to achieve them. If not, they will never reach them.

Assessment activity 3.3 (P1, P4, M1, D1)

Using the information you obtained in Assessment activity 3.2:

- Produce a health improvement plan for the person who completed your questionnaire.

- Explain how the plan meets the person's health and wellbeing needs.

- Justify how the plan takes into account the person's circumstances and preferences.

You should present your plan and the justification in the form of a report.

Topic check

1 What is a holistic assessment?
2 Explain how task-focused care differs from individualised care.
3 Identify three different methods a care worker can use to assess an individual's care needs.
4 Describe the main stages of the care planning cycle.
5 Explain why care planning goals should be SMART.
6 What does care plan evaluation involve?

Assessment summary

The overall grade you achieve for this unit depends on how well you meet the grading criteria set out at the start of the chapter (see page 43). You must complete:

- all of the P criteria to achieve a **pass** grade
- all of the P and the M criteria to achieve a **merit** grade
- all of the P, M and D criteria to achieve a **distinction** grade.

Your tutor will assess the assessment activities that you complete for this unit. The work you produce should provide evidence which demonstrates that you have achieved each of the assessment criteria. The table below identifies what you need to demonstrate to meet each of the pass, merit and distinction criteria for this unit. You should always check and self-assess your work before you submit your assignments for marking.

Remember that you MUST provide evidence for all of the P criteria to pass the unit.

Grading criteria	You need to demonstrate that you can:	Have you got the evidence?
P1	Outline the everyday needs of individuals	
P2	Explain factors which affect the everyday needs of individuals	
P3	Carry out an assessment of the health and wellbeing of an individual	
P4	Produce a plan for improving the health and wellbeing of an individual	
M1	Explain how the plan meets the health and wellbeing needs of the individual	
D1	Justify how the plan takes into account the individual's circumstances and preferences	

Always ask your tutor to explain any assignment tasks or assessment criteria that you don't fully understand. Being clear about the task before you begin gives you the best chance of succeeding. Good luck with your Unit 3 assessment work!

4 Ensuring safe environments in health and social care

Unit outline

Safeguarding and health and safety issues within the care environment should be a high priority for everyone who works in a care setting. This unit introduces you to safeguarding and health and safety issues in the care environment. It looks at the reasons why people who use care services can require safeguarding, and at the range of health and safety hazards that can be present within a care environment. The safeguarding and health and safety laws and guidelines that apply within the health and social care sectors will also be introduced and explained.

Learning outcomes

1. **Know potential hazards in health and social care environments.**
2. **Know the main principles of health and safety legislation applied to health and social care environments.**
3. **Understand risk assessment processes related to health and social care**

Grading guide

To achieve a **pass**, you must show you can:	To achieve a **merit**, you must show you can:	To achieve a **distinction**, you must show you can:
P1 Identify potential hazards that might arise in health and social care environments		
P2 Outline the main features of current health and safety legislation as applied in health and social care		
P3 Explain risk assessment processes in the context of everyday activities in health and social care	**M1** Carry out a risk assessment of an indoor space used for everyday activities	**D1** Discuss possible ways of reducing risk to users of the indoor space

Health, safety and safeguarding

Getting started

This topic introduces you to a range of health and safety hazards that exist in health and social care environments. When you have completed this topic, you should:

- know and be able to describe a range of potential health and safety hazards in care settings
- know the health and safety responsibilities of employers, employees and service users in care settings.

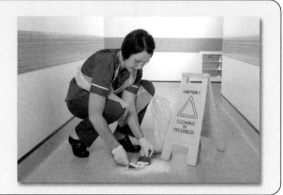

Key terms

Flammable: easily set on fire and capable of burning

Hazard: anything that can cause harm

Noxious: unpleasant and possibly harmful

Perpetrator: a person who carries out a wrongdoing

Pollution: contamination of natural surroundings (including air and water) by poisonous or harmful substances

Risk: the chance of harm being done by a hazard

Safeguard: protect

Hazards in health and social care environments

Health, social care and early years services are provided in a range of care settings. The facilities provided in a care setting should enable care practitioners to provide high-quality care in a safe and effective way. However, care settings are also places that contain **hazards** and potential health and safety **risks**.

Examples of hazards in care settings include:

- *faulty electrical appliances*, overloaded sockets and frayed flexes that can lead to fires, burns and electrical shocks
- *faulty gas appliances and gas leaks* that can cause fires, explosions, breathing difficulties, unconsciousness and asphyxiation
- *water leaks* that can cause accidents and injuries if people slip or trip.

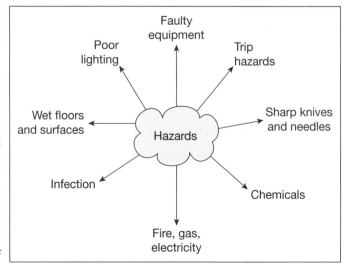

Figure 4.1 Potential hazards in care settings

Environmental hazards

The areas in care settings where health and safety risks are often highest are:

- kitchens
- lounges and bedrooms
- bathrooms
- communal areas such as halls, entrance areas and stairs
- bedrooms
- play areas (inside and outside).

A range of hazards is present in each of these areas. These include:

- *kitchen hazards* such as sharp knives, hot cooking appliances, pot handles sticking out over the edge of a cooker, slippery floors and contaminated food
- *living room and bedroom hazards* such as worn or badly fitted carpets, loose rugs, poorly placed furniture, floor-length curtains, clothes or bed linen left on the floor, trailing flexes, poor lighting, electrical appliances, fires without guards
- *bathroom hazards* such as hot water, wet slippery surfaces and floors, electrical items near water
- *working areas* that are cramped and draughty, with poor lighting
- *stairs* that lack hand rails, are steep or have poorly fitted, loose carpets.

Poor maintenance of buildings, which results in leaking roofs, broken steps, handrails and lifts, or damaged fixtures and fittings, can also make a care setting hazardous to people who are frail and vulnerable or those who are unfamiliar with the environment.

Equipment hazards

Care practitioners use a range of equipment, such as hoists, bath boards, wheelchairs and electronically operated beds, to make their work easier and safer. Personal protective equipment such as aprons, gloves and masks are also examples of health and safety equipment. The equipment used by care practitioners needs to be in good condition and should only be used by people who have received appropriate training. Examples of equipment hazards in care settings include:

- mobility aids that are the wrong size or which do not work properly
- faulty or damaged lifting equipment
- broken, dirty or damaged toys or play equipment
- brakes and hydraulics on beds that do not work properly
- blades and syringe needles that are stored or disposed of incorrectly
- unlabelled, incorrectly labelled or leaking bottles and containers
- old and faulty electrical and gas-fuelled appliances
- excessively full or faulty waste disposal equipment.

Care practitioners should always check the equipment to ensure that it is safe and free of hazards. They should not use equipment which is faulty or which they have not been trained to use. Faulty, unsafe equipment should be reported and removed from the care setting.

Infection hazards

Care workers should always follow basic infection control procedures. People who use care services are vulnerable to infection because of their poor physical health, and can suffer serious complications or additional health problems if they contract an infection. Basic infection control procedures include:

▶ maintaining good standards of personal hygiene (relating to dress, hair care, footwear and oral hygiene)

▶ using personal protective clothing such as aprons, gloves and masks appropriately

▶ following standard health, safety and hygiene precautions in the workplace

▶ washing hands regularly and thoroughly.

 Case study

Audrey has been a volunteer nursery assistant at the Elim Pre-School Group for 2 years. She works at the nursery every Tuesday and brings Buster, her Labrador dog, with her. The children like Buster a lot and spend time patting and stroking him. Buster is very placid, used to children and seems to enjoy padding about in the nursery. Buster is usually very obedient and spends a lot of time sleeping. However, following a visit by an environmental health inspector from the local authority, Audrey has been told not to bring Buster to the nursery any more. She is quite upset about this, as she doesn't understand how Buster could be a health and safety risk.

1. Identify reasons why Buster is a health and safety risk at the nursery.

2. Explain how Buster's presence might lead to food hygiene problems at the nursery.

3. Suggest how health and safety risks can be minimised to allow children to touch and play with pets.

Chemical hazards

A range of potentially hazardous substances are present in care settings. These include cleaning agents, such as disinfectants and detergents, medicines, art and craft materials (e.g. paints, glues and clay) and sterilising fluids. Substances can be hazardous because they are toxic (poisonous), corrosive (burning) or irritants. Hazard symbols (see Figure 4.2) should be printed on bottles, packets and canisters to indicate the kinds of dangers they pose.

Care organisations have to ensure that all hazardous substances are correctly stored and handled (see Topic 4.2).

Figure 4.2 Hazard warnings

Fire hazards

There may be a number of different fire hazards in a care setting, including:

- ▶ faulty electrical and gas appliances, gas leaks and open fires
- ▶ blocked fire exits and escape routes
- ▶ fire alarms that don't work or which people can't hear
- ▶ unsafe, loose or **flammable** furnishings (these must now be fire resistant)
- ▶ people smoking cigarettes, cigars or pipes indoors or using lighters and matches (despite warnings not to!).

Every care setting should have a fire policy, an evacuation procedure and a range of safety features, including marked fire exits, smoke alarms and no smoking signs, to minimise the risk of fire. Care workers usually receive basic fire safety training as part of their induction when they start their job. Fires and gas leaks are very dangerous and, although it is very rare for a hospital or care home to have to evacuate in-patients or residents, all care workers should be prepared for this unlikely possibility.

Personal safety and security hazards

Care settings are typically thought to be safe environments where people are cared for and not harmed. However, because of the threat of intruders and increasing levels of violence and aggression towards care workers, the security of buildings and personnel needs to be taken very seriously. In most care settings security provisions are designed to protect:

- ▶ people
- ▶ property
- ▶ personal details and confidentiality
- ▶ clients from leaving buildings unless it is safe for them to do so.

Care organisations try to prevent security breaches by:

- ▶ developing security policies and procedures
- ▶ training staff to avoid and deal with aggression and violence
- ▶ giving all staff identification badges and personal security alarms to wear
- ▶ using a sign in/out system to record the whereabouts of staff at all times
- ▶ having security guards and receptionists who check the identification of everybody entering a care setting
- ▶ using identity card systems, CCTV monitors and electronic code pads to restrict entry by unauthorised people.

Poor staff training and inadequate security in a care setting puts the health and safety of everybody present at risk. The Health and Safety at Work Act 1974 places a duty on workers to take care of their own security, the security of others and to report security hazards to managers.

Pollution hazards

Pollution in care settings usually involves the release of a substance, such as human sewage or chemicals, into the air or water system. An old or heavily used sewerage system can result in toilets or sinks becoming blocked and overflowing. Similarly, where medical gases, solvents or other **noxious** (poisonous or harmful) substances are used, there should be an adequate monitoring and ventilation system to prevent and deal with any leakages.

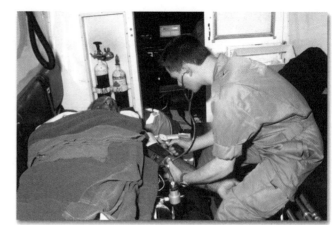
Medical gases can be hazardous as well as helpful.

Abuse and neglect

Some people who use care services are vulnerable to abuse and neglect because of their age (young or old), disability or special care needs. Part of the care worker's role is to protect vulnerable people and to ensure that each individual's best interests are **safeguarded**. A vulnerable person might be at risk of:

▶ physical abuse

▶ sexual abuse

▶ emotional and psychological abuse

▶ financial exploitation

▶ neglect.

Care workers who are poorly trained, unsupervised and overworked, or who lack support from colleagues and managers can become **perpetrators** of neglect and abuse. The risk of abuse and neglect in care settings can be reduced by:

▶ ensuring care standards are monitored

▶ providing regular training and updating

▶ ensuring care workers have enough support to provide good-quality care

▶ developing an easy-to-use complaints system.

Case study

Charlotte Cohen, aged 80, lives in a residential home. Over the last 6 months she has become more confused and has started to wander around the home and going out unexpectedly. The staff now describe Charlotte as 'a bit of a handful' and have asked for an additional member of staff to look after her. In the meantime, the care workers at Charlotte's home have taken to keeping her in her room for most of the day. They do this by wedging the door open and then placing a small table across the opening to stop her from getting out. Charlotte complains loudly about this every morning and tries to remove the table, but eventually gives up. The staff have told her daughter they 'don't have the time' to stay with Charlotte all day and that 'it's for health and safety reasons – at least we know where she is'.

1. Do you think the care workers at Charlotte's residential home are guilty of abuse?

2. What factors have led to this situation occurring?

3. What effects do you think this treatment is likely to have on Charlotte?

Health and safety responsibilities

Employers, employees and service users all have health and safety responsibilities in care settings. Employers are responsible for providing:

▶ a safe and secure work environment

▶ safe equipment

▶ information and training about health, safety and security.

Care organisations (employers) must provide a work environment that meets expected health and safety standards. They must make it possible for care practitioners to work safely and for service users to receive safe care. Employees (care workers) have a responsibility to:

▶ work safely within the care setting

▶ monitor their work environment for health and safety problems that may develop

▶ report and respond appropriately to any health and safety risks.

Both employers and employees have to work within a range of health and safety laws (see Topic 4.2) in order to provide safe care for service users. People who receive care are expected to behave in a reasonable, safe way in order to protect their own health and safety as well as that of others. This means that they must follow all health and safety instructions (e.g. No Smoking!) and abide by the health and safety policies of the care setting.

Assessment activity 4.1 (P1)

You are the health and safety coordinator in a residential care home for older people. The care home manager has asked you to produce a poster identifying potential hazards in the different parts of the care home environment.

You could base your poster on a care home that you are familiar with or create a poster based on a hypothetical care home that has a kitchen, bathrooms, bedrooms, corridors, stairs, garden and a residents' lounge area.

Topic check

1 What is the difference between a 'hazard' and a 'risk'?

2 Describe three types of health and safety hazard that might be found in a care home kitchen.

3 Explain why loose carpets and rugs are a health and safety hazard in a care home for older people.

4 Identify three different fire hazards that could be found in a care setting.

5 Give three examples of unsafe equipment that would present health and safety hazards in a care setting.

6 Identify three different types of hazardous substances that can often be found in care settings.

7 Outline the health and safety responsibilities of employers and employees in a health and social care environment.

Health and safety legislation

> ## ▶ Getting started

This topic introduces you to a range of health and safety laws that apply to health and social care environments. When you have completed this topic, you should:

- know about health and safety laws that apply to care settings
- be able to describe the main principles of these health and safety laws.

🔑 Key terms

Compliance: agreeing to or meeting the requirements of the law

Health and Safety Executive: the government agency responsible for monitoring and enforcing health and safety laws in the workplace

Legislation: written laws, also known as statutes, Acts of Parliament and regulations (e.g. the Health and Safety at Work Act 1974)

Prohibition: a restriction or refusal to approve or agree to something

Risk assessment: the process of evaluating the likelihood of a hazard actually causing harm

Legislation and guidelines

The health and safety responsibilities of employers and employees in health and social care environments result from the wide range of legislation that governs health and safety in workplaces generally. A number of health and safety laws specific to care settings also exist. **Legislation** is necessary to ensure that:

- care is provided through safe working practices
- care practitioners are able to work in a safe environment.

The health and safety laws that apply to care settings are monitored and enforced by the Health and Safety Executive.

The Health and Safety Executive

The **Health and Safety Executive** is the body that monitors standards and enforces health and safety law in the workplace in England, Wales and Scotland. The Health and Safety Executive Northern Ireland has this responsibility in Northern Ireland. The Health and Safety Executive was created by the Health and Safety at Work Act 1974. One of its key tasks is to investigate all accidents in the workplace. The website of the Health and Safety Executive (www.hse.gov.uk) says that, 'Our mission is to prevent death, injury and ill-health in Great Britain's workplaces'.

The Health and Safety Executive can:

▶ enter premises to conduct investigations or carry out spot checks on health and safety

▶ conduct investigations into accidents and safety **compliance**

▶ take samples and photographs to assess health and safety risks

▶ ask questions about health and safety procedures and risk control

▶ give advice on how to minimise risk

▶ issue instructions that must be carried out by law

▶ issue improvement and **prohibition** notices.

The Health and Safety Executive is most likely to visit care settings where:

▶ there is evidence that health and safety is poor

▶ there are hazardous substances that should be properly stored and controlled

▶ a specific incident (e.g. accident, death or illness) has occurred.

The purpose of Health and Safety Executive visits and investigations is to check that standards of workplace health, safety and welfare are satisfactory and to give advice on how risks to people being injured or becoming ill in the workplace can be minimised.

The Health and Safety at Work Act 1974

This is the main piece of health and safety law in the UK. It affects everyone present in a care setting, but focuses mainly on employers and employees. Under this Act, care practitioners share responsibility for health and safety in care settings with the care organisation that employs them (see Topic 4.1 also). To meet their legal responsibilities, care organisations:

▶ carry out health and safety **risk assessments**

▶ develop health and safety procedures, such as fire evacuation procedures

▶ provide health and safety equipment, such as fire extinguishers, fire blankets and first aid boxes

▶ ensure that care settings have safety features, such as smoke alarms, fire exits and security fixtures (e.g. electronic pads on doors and window guards), built in to them

▶ train their employees to follow health and safety procedures and use health and safety equipment and safety features appropriately

▶ provide a range of health and safety information and warning signs to alert people to safety features (e.g. fire exits and first aid equipment) and to warn them (e.g. about prohibited areas and not smoking).

Care practitioners carry out their legal responsibilities by:

▶ developing an awareness of health and safety law

▶ working in ways that follow health and safety guidelines, policies and procedures

▶ monitoring the care environment for health and safety hazards

▶ dealing directly with hazards that present a health and safety risk, where it is safe to do so

▶ reporting health and safety hazards or the failure of safety systems or procedures to a supervisor or manager.

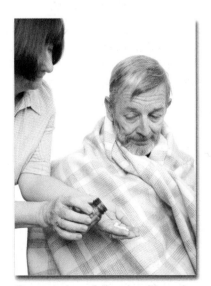

Care workers follow health and safety procedures carefully when dispensing medication.

The Health and Safety at Work Act 1974 enforces minimum standards of workplace health and safety and establishes a framework for safe working.

Food safety legislation

The Food Safety Act 1990 states that people working with food must practise good food hygiene in the workplace. Food provided for people who use services and for visitors must be safely stored and prepared and must not be 'injurious to health'. Local authority environmental health officers enforce this law.

The Food Safety (General Food Hygiene) Regulations 1995, 2005 and 2006 refer to the need to identify possible risks surrounding food hygiene, and to put controls in place to ensure any risk is reduced. These regulations also specify how premises that provide food should be equipped and organised.

Safety training for employees

Infection control

Safe lifting and handling

Good standards of heating and ventilation

The HASWA 1974 requires...

Fire safety training and procedures

Safe disposal of waste

High standards of hygiene

Correct food preparation techniques

Figure 4.3 Health and Safety at Work Act 1974 requires...

Manual handling

The Manual Handling Operations Regulations 1992 cover all manual handling activities, such as lifting, lowering, pushing, pulling or carrying objects or people. A large proportion of workplace injuries are due to poor manual handling skills. Employers have a duty to assess the risk of any activity that involves manual handling. They must put in place measures to reduce or avoid the risk. Employees must follow manual handling procedures and co-operate on all manual handling issues.

Reporting health and safety issues

Care practitioners are expected to report diseases, illnesses and conditions that are infectious or present a significant risk to health, safety or hygiene. The Reporting of Injuries, Diseases and Dangerous Occurrences Regulations (RIDDOR) 1995 say that by law, the following situations must be recorded and reported to the Health and Safety Executive:

▶ death in the workplace

▶ injuries that lead to 3 or more days off sick

▶ a range of infectious diseases and illnesses including malaria, tetanus, typhoid, typhus, measles and salmonella.

 Activity

The Food Standards Agency provides comprehensive and up-to-date information and advice on food hygiene through their eat well website (www.eatwell.gov.uk). You can find out about ways of preventing food poisoning by reading the Germ Watch section of the site.

Environmental problems such as overflowing drains, the presence of hazardous chemicals (including cleaning substances) and gases must also be recorded and reported on.

Health and safety training

The Management of Health and Safety at Work Regulations 1999 places a responsibility on employers to train staff in relation to health and safety legislation, fire prevention and moving and handling issues. They also require employers to carry out risk assessments and to remove or reduce any health and safety hazards identified. Employers must write safe working procedures based on risk assessments carried out.

Chemicals and hazardous substances

The Control of Substances Hazardous to Health (COSHH) Regulations 2002 state that all hazardous substances must be correctly handled and stored to minimise the risks they present. A COSHH file must be kept in each care setting, providing details of:

▶ the hazardous substances that are present

▶ where they are stored

▶ how they should be handled

▶ how any spillage or accident involving them should be dealt with.

The COSHH file should provide details about the health and safety risks and effects of each hazardous substance, as well as information on how to deal with them in an emergency.

Assessment activity 4.2 (P2)

The manager of a day care nursery has decided to improve the training programme for new staff and students who come to the nursery on work placement. She wants to ensure that new staff and students have a good understanding of health and safety law.

• The manager has asked you to research and produce an information booklet that outlines the main principles of health and safety legislation and guidance for health and social care environments.

• You should focus your examples and explanation on how the principles of health and safety legislation might apply to a nursery setting.

Topic check

1 What responsibilities do employers have for health and safety under the Health and Safety at Work Act 1974?

2 Describe the health and safety responsibilities that employees have under the Health and Safety at Work Act 1974.

3 Which organisation is responsible for monitoring and enforcing health and safety law in the care workplace?

4 What responsibilities does the Food safety Act 1990 place on care workers?

5 Identify the types of incidents that must be reported under RIDDOR 1995.

6 Describe the main principles of the COSHH Regulations 2002.

Risk assessment in health and social care environments

Getting started

This topic focuses on the process of risk assessment in health and social care environments. When you have completed this topic, you should:

■ be able to define risk assessment and explain what it involves

■ know the main stages of risk assessment.

CAUTION
CLINICAL WASTE

Key terms

Evaluate: make a judgement about something

Health and safety officer: an employee with the main responsibility for managing issues relating to health and safety at work

Risk assessment: the process of evaluating the likelihood of a hazard actually causing harm

Assessing risk

By law, care organisations are required to carry out formal risk assessments of their care settings. **Risk assessment** aims to identify potential risks to the health, safety and security of care practitioners, people who use care services and visitors to a care setting.

Risk assessment recognises that care activities, equipment and the care setting itself can be hazardous, but that steps can be taken to minimise or remove the level of risk to people. The ultimate aim of a risk assessment is to ensure that people use care settings without coming to any harm. The Health and Safety Executive has identified five stages of a risk assessment. These stages and their purpose are identified in Figure 4.4.

Figure 4.4 The five stages of risk assessment

Stage	Key questions	Purpose
1. Identifying the risk	• What are the hazards?	• To identify all hazards that could cause a risk
2. Estimating the risk	• Who is at risk?	• To **evaluate** the risk of hazards causing harm
3. Controlling the risk	• What needs to be done? • Who needs to do what?	• To identify risk control measures and responsibilities for reducing or removing the risk
4. Monitoring risk control measures	• Are the risk control measures being implemented?	• To monitor the implementation and effectiveness of risk control measures
5. Reassessing the risk	• Is risk controlled? • Can the risk be reduced still further?	• To evaluate the effectiveness of current risk control strategies • To identify new risks or changes to risk levels • To consider new strategies for controlling risk

The Management of Health and Safety at Work Regulations 1999 place a legal duty on employers to carry out risk assessments in order to ensure a safe and healthy workplace. The risk assessments that are produced should clearly identify:

▶ the potential hazards and risks to the health and safety of employees and others in the workplace

▶ any preventive and protective measures that are needed to minimise risk and improve health and safety

Many larger care organisations employ people in **health and safety officer** roles to carry out risk assessments and manage health and safety issues generally. In smaller care organisations this might be the responsibility of one or more of the managers or a senior practitioner.

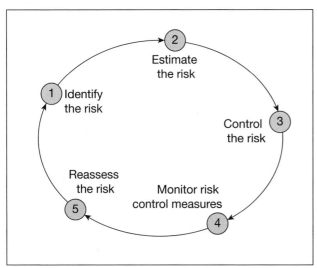

Figure 4.5 Stages of risk assessment

Case study

Kamylah, aged 17, has recently started a work experience placement at the White Horse care project for disabled adults. She is currently shadowing Paula, an experienced care worker. Kamylah has been reading though the health and safety policies and procedures and has spent some time socialising with residents since she started a couple of days ago. She mentioned to Paula that she would now like to get involved in providing care for residents. Paula responded by saying that Kamylah could help her give Colin, one of the residents, a bath this afternoon.

Colin, aged 25, has complex physical and learning disabilities. He is unable to talk but can understand simple speech. Colin is able sit up in the bath but can't get in or out without support. A staff member also has to run the bath, sort out towels, clothes and bathroom equipment. With encouragement Colin is able to wash and dry himself, but needs to be monitored while he is in the bath.

1. What health and safety hazards should Paula and Kamylah bear in mind in this situation?

2. Who is at risk and why in this situation?

3. What needs to be done and who needs to do it to minimise the health and safety risks involved in giving Colin a bath?

Risk assessment by care workers

Care practitioners can also carry out their own ongoing risk assessments in their everyday work. Basically this involves:

▶ being alert to possible hazards

▶ understanding the risks associated with each hazard

▶ reporting any health and safety concerns that are identified.

Risk areas that need to be assessed and planned for by care practitioners as part of their everyday work include risks associated with:

▶ moving and handling people and equipment

▶ hazardous chemicals (such as cleaning fluids, disinfectants and sterilising fluids)

▶ medicines

▶ infection control

▶ personal security.

Care workers need to be aware that the everyday activities they take part in, such as providing personal care, food preparation and eating, as well as leisure activities, all have some degree of risk associated with them. Basic risk assessment skills help care workers to identify and minimise risks in these situations.

Security issues

Care settings should have a range of security measures in place. Some of these relate to procedures for gaining entry to the care setting and moving around within it. Large hospitals and many residential services may only allow access to authorised people and have security staff checking and controlling who is coming in and out of buildings. Care organisations also need to ensure that their buildings are fitted with high-quality security measures. Doors and windows must be adequately secured. Sometimes adjustments to door handles and windows may need to be made. A keypad or card entry system may be used to control access to buildings or to parts of buildings. It is essential that staff members don't loan their entry cards or give the keypad code to other unauthorised people where these systems are used. This may be a disciplinary offence and will compromise security.

Staff should make regular checks of ground-floor windows and doors to ensure that they are safe and secure and that they have not been tampered with or left wedged open. The policies and procedures of care organisations should encourage staff to always report any concerns they have to the senior person about visitors to the care setting, or any apparent attempts to break into the building. Despite security measures, intruders can still be a problem for some care organisations. It is appropriate for care workers to politely challenge any unfamiliar people seen on the premises, and to alert their colleagues to the presence of any suspicious or unexpected person. However, personal safety is important and if a care worker has any serious suspicions or becomes aware of an intruder it is advisable to seek help quickly and call onsite security staff and/or the police.

Activity

Using a scale of 1–5, where 5 is very possible/probable, 4 is possible, 3 is a moderate risk, 2 is a low risk and 1 is the lowest, not very likely risk:

a) identify the main hazard in each of the following situations

b) estimate the risk

c) briefly describe how the risk could be minimised.

1. The playgroup kitchen floor has just been washed and is still wet.

2. A laundry bag half full of dirty linen has been left at the top of the stairs outside a hospital ward.

3. An elderly resident's window has been left wide open to air her room in a nursing home.

4. The scissors have been left out on the craft room table at the learning disability day centre.

5. A workman fitting a new security pad to the front door of the nursery has left the door wide open and unattended while he goes to his van for some tools.

Case study

Look at the picture of Dave's Diner. This is a popular meeting place for young people with learning disabilities who attend a nearby day centre.

1. Carry out a risk assessment of Dave's Diner. Summarise your thoughts in a table using the following headings: Hazards; Risk (1–5); Action to reduce risk; How often should risk be checked?

2. Make some recommendations on the kinds of improvements that should be made to make Dave's Downtown Diner a safe environment.

Assessment activity 4.3 (P3, M1, D1)

Imagine that you are a care worker who has recently completed a health and safety course in which you learnt about the importance of risk assessment. The final part of your course involves putting this learning into action. You need to:

• Explain how and why it is important to carry out risk assessment processes in relation to everyday activities in health or social care.

• Carry out a risk assessment of an indoor space used for everyday activites. Carefully record the information you obtain in a suitable format.

• Discuss possible ways of reducing the risks to users of the indoor space that you have identified.

Topic check

1 Using your own words, explain what a risk assessment involves.

2 Which regulations make carrying out a risk assessment in a care setting a legal requirement?

3 Why is it important to carry out regular risk assessments in care settings?

4 What are the five steps involved in a risk assessment?

5 Who usually carries out risk assessments in health and social care settings?

6 How can a care worker carry out risk assessments as part of their own care practice?

Assessment summary

The overall grade you achieve for this unit depends on how well you meet the grading criteria set out at the start of the chapter (see page 81). You must complete:

■ all of the P criteria to achieve a **pass** grade
■ all of the P and the M criteria to achieve a **merit** grade
■ all of the P, M and D criteria to achieve a **distinction** grade.

Your tutor will assess the assessment activities that you complete for this unit. The work you produce should provide evidence which demonstrates that you have achieved each of the assessment criteria. The table below identifies what you need to demonstrate to meet each of the pass, merit and distinction criteria for this unit. You should always check and self-assess your work before you submit your assignments for marking.

Remember that you MUST provide evidence for all of the P criteria to pass the unit.

Grading criteria	You need to demonstrate that you can:	Have you got the evidence?
P1	Identify potential hazards that might arise in health and social care environments	
P2	Outline the main features of current health and safety legislation as applied in health and social care	
P3	Explain risk assessment processes in the context of everyday activities in health and social care	
M1	Carry out a risk assessment of an indoor space used for everyday activities	
D1	Discuss possible ways of reducing risk to users of the indoor space	

Always ask your tutor to explain any assignment tasks or assessment criteria that you don't understand fully. Being clear about the task before you begin gives you the best chance of succeeding. Good luck with your Unit 4 assessment work!

5 Vocational experience in a health or social care setting

Unit outline

This unit introduces you to the process of applying for, carrying out and reflecting on a practical care work role. You will need to prepare placement application documents, prepare for and take part in an interview and also demonstrate effective interpersonal skills during a period of work experience. This unit enables you to draw on and apply knowledge and understanding from all of the other units in the qualification.

Learning outcomes

1 **Be able to complete the application process for a period of work experience in a health or social care setting.**
2 **Be able to complete a period of work experience in a health or social care setting.**
3 **Be able to demonstrate interpersonal skills in a health or social care setting.**
4 **Be able to reflect upon own performance in a health or social care setting.**

Grading guide

To achieve a **pass**, your evidence must show that you are able to:	To achieve a **merit**, your evidence must show that you are able to:	To achieve a **distinction**, your evidence must show that you are able to:
P1 Complete an appropriate letter of application, with an attached CV, to a local health and social care setting		
P2 Plan appropriately for an interview at your work experience placement	**M1** Demonstrate appropriate interview skills	**D1** Assess the strengths and weaknesses of your interview skills
P3 Carry out a period of work experience, using relevant skills, in a health or social care setting	**M2** Discuss your overall performance during the period of work experience	**D2** Produce an action plan to show how you could have improved your performance
P4 Demonstrate appropriate interpersonal skills in a health or social care setting	**M3** Discuss own interpersonal skills used in a health and social care setting	
P5 Complete a reflective logbook during your period of work experience in a health or social care setting		

Applying for a work placement

Getting started

This topic introduces you to the different methods of applying for a work placement in a health and social care organisation. When you have completed this topic, you should:

- know about different methods of applying for a work placement
- be able to write a letter of application and a CV using **ICT**
- know about the different types of care organisations that offer work placements.

Key terms

Aptitude: a person's potential or natural ability to learn or develop particular skills

Covering letter: a short, concise letter written to accompany other documents

Curriculum vitae (CV): a written summary of a person's academic and work history

ICT: Information and Communications Technology

Private sector care organisations: care businesses or independent practitioners who charge a fee for the care services they provide

Proof read: reading a copy of a written document to check for and correct any errors

Speculatively: with a view to trying something without knowing whether or not you will succeed

Statutory care sector organisations: government run care organisations, including the NHS and local authority care services

Voluntary care sector organisations: not-for-profit organisations that often use volunteers (as well as employed staff) to provide care services

Applying for a work placement

One of the main reasons that students choose to take a BTEC First Health and Social Care course is that it offers an opportunity to experience the real world of care work. For many, this is something to look forward to and the highlight of the course. However, in the same way that all care workers have had to apply for their jobs, BTEC First Health and Social Care students have to understand and follow the application procedures of care organisations in order to obtain a work placement.

Most care organisations require applicants for jobs or work placements to make a written application and then, if selected, to attend an interview. Applicants for a work placement may be asked to write and send:

▶ a letter of application
▶ a **curriculum vitae (CV)**
▶ an application form.

People who work in health and social care settings are very busy. Their main priorities are providing care for people who use services, supporting care workers who provide care and ensuring that care settings are run as smoothly as possible. The working life of care managers and care workers is often quite pressurised and hectic. As a result, the people who receive and read your application for a work placement will expect you to produce concise documents that contain information relevant to your request for a work placement.

Letters of application

Letters of application are often used as a way of applying for a work placement. When writing a letter of application, it is important to:

▶ send the letter to a named person, using their correct title and address

▶ write neatly, clearly and legibly

▶ write in a concise way and include relevant information about yourself

▶ use the right tone, avoiding the use of slang, jokes or demanding language

▶ **proof read** your letter, checking the spelling, punctuation and layout carefully before you send it.

Michelle Crossley
22 Highbury Road
Endsworth
Wiltshire
BA44 8GY

Mrs A Khalid
Sunshire Day Nursery
Holdham Road
Bath
Wiltshire
BA4 9GH

7 October, 2010

Dear Mrs Khalid,

I am writing to find out whether it would be possible to arrange a work experience placement at Sunshine Day Nursery. I have chosen Sunshine Day Nursery because I would like to gain experience working with children aged 3–4. I am currently taking a BTEC First Diploma in Health and Social Care and need to gain 60 hours of work experience from January 2011.

I completed a work placement in a nursery while I was at school and gained a very good report for this. I would like to gain more experience, particularly working with children who have learning disabilities. I know that your nursery has a very good reputation for caring for children with special needs. This is why I feel that I could learn a lot from spending time at Sunshine Day Nursery.

As well as experience of working with children, I also have a current First Aid certificate and recently passed a Food Hygiene certificate. I am used to working hard, am able to work well with other people and have good communication skills. My previous work placement supervisor described me as 'hardworking, enthusiastic and very respectful of children and their parents'. I am a reliable and positive person and would welcome an opportunity to provide you with more details about my background or to talk to you about the possibility of arranging a work placement.

I hope you will consider offering me a work placement at Sunshine Day Nursery and look forward to hearing from you.

Yours sincerely

Michelle Crossley

Figure 5.1 An example of a letter of application

The person to whom you are writing will want to know:

▶ your name, age and contact details

▶ the course you are studying

▶ how a work placement with them is relevant to your course and your career interests

▶ what you consider to be your main skills, **aptitudes** and personal qualities

▶ whether you have any relevant previous experience

▶ whether you have any disabilities, health problems or specific difficulties that may affect you on a work placement

▶ how long you want a work placement for and when (days and times) you would be able to attend.

You will need to think about some of these issues before you write any letters of application. It is also a good idea to practise writing letters of application, as the way you express yourself and make your points will improve the more you do this.

Curriculum vitae (CV)

A person's curriculum vitae (CV) is a concise, chronological record of their work and education history and their achievements, which also outlines key points about them as a person.

Activity

Identify a local care organisation with which you would like to have a work placement. Using the guidance provided in this unit, write a letter to the organisation applying for a work placement. Ask your tutor or a class colleague to read your letter and identify its strengths and weaknesses.

Activity

Write a curriculum vitae for yourself. Try to ensure that you follow the principles outlined above when compiling your CV. You should create and produce your CV using information technology. Ensure that it is easy to follow and contains information relevant to the needs of care employers.

Personal details
Michelle Crossley
22 Highbury Road
Endsworth
Wiltshire
BA44 8GY

Telephone: 01247 333987
Mobile: 0787 866 555
Email: michelle92crossley@hotmail.co.uk

Personal profile
I am a 17-year-old student at Endbury College where I am studying for a BTEC First Health and Social Care qualification. I would like to work with children and young people who have learning disabilities. I am a well organised, hard working and enthusiastic student. I am able to work well with others, always do my best for other people and am a reliable and respectful person.

Qualifications

2009	BTEC First Diploma in Health and Social Care (equivalent to 4 GCSEs) I am studying this qualification at the moment. It includes units on communication, individual rights, individual needs, creative activities, cultural diversity and diet.
	GCSE Mathematics
2008	GCSE English Language (C), GCSE Home Economics (D), GCSE Sociology (C) Food Hygiene certificate First Aid at Work certificate

Work skills
Childcare play and activities: Organising and helping with play activities for pre-school children in Big Ted's Nursery. Comforting children when upset and providing snack-time drinks and biscuits.
Customer service: Answering the telephone, talking with parents and providing information about activities and the children's day.

Work experience

2008	Six-week summer job as nursery assistant at Big Ted's nursery, Endsworth
2008	Two-week work experience placement at Big Ted's nursery, Endsworth
2006 to date	Helping Grandma with household jobs (washing, ironing, cleaning) after she had a stroke.

Interests
I am a junior tennis coach at a local leisure centre. I teach children under 10 basic tennis skills and make their lessons fun. I am also a keen tennis player and have represented my school and a local tennis club in several competitions. I also enjoy going to films and clubs with friends.

Referees
Mrs A Jamieson, Programme Tutor, Endbury College, Edge Lane, Endsworth, Wiltshire, BA44 1QQ

Ms P Lally, Nursery Manager, Big Ted's Nursery, 15 High Street, Endsworth, Wiltshire, BA44 8HP.

Figure 5.2 Example of a CV and covering letter

There are many different ways of setting out a CV, but it is important to ensure that it is:

▶ easy to follow and concise

▶ relevant to the job or work placement

▶ word processed and spell checked

▶ truthful.

Your CV is a way of advertising your strengths, ambitions and achievements. It needs to be well organised and well presented to make a good impression on those who read it. It should be short and focused on relevant information, as most employers and work placement recruiters don't have time to read long, rambling CVs and won't be interested in people who don't seem to have the kind of skills, qualities or experience they are looking for. It is essential that your CV is truthful. Lying about qualifications, previous jobs or other matters is unacceptable and leads to questions about your honesty and trustworthiness. Being found out may well lead to you being told to leave your work placement.

Application forms

Care organisations often produce an application form that they ask all applicants for jobs or work placements to complete. Application forms typically begin with some basic questions about the applicant (name, address, contact numbers). They then tend to have a few boxes where applicants provide details of their work history and education (schools attended, qualifications achieved). Most application forms end with a blank box (or even a whole page) where the applicant is asked to write a statement describing the reasons they have applied for a job or work placement and how their skills, qualifications or previous experiences make them a suitable candidate.

▶ It is always best to photocopy an application form so that you can practise your answers before you complete the version you will send.

▶ Follow the instructions on the form and complete it in the way that you are asked to (e.g. use block capitals where requested and blue or black ink if required).

▶ Answer every question unless it is not applicable to you. Where this is the case put n/a.

▶ Write clearly and legibly.

▶ Proof read the form before you send it off, checking your spelling, grammar and punctuation.

▶ Provide information that is directly relevant to the job or work placement – don't write about irrelevant things.

▶ Always tell the truth – don't lie or try to hide the truth about your qualifications or previous experiences.

▶ Provide the names of referees who know you well and who have given you permission to use their names.

▶ Make a photocopy of your completed form in case you get an interview and need to refer to it again.

▶ Send or deliver your unfolded application documents in an unused A4 envelope that is addressed to the person responsible for work placements.

 Activity

Find a vacancy for a nursery assistant or care assistant post in your local newspaper. Obtain an application form from the organisation advertising the vacancy. Complete the form with as much information as you can. When you have finished, review the form critically.

● Are there any questions you have not answered?

● Does the form ask about anything you don't understand?

● Which parts of the form were hardest to complete?

● What kind of help with the form might you need if you were actually going to apply for this job?

Covering letters

It is good practice to write and send a **covering letter** with a CV or application form when you are applying for a job or a work placement. Your letter should:

▶ make it clear that you are applying for a work placement

▶ indicate that you have enclosed a number of documents in support of your application

▶ thank the reader for considering your application

▶ say that you look forward to hearing from the reader in due course.

As with the other application documents, you should proof read your covering letter to ensure that there are no spelling, punctuation or grammatical errors.

Using email and texting

It is appropriate to email a letter, CV or application form to an employer or placement provider when they say this is okay and provide an email address through which applicants can contact them. If the organisation doesn't specifically say that you can email or text them, you should either write or phone to make contact.

Work placement providers

Health and social care services are provided by a number of different types of care organisation (see Unit 10 for more details). The three main types of care organisations that provide services and which may be able to offer a work placement are statutory, private and voluntary organisations.

Statutory sector organisations

Statutory sector care organisations, such as the NHS, Sure Start children's centres, primary schools and local authorities, are provided and run by the government. There may be a range of different placement opportunities in local statutory care services (see Figure 5.3).

Figure 5.3 Examples of work placement opportunities in the statutory sector

Area of work	Examples of placement opportunities
Primary health care	• Clerical or support work in a GP practice • Shadowing primary health care workers, such as community nurses
Secondary health care	• Clerical or support work in in-patient or out-patient hospital units • Play or childcare work in hospital nurseries or children's units • Shadowing care staff, such as nurses, care assistants or therapy staff
Community-based early years	• Assisting in local playgroups, nurseries or crèche services • Shadowing nursery teachers, nursery nurses or nursery assistants
Early education services	• Assisting in reception or foundation-stage classes in primary schools or nurseries • Shadowing teachers, classroom assistants or other support workers
Community-based social care	• Clerical or support work in day centres or other social care settings • Shadowing social workers or social care support workers

Statutory care organisations are unlikely to advertise placement opportunities. You may need to identify an organisation where you would like to gain some work experience, research possible placement opportunities and approach them **speculatively**. This means you have to use your initiative to get the placement you want. Alternatively, your school or college tutor or work placement coordinator may have a range of placement opportunities they can tell you about, or may be able to provide guidance on how to approach local statutory organisations for a placement.

Private sector organisations

There are likely to be a range of **private sector care organisations** and private practitioners in your local area. These might include:

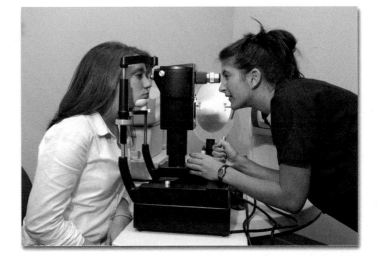

- a clinic or hospital

- high street opticians, dentists or pharmacies

- an osteopath, physiotherapist or chiropodist

- a residential care home, nursing home or home
  care agency

- nurseries and playgroups.

Private sector organisations may be able to offer work placements supporting or shadowing care workers. Again, they do not advertise placement opportunities and need to be approached speculatively or through your tutor or work placement coordinator. It is important to remember that private sector organisations and practitioners are in business and need to make money from the services they provide. They will expect any students on placement to make a positive impression on their customers.

Case study

Jacqui, aged 17, has obtained a work placement at Woodside Pharmacy. Her placement supervisor is Yasmin Bhatt, a qualified Pharmacist who is also the owner of Woodside Pharmacy. Jacqui has never had a part-time job before and knows nothing about working in a pharmacy. Yasmin has told her that she needs to arrive punctually for work by 8.30 a.m., should dress smartly and always have clean hair and nails. She has arranged for Jacqui to shadow Dawn Fowler, an experienced pharmacy assistant, for the first week of her placement. During her first week, Dawn plans to show Jacqui how to talk to customers, how to find medicines in the shop and how to use the till. Yasmin will review Jacqui's progress at the end of her first week on placement.

1. Why do you think Yasmin insists on Jacqui arriving punctually?

2. What kind of clothes should Jacqui wear to create a positive, professional impression?

3. Describe the kinds of skills that Jacqui could develop during her work placement at the pharmacy.

Voluntary sector organisations

Voluntary sector care organisations are run on a not-for-profit basis and usually have a positive attitude towards people who wish to volunteer with them. Services in your area provided by voluntary sector organisations might include:

- ▶ day centres for older people, people with learning or physical disabilities or people with mental health problems

- ▶ residential services for people with disabilities, who are frail or who have mental health problems

- ▶ playgroups and nurseries for pre-school children

- ▶ activity clubs and youth clubs for older children and teenagers.

Speculative applications through letters or phone calls may be needed to find out whether a local voluntary group or organisation is able to offer work placement opportunities. Again, it is likely that your tutor or work placement coordinator will be familiar with the range of local voluntary organisations.

Finding out what suits you

You may already have a clear idea about the kind of care organisation or placement environment you would like to gain some work experience in. This might be because you already know which area of care you would like eventually to work in or which client group you would like to work with. However, it is important to keep an open mind as your interests may change and your skills may, in fact, be better suited to another area of care work. Talking to your tutor, class colleagues and care workers about your interests and abilities, and gaining experience in a couple of different care settings can help you to choose the kind of work placement to which you are best suited.

Case study

Angela is a 17-year-old BTEC First student. Angela's mum works as a nurse in the medical unit for older people at the local general hospital. She tells Angela about her work from time to time and thinks that Angela would enjoy and be suited to working with older people. Angela doesn't think so! She would like to work in the intensive care unit with premature babies or in a setting with children who have been abused. Angela says that she is passionate about protecting vulnerable children and that this is the kind of care work she would eventually like to do. Angela's tutor has explained to her that she needs to think a bit more about the kind of work placement that would suit her now. She has pointed out that it would be very unusual for a student to gain a work placement in either an intensive care unit or working with abused children and that these areas may be too emotionally difficult for Angela at this point in her life.

1. How could Angela go about seeking the kind of work placement she wants?

2. What kinds of information would care organisations expect Angela to provide about herself?

3. Do you think that Angela's preferred placement settings are appropriate for a 17-year-old BTEC First student?

4. What other kinds of work placement could Angela consider to gain experience with

   a) people who are 'vulnerable'

   b) caring for children?

Assessment activity 5.1 (P1)

In preparation for your work experience, you must apply for a post at a local day centre for older people. Produce a letter of application and a current CV.

Topic check

1 Identify three different ways of applying for a work placement.
2 Describe three features of a good letter of application.
3 Explain why it is important to be honest and concise when writing a CV.
4 What kinds of information have to be provided when completing an application form for a work placement?
5 Explain what a covering letter is and describe what it should contain.
6 Identify an example of a work placement opportunity that may be available in a local statutory sector organisation.

Obtaining a work placement

Getting started

This topic introduces you to ways of preparing for a work placement interview and to the skills needed to succeed in obtaining a placement. When you have completed this topic, you should:

- know about a range of interview skills
- be able to prepare for a work placement interview
- be able to demonstrate effective communication skills in an interview.

Key terms

Body language: another term for non-verbal communication

Dress code: the expected way of dressing or the standard of dress expected in a workplace

Posture: the way a person positions or arranges their body

Punctuality: being on time

Preparation for interview

It is hoped that your written application for a work placement will lead to attend an interview. To prepare yourself for the interview you will need to:

▶ Develop your telephone skills so that you make a positive impression when you phone to confirm that you will be attending the interview. Alternatively, somebody from the care organisation might phone to let you know you have an interview. In either case, you should speak clearly but not too quickly, check who you are speaking to and confirm the time and date of your interview in a friendly, confident way. Remember to write down the caller's name, contact number and the interview details if somebody phones you. It always leaves a good impression if you thank the person for calling before you hang up.

▶ Make transport arrangements to get to your interview. This might involve finding out about and planning bus or train journeys. If so, you will need to know how long the journey takes and where to get on and off. If you are travelling by car you will need to work out a route and find out what traffic conditions are like when you will be travelling. If you have never been to the interview location before, it is very useful to do a practice journey a few days beforehand and to allow yourself plenty of time to get there. You must not arrive late as this will create a bad impression!

- Find out about the **dress code** of the care organisation. This will enable you to dress appropriately for the interview. People often make initial judgements about an interview candidate's suitability for a job or work placement on the basis of their appearance. A scruffy, unkempt appearance suggests the person is disorganised and doesn't really care what others think about them. People who present themselves well and who have made an effort to dress appropriately suggest they can fit in and think about how others respond to them.

- Find out about the interview procedure. It is helpful to know how many people will be interviewing you, how long the interview will last and whether there are any tasks (such as a presentation) involved in the interview process. Knowing what is going to happen should help you to prepare for the interview and should help you to feel less nervous on the day.

 Over to you!

1. What would you wear if you were invited to attend an interview for a work placement at:
   a) your local GP practice?
   b) a nursery school for the under fives?
   c) a youth club for 11–14 year olds?
2. Explain why you would or wouldn't dress differently for each of these interviews.

The interview

Figure 5.4 identifies the ingredients or elements of an effective interview. Your work placement interview should go well if you can put these things into practice.

Punctuality

The number one, golden rule of interviews is to be punctual. That is, arrive on time – don't be late! If you are unavoidably late or simply cannot attend the interview, you should contact the placement setting and let them know as soon as you can.

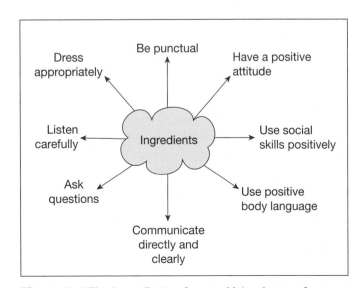

Figure 5.4 The ingredients of a good interview performance

Using social and personal skills

Social and personal skills relate to the way you behave and treat others. Being considerate, polite and friendly towards other people are positive qualities that will help you to obtain a placement in a care setting. Being impatient, rude or inconsiderate about other people's needs or feelings is likely to create a negative impression. You should always avoid swearing, being argumentative, rude or stroppy during interviews. The way you behave and respond to others should convince an interviewer that you have the social and personal skills needed for care work.

Demonstrating communication skills

Communication skills are central to care work. Smiling, being relaxed but using appropriate **body language**, shaking hands at the start and end of the interview, making good eye contact, speaking clearly and confidently and listening carefully will help you to show that you have the kinds of communication skills needed for care work.

Listening

The importance of listening during interviews, and in care work generally, should not be underestimated. Paying close attention to the interviewer's questions and to what they say about the placement setting will help you answer their questions and ask some of your own. Listening skills are an important part of care work, so it is a good idea to demonstrate that you have them at your interview.

Activity

Where would you like to have a work experience placement? Imagine that you have been invited for interview. Plan five questions that you would like to ask at the end of your interview about the placement and the learning opportunities it provides.

Asking and answering questions

Interviews are based around a series of questions and answers. Most of the questions are asked by the interviewer. However, towards the end of the nterview you will probably be asked whether you have any questions to ask. This is an ideal opportunity to show interest in the placement organisation, the care environment and the type of work experience that could be gained there. Plan some questions in advance of the interview and use them to find out more about the organisation and what you might be able to do and learn there.

Appearance and attitude

A person's appearance says something about whether they can be bothered to make an effort and whether they have thought about the situation they are facing. An inappropriate appearance (e.g. short skirt, lots of exposed flesh) will not make a good impression with an interviewer. Fitting in with the organisation's dress code is much more likely to do this. Similarly, a person's attitude can make the difference between them getting a placement and receiving a rejection letter. Having a 'can do' attitude where you express enthusiasm, initiative and a willingness to learn and have a go at new things conveys a positive attitude and leaves a positive first impression.

Non-verbal communication

Sitting up straight, using an open **posture**, smiling and making good eye contact all give positive non-verbal 'messages' to an interviewer (see Unit 1 for more on non-verbal communication).

Assessment activity 5.2 (P2, M1, D1)

In preparation for your work experience, you must participate in a simulated job interview.

Case study

Baljinder is 16 years old and has recently started her BTEC First Health and Social Care course. Her local day nursery has replied to Baljinder's application for a work experience placement. She has been invited to attend an interview in a fortnight. Baljinder is becoming quite anxious about this, as she has never attended a job-related interview before.

1. Identify three key points Baljinder needs to be aware of in order to succeed in her interview.

2. Describe ways in which Baljinder can demonstrate that she has effective communication and interpersonal skills.

3. What advice would you give to Baljinder about the way she dresses and presents herself for the interview?

Topic check

1 Identify three things that you should do to prepare for a work placement interview.
2 Why is it important to make and check transport arrangements before your work placement interview?
3 What does the term 'dress code' mean and why is it important to find out about this before a work placement interview?
4 What is the golden rule of interviews?
5 Describe how you could demonstrate effective communication skills during a work placement interview.
6 Explain how a person's attitude can affect the outcome of a work placement interview.

Using interpersonal skills on placement

Getting started

This topic introduces you to ways of using and demonstrating your interpersonal skills during a work placement. When you have completed this topic, you should:

- know about a range of interpersonal skills
- understand the importance of interpersonal skills in health and social care work
- be able to demonstrate use of verbal and non-verbal communication skills.

Key terms

Advocate: a person who speaks on behalf of another person

Interpersonal: describes a relationship or interaction occurring between two or more people

Non-verbal communication: communication without using words, e.g. through gestures, eye contact, facial expressions and body language

Paralanguage: the pitch, volume, tone and 'um' and 'uh-huh' sounds that affect the meaning of what a person says

Proximity: how close one person is to another

Verbal communication: the use of words (spoken and written) to communicate

The communication cycle

Care workers need to have excellent communication skills. One of the reasons for this is that care workers talk with people who use services, with their relatives and with other care workers on a regular basis about the needs, care preferences and problems of service users. A care worker must be a good listener but must also be able to make themselves understood to people from diverse backgrounds. Unit 1 explained the importance of the communication cycle in this process (see Figure 5.5).

The **interpersonal** skills that care workers use are based on repeated, skilful use of the communication cycle. As you gain experience and observe other care workers using communication skills, you will be able to identify and incorporate effective communication skills into the way you approach, support and interact with others in care settings.

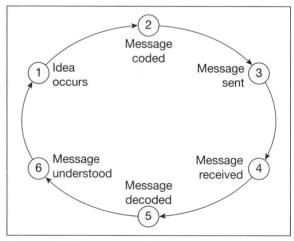

Figure 5.5 The communication cycle

Using interpersonal skills

Unit 1 provides detailed coverage of interpersonal skills in care work. You should remind yourself of the basic points by rereading the relevant sections of Unit 1.

During your work placement you will need to show that you can communicate effectively in:

▶ one-to-one situations   ▶ informal situations

▶ group situations   ▶ formal situations.

To be effective, you will need to use a range of verbal, non-verbal and listening skills. Figure 5.6 provides a summary of the issues you should know about.

Figure 5.6 Verbal, non-verbal and listening skills

Type of communication	Example	Do try to...	Avoid...
Verbal communication	Speech/talking Writing	• Speak clearly • Use the right tone of speech • Pace your speech to suit the listener • Write clearly and legibly • Be concise • Get the information across clearly	• Mumbling • Using jargon or slang • Shouting • Speaking too quickly • Sounding annoyed or irritated • Abbreviations, jargon and slang • Scruffy, unclear writing • Poor spelling
Paralanguage	'Ums' and 'ahhs'	• Use paralanguage appropriately – to encourage the person who is talking	• Using too much paralanguage • Interrupting the speaker with your own paralanguage
Non-verbal communication	Body posture Gestures Eye contact Facial expression Touch **Proximity**	• Be aware of your own non-verbal communication • Try to notice the other person's non-verbal communication • Make an effort to use non-verbal communication in a supportive and encouraging way	• Use your body in a threatening or hostile way • Use inappropriate eye contact, gestures or touch • Get too close, thus making other person uncomfortable
Listening skills	Active listening	• Listen actively to verbal and non-verbal aspects of communication • Respect silences, giving the person time to think • Check your understanding of what the person has said	• Be impatient and interrupt the speaker • Let your attention wander • Give advice or your opinion as soon as the person stops talking

 Activity

Imagine that you are on work placement at a local residential home for older people. What communication skills will you need to use in order to:

• introduce yourself to the care workers who are employed at the residential home?

• find out about the dietary needs and preferences of one of the residents?

• pass on information about a resident's dietary choices to the catering manager?

• take a phone call from a local GP about one of the residents?

• reassure a resident who seems frightened when you sit near her?

Supporting communication

The people you work with during your work placement may have a range of communication support needs. You should always check and take appropriate action to ensure that each person has access to:

▶ adaptive equipment or communication aids, such as glasses, hearing aids and electronic communication devices if they normally require or choose to use them

▶ specialist support staff such as interpreters, **advocates** and speech and language therapists if they have speech or language problems, or if they are unable to communicate or express their views independently.

Providing appropriate support increases the likelihood that a person will be able to communicate and interact effectively.

Being an active listener

It is important to present yourself in a positive way to the people you work with. This increases the likelihood that they will actually want to communicate with you and that they won't feel anxious when they really need to. For example, you should:

▶ make time for people, even if it is only to say hello at the start of a shift or goodbye before you leave

▶ be approachable and behave in ways that make people feel able to talk to and trust you.

Wearing your uniform in an appropriate way, having your ID badge available to show who you are and being presentable all help to establish trust.

You can be a more effective, active listener by:

▶ providing each individual with the support they need to communicate their views, wishes and preferences

▶ positioning yourself appropriately to maximise communication and listening during each interaction

▶ using appropriate body language, eye contact and listening skills during your interactions

▶ responding appropriately to any questions or concerns that an individual expresses

▶ recognising your own limits and referring matters outside of your area of competence to appropriate people.

Activity

Identify a work placement where you would like to gain some work experience. Based on what you already know about the care setting and the type of care work that happens there, identify a situation where you would need to use:

• verbal communication

• non-verbal communication.

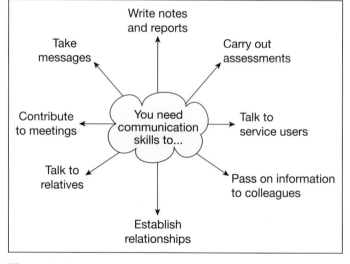

Figure 5.7 Tasks requiring communication skills

Over to you!

Are your communication skills good enough to enable you to follow instructions (listening), write in a person's notes (verbal communication) and provide reassurance through the use of posture and touch (non-verbal communication) on work placement?

Which aspects of your interpersonal skills do you think you need to develop further?

Case study

Mrs Ida Williams, aged 78, is being admitted for a 3-week respite period to the residential home where you are on work placement. You have been given the job of showing her around. You know that Mrs Williams has poor hearing and is sometimes confused. When she arrives, Mrs Williams is with her daughter and a social worker. When you introduce yourself to Mrs Williams, her daughter answers by saying, 'You're wasting your time. She doesn't communicate any more.'

1. Suggest reasons why Mrs Williams may communicate less than she used to.

2. What could you do to help Mrs Williams to communicate effectively during her stay?

3. How could you use your knowledge and understanding of non-verbal communication skills in your interactions with Mrs Williams?

Topic check

1. What happens during the 'communication cycle'?

2. Identify two different kinds of situations in which you will be expected to communicate during work placement.

3. What does the skill of 'active listening' involve?

4. Explain why a care worker may need to be tactful and diplomatic when communicating with people who use care services and their relatives.

5. Which aspects of your communication skills do you have confidence in?

6. Which aspects of your communication skills do you need to develop further?

Reflecting on your performance

Getting started

This topic focuses on your performance during work placement. It introduces you to ways of reflecting on your placement experiences. When you have completed this topic, you should:

■ be able to identify the strengths and weaknesses of your work placement performance

■ be able to reflect constructively on your achievements and areas for development.

 Key terms

Career development: ways of progressing at work

Constructive criticism: comments or feedback that aim to help a person improve their performance or ability

Initiative: the ability to act independently

Reflect: think about an experience or issue in a careful, considered way

Reflecting on your work placement performance

You will not be working on your own or without support during your work experience placement. You should have a supervisor in the work placement setting and your tutor will probably monitor your progress by visiting and keeping in touch with your supervisor. Your supervisor and tutor should both be able to give you feedback on your performance and on how you can improve your skills and contribution to the care team you are working with. You should also **reflect** on your achievements, strengths and weaknesses and ways of improving your performance during your period of work placement.

It is important to remember that you are a learner and are not expected to know everything or already have effective care-giving skills during what may be your first work experience placement in a care setting. You should focus on finding out about and improving your knowledge of the setting and, under supervision, developing some of the care skills needed to work in your placement area. Reflecting on and reviewing what you are achieving and

Figure 5.8 Gibbs' reflective cycle

what you would like to improve on is a very good way of improving your work placement performance. It can be helpful to try and use Gibbs' reflective cycle (Figure 5.8) as a way of thinking about challenging or difficult situations that you experience during work placement. It may help you to learn something useful from what you might otherwise think of as a 'bad experience'.

What have you achieved?

By assessing your own performance and using feedback from your work placement colleagues, you should be able to reflect on and review:

▶ the knowledge and skills you have gained during your work placement

▶ whether and in what ways your self-confidence has changed

▶ how your knowledge and understanding of the placement setting has changed

▶ how your knowledge and understanding of individuals' medical conditions and social problems have developed

▶ the range of care-related activities you have undertaken

▶ your effectiveness in providing care services and support for people.

It is important to be as honest with yourself as possible when reflecting on your work placement performance. While it is nice to enjoy the positive feelings that come with doing something well and receiving positive feedback from others, thinking about the things that didn't go so well, and being open to **constructive criticism**, are also important for your learning and development.

Your work placement supervisor and tutor may arrange review or progress meetings that provide you with opportunities to reflect on your performance. There are also many informal opportunities to do this, when you discuss how things are going and what you have been doing with your colleagues in the care setting. It is important to both identify your achievements and be aware of areas you could improve on when appraising your performance.

 Activity

Produce a performance appraisal form that you can complete on a weekly basis during your period of work placement. You might want to create and complete this using information technology packages. Your performance appraisal form could include questions such as:

• What care activities have I been involved in this week?

• How well did I contribute to these activities?

• What did I learn from taking part in each of these activities?

• What have I done well this week?

• Which aspects of my performance could I improve on?

• What can I do to improve my performance over the next few weeks?

Case study

Joanne is a BTEC First Health and Social Care student. She has completed two units of her BTEC First diploma course so far. Joanne is also a member of her local St John's Ambulance Brigade and is a qualified and experienced first aider. Joanne has two GCSEs and has also completed a food hygiene certificate at a local college. She is looking forward to her work experience placement at a local pre-school nursery. Her tutor has asked her to reflect on the knowledge and skills she currently has and on her achievements to date.

1. What would you list as Joanne's achievements to date?
2. Does Joanne have any knowledge or skills relevant to her work experience placement?
3. If you were Joanne and you were asked in a work placement interview why the nursery should offer you a placement, what would you say?

Personal strengths and weaknesses

Reflecting on your work placement experiences should make you aware of your personal strengths and weaknesses (see Figure 5.9). You should complete a diary or work placement logbook to record your work experience activities. When you do this, you should make a point of noting where your skills and performance are strong and where there are weaknesses that need addressing. When you become aware of weaknesses in the way you work, it is best to discuss these with your supervisor rather than ignore or try to hide them. Your supervisor and placement colleagues may be able to suggest ways of improving on these aspects of your work skills or care practice. Remember that improving your skills will benefit the people you are providing care for.

Recording your work placement reflections is a way of learning from your experiences. You will benefit from this if you think about how you can build on the strengths that you have and improve on the areas that you identify as weaknesses. Effective care workers are always seeking to learn from their experiences and try continually to develop and adapt their knowledge and skills to meet the needs of the people they work with.

Figure 5.9 Reflecting on strengths and weaknesses

Performance area	Start of placement		End of placement	
	Good	**Improvement needed**	**Good**	**Improvement needed**
Punctuality				
Confidence				
Using **initiative**				
Ability to follow instructions				
Ability to receive constructive criticism				
Use of verbal communication skills				
Use of non-verbal communication skills				
Use of listening skills				
Practical caring skills				

Thinking about the future

Many students who complete a BTEC First Health and Social Care course go on to work in the health and social care sector. It is hoped that you will be one of them! Your work placement experiences may have given you some ideas about what you would and wouldn't like to do as part of your future career in care. The health and social care sector offers a huge range of different job roles, and lots of opportunities for career development and progression. It may be helpful, towards the end of your work placement, and later towards the end of the course as a whole, to discuss your **career development** plans with people who work in care.

You may already have some ideas about the area and type of work you wish to progress to. People who have experience in the care field may be a good source of advice, guidance and information when you are considering your progression options. It might also be helpful to obtain careers guidance from a trained careers counsellor. They should be able to identify the range of opportunities that are available to you. It is best to be honest with yourself about your capabilities and interests so that you make good choices. As you gain experience and confidence, you will be able to develop a career that suits your interests and enables you to use your abilities and skills.

Activity

Do you already have some ideas about the kind of care setting you would like to work in or the type of job role you would like to perform in the future? You can investigate progression opportunities in the areas and job roles you are interested in by searching internet sites such as NHS Careers (www.nhscareers.nhs.uk), Social Work Careers (www.socialworkcareers.co.uk) and Childcare Careers (www.childcarecareers.gov.uk).

Assessment activity 5.3 (P3, P4, P5, M2, M3 and D2)

To meet the assessment criteria for this unit, you need to complete a reflective logbook about your work placement. Your entries in the logbook should:

- identify the activities you have taken part in
- describe the practical and interpersonal skills you have used
- reflect on your feelings about your placement experiences and your own performance
- identify and describe the knowledge and skills you have developed during your period of work placement.

Using your logbook and personal reflections you should also produce a report that:

- reviews your overall performance during the period of work experience
- includes an action plan that shows how you could improve your performance.

Where possible you should also obtain witness statements from your supervisor or work colleagues to confirm that you have demonstrated effective interpersonal and practical skills.

Topic check

1 What does the skill of 'reflection' involve?
2 Identify three things that you should reflect on when you review your own work placement performance.
3 What is the purpose of constructive criticism?
4 Why is it important to use your initiative during work placement?
5 Identify three skills that you will need to use and try to improve on during your work placement.
6 How can you find out about progression opportunities in the areas of care work which you are interested in?

Assessment summary

The overall grade you achieve for this unit depends on how well you meet the grading criteria set out at the start of the chapter (see page 97). You must complete:

- all of the P criteria to achieve a **pass** grade
- all of the P and the M criteria to achieve a **merit** grade
- all of the P, M and D criteria to achieve a **distinction** grade.

Your tutor will assess the assessment activities that you complete for this unit. The work you produce should provide evidence which demonstrates that you have achieved each of the assessment criteria. The table below identifies what you need to demonstrate to meet each of the pass, merit and distinction criteria for this unit. You should always check and self-assess your work before you submit your assignments for marking.

Remember that you MUST provide evidence for all of the P criteria to pass the unit.

Grading criteria	You need to demonstrate that you can:	Have you got the evidence?
P1	Complete an appropriate letter of application, with an attached CV, to a local health and social care setting	
P2	Plan appropriately for an interview at your work experience placement	
M1	Demonstrate appropriate interview skills	
D1	Assess the strengths and weaknesses of your interview skills	
P3	Carry out a period of work experience, using relevant skills, in a health or social care setting	
M2	Discuss on your overall performance during the period of work experience	
P4	Demonstrate appropriate interpersonal skills in a health or social care setting	
M3	Discuss own interpersonal skills used in a health and social care setting	
P5	Complete a reflective logbook during your period of work experience in a health or social care setting	
D2	Produce an action plan to show how you could have improved your performance	

Always ask your tutor to explain any assignment tasks or assessment criteria that you don't understand fully. Being clear about the task before you begin gives you the best chance of succeeding. Good luck with your Unit 5 assessment work!

6 Cultural diversity in health and social care

Unit outline

The United Kingdom is a country with a growing and increasingly diverse population. Health and social care workers need to know about and understand cultural diversity because it affects individual's rights and the quality of care services. This unit introduces you to the diversity of individuals in UK society and shows how an understanding of diversity helps to promote equality of opportunity for people who use care services. You will also gain an overview of equality law and rights, and the responsibilities of care organisations and their employees.

Learning outcomes

1 **Know the diversity of individuals in society.**
2 **Understand beliefs and practices in different religious or secular groups.**
3 **Understand factors that influence the equality of opportunity for individuals in society.**
4 **Know the role of legislation, codes of practice and charters in promoting diversity.**

Grading guide

To achieve a **pass**, you must show you can:	To achieve a **merit**, you must show you can:	To achieve a **distinction**, you must show you can:
P1 Identify social, cultural and political factors that create diversity within society.		
P2 Explain the beliefs and practices of individuals from two contrasting religious groups/secular groups	**M1** Compare the similarities and differences in the practices and beliefs of individuals from two contrasting religious or secular groups	
P3 Explain factors that may influence the equality of opportunities for individuals	**M2** Discuss how discriminatory practice can be avoided	**D1** Assess the possible effects of discrimination on the physical, intellectual, emotional and social health/wellbeing of individuals
P4 Outline one piece of relevant legislation and one code of practice or charter for a chosen health or social care environment that aims to promote diversity	**M3** Describe how the legislation and code of practice or charter promotes diversity	**D2** Assess the effectiveness of the chosen legislation and code of practice or charter in promoting diversity

Diversity in society

 Getting started

This topic focuses on the diversity of individuals in UK society. When you have completed this topic, you should:

- know about forms of social and political diversity in the UK population
- be able to explain how diversity can affect care provision in the UK.

Key terms

Disability: a condition or problem that restricts a person's ability to do something

Life chances: opportunities each person has to improve his or her quality of life

Multicultural: the presence of two or more cultures in one country

Secular: non-religious

Social diversity: when a population is socially mixed, consisting of people from many different backgrounds

Unfair discrimination: treating someone differently for unfair or arbitrary reasons

Diversity of individuals in society

Every individual has unique qualities and experiences. These make us all different in some way. At the same time, people share a range of characteristics, qualities and other features that make them similar to others. For example, a person may be similar to others in terms of their:

- ethnicity
- gender
- religious or **secular** beliefs
- socials class
- sexuality
- age
- family structure and background
- **disability**.

An individual's personal development and behaviour are influenced by the way they identify with and respond to these social factors. However, even though there is **social diversity** in the UK, some people suffer **unfair discrimination** because of their social differences. Social and cultural difference can affect an individual's opportunities, experiences and **life chances**.

Ethnicity

An individual may be classified as belonging to a particular ethnic group because of their place of birth, background or skin colour, for example. People also identify themselves with particular ethnic groups when they say they are 'black', 'white', 'Bengali' or 'Scottish', for example. Prejudice and unfair treatment because of a person's ethnicity is known as racial discrimination.

Gender

When you are asked to identify your 'gender' on an official form, you are being asked to say whether you are male or female. This in itself isn't controversial. However, when men and women are treated differently for no reasons other than their gender, sex discrimination can occur. This is usually based on prejudice and is often called sexism.

Religious and secular beliefs

Some people are born into a religious faith because their family follows a particular religion and socialises them into it. Other people acquire religious beliefs themselves later in life. Religion can have a big influence on an individual's lifestyle. Some people base their everyday life around prayer and religious 'rules' for living (see Topic 6.2). Others have no religion at all and live a completely secular life. However, religion does tend to cause strong feelings (for and against) and can lead to discrimination because a person belongs, or doesn't belong, to a particular faith community.

Over to you!

How would you define your ethnicity and your religious beliefs? What impact has either of these features of your life had on your opportunities or way of life so far?

Social class

A person's social class is determined by their occupation, income, education and their attitudes and values (or those of their parents). Social class is linked to both an individual's opportunities in life and their health and wellbeing. People with a similar social class background tend to live similar lives. Discrimination can occur where people act on their class-based prejudices. For example, an employer with class-based prejudices may avoid interviewing job applicants from certain social classes because they favour and prefer to work with people from their own class.

Sexuality

A person's sexual orientation may be gay, lesbian, heterosexual or bisexual. People who identify themselves as gay/lesbian or bisexual have tended to experience prejudice (homophobia) and unfair discrimination because of their sexuality. In particular, some people judge non-heterosexual relationships as 'abnormal' and believe it is okay to deny gay and lesbian people the same basic rights as heterosexual people.

Age

The UK population consists of a number of different age groupings. Infants, children, adolescents, adults and older people are examples of age groupings. In situations where an age group is given preference, an advantage or is more highly valued than others, ageism may occur. This kind of prejudice may lead to age discrimination, where a person is treated unfairly purely because of their age. Assumptions about the needs and abilities of older people sometimes lead to this happening.

THE FIRST THING SOME PEOPLE NOTICE IS HER AGE.

AGE

Family structure

There is a range of different family structures in the UK. These include nuclear families, extended families, lone-parent families, blended families and foster families. In some families parents are married, while in others they cohabit and remain unmarried. Where an individual makes judgements or holds prejudices about a person's family background, unfair discrimination can occur. For example, some people assume that it is 'better' to come from a two-parent family, and assume that lone-parent families are less stable and less able to raise children successfully. Negative assumptions and prejudices about lone-parent families sometimes lead to them being seen as 'problem families'.

Over to you!

Do you think there are any advantages to living in a nuclear or extended family compared with a lone-parent family?

Case study

Egil Johnsen, aged 38, has recently moved from Norway to live with Joanna, aged 35, and her daughter Eve, aged 3. Joanna and Egil are expecting their first child together in 3 months' time. They have decided to get married and live in the UK near to Joanna's parents and her sister. Joanna thinks that she will need help and support from other members of her family when the baby is born. Egil is happy to move to the UK but says he will miss his brother and sister who live in Norway. He is also going to miss his daughter, Anna, who lives with his former wife, Erica, and her new partner. Egil is excited about 'this new kind of family life' but also admits it makes his life quite complicated.

1. What kind of family structure will Egil, Joanna, Eve and their new baby live in?

2. Identify the people who are members of Joanna's extended family.

3. Explain how the case study illustrates the diverse range of family structures in the UK.

Disabilities

A disability is a condition or problem that limits a person's mobility, hearing, vision, speech or mental function. A person may be born with a disabling condition or problem, or may acquire their disability as the result of an accident, illness or some form of trauma. Some people have more than one disability. A disabled person may be treated unfairly or less favourably than an able-bodied person because of deliberate prejudice against disabled people or because others don't understand the particular needs of a disabled person. Prejudice against disabled people is known as disablism. Where people act on their disablist prejudices, disability discrimination may occur.

Diversity and care provision

People who use health and social care services are entitled to expect that they will be treated equally and fairly, regardless of their personal characteristics or cultural background. Health and social care organisations and individual care practitioners need to understand cultural diversity and have to find ways of promoting equality of opportunity and fair treatment for all. Laws protecting individuals' rights, and the strategies used to promote diversity and ensure fair treatment for all service users, are discussed in Unit 2 and Topic 6.4 of this unit.

Activity

Which aspects of cultural diversity would be promoted and respected if the following activities were carried out in care settings?

- Providing pamphlets and information in local community languages in a GP surgery.
- Celebrating **multicultural** festivals in a nursery.

- Employing male workers to work with children in a playgroup.
- Encouraging applications from disabled people for social work jobs.
- Including a question about sexual orientation on the equal opportunities monitoring form in a job application pack.

Assessment activity 6.1 (P1, P2, M1)

Imagine that you are one of the student representatives on your school or college's Equal Opportunities Committee. Following a recent review of the policies and the way they are explained to students, the committee has decided that some new display material should be developed.

- You have been asked to update the poster displays on cultural and religious diversity in society that are used in the entrance area of your school or college.
- Your poster or display should illustrate key features of cultural and religious diversity in the UK, explaining and comparing beliefs and practices of two contrasting religious or secular groups.

Topic check

1 Identify five different forms of cultural diversity in the UK population.
2 Explain what the term 'prejudice' means.
3 Describe one form of prejudice that can lead to unfair discrimination against people.
4 How are older people sometimes unfairly discriminated against?
5 Describe how a person's family background might be used to discriminate against them.
6 Explain how cultural diversity affects the provision of health and social care services in the UK.

Religious and secular beliefs and practices

 Getting started

People within the UK population have a diverse range of religious beliefs and practices. When you have completed this topic, you should:

- know about a range of different religious and secular beliefs and practices in UK society
- be able to describe key aspects of the beliefs and practices of a range of different faith communities.

 Key terms

Altruism: unselfish concern for the welfare of others

Ayurvedic medicine: a 5000-year-old natural healing system that treats illness as a problem of imbalance

Karma: this is the idea that a person's actions in this life will determine their destiny when they are reincarnated (reborn) in their next life

Nirvana: a state of being free from suffering

Revered: respected and honoured

Beliefs and practices

There is a range of beliefs about God and religion in UK society. Most religions are based on sets of beliefs, symbols and practices (e.g. praying) that accept the existence of one or more gods. Secular beliefs tend to focus on other issues, some of which reject the existence of God. People who use health and social care services may have a religious faith or may hold other secular beliefs that are equally as important to them.

Buddhism

Buddhist religion is largely based on the teachings of Siddhartha Gautama (Buddha) who lived in Nepal around 580BC. Buddhist beliefs are found throughout the world, but are most popular in Asia.

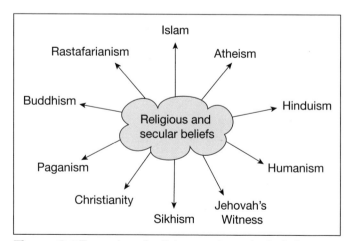

Figure 6.1 Examples of religious and secular beliefs

Buddhism is different from some other religions because Buddha was a human being rather than a god. He is special and **revered** by followers of Buddhism because he achieved enlightenment. Buddha means 'the awakened one'. Buddhist teachings and practice are based on ethical conduct and **altruism**.

Buddhist beliefs vary according to the branch of Buddhism the person practices. However, they may include beliefs about:

▶ reincarnation – the belief that after a person dies their soul is born into a new body

▶ samsara – the belief that life is a cycle of birth, life, death and rebirth

▶ **nirvana** – the belief that enlightenment breaks the cycle of suffering and rebirth when nirvana is reached.

The aim of people who practise Buddhism is to escape the cycle of suffering and rebirth that most people are trapped in, and to achieve nirvana. Buddhist practices can include:

▶ meditation

▶ eating a vegetarian diet

▶ physical exercise (such as breathing exercises)

▶ non-violence and non-aggression towards others

▶ rejection of material possessions

▶ rejection of personal and material greed.

The key religious festival that Buddhists celebrate is Wesak (Buddha Day). This falls on the day of the full moon in May or June when Buddha is said to have been born, gained enlightenment and passed away (same day, different years!). Buddhists celebrate this day by sharing a meal, giving and receiving presents and going to the temple to meditate and receive teaching.

Christianity

Christianity originated in the Middle East about 200 years ago. It is based on the teachings of Jesus Christ. There are a variety of different forms of Christian belief, e.g. Catholic, Protestant, Anglican and Evangelical Christianity. All of these different forms of Christianity believe Jesus to be the Son of God who helped poor, oppressed people and who died to save humankind.

Christians believe in one God, but usually see God as a trinity – Father, Son (Jesus) and the Holy Spirit. Christian beliefs suggest that the Holy Spirit can enter into and inspire believers to live and work for God and their own salvation. The religious beliefs of Christians vary slightly according to the branch of Christianity they are part of, but generally Christians believe that:

▶ human beings have one life on earth and ascend into heaven or descend into hell after their death

▶ the Bible holds the word of God and is a guide to worship, beliefs and practices: the Old Testament teaches about life before Jesus; the New Testament tells of Jesus' life and experiences.

 Activity

Christian churches often use their facilities to provide care and support services for local people. Identify the location of as many churches as you can in your local area. Find out whether they offer any care services, such as playgroups, lunch clubs or activity sessions for local people. Produce a table summarising your findings.

The religious practices of Christians vary, but include:

▶ praying to God in church or privately

▶ celebrating Christmas (Jesus' birth) and Easter (Jesus' death and resurrection) as well as a range of other festivals with special meals and other celebrations

▶ no special diet, though some fasting during lent and on other holy days for some Christians

▶ worshipping and resting from work on Sundays.

Some Christians do not believe in using contraception, believe abortion is sinful and avoid drugs and alcohol. Many Christians pray when unwell and wish to receive 'last rites' from a priest when dying, as this is believed to help them go to heaven.

Jehovah's Witnesses

Jehovah's Witnesses are evangelical Christians. They actively seek to recruit and convert others to their form of Christianity. The Jehovah's Witness faith originated in 1875 when Charles Taze Russell claimed that Christ had returned invisibly to Earth in 1874. Jehovah's Witnesses base their lives on the Bible, which they see as the word of God. People who belong to this religious community believe that:

▶ God the father (Jehovah) is the only true God

▶ Jesus Christ was created by but is inferior to God

▶ the Holy Spirit is God's active force

▶ Jesus died on a stake or pole, not on a cross – they see the cross as a pagan symbol

▶ there is no afterlife as such, but each person can be remembered by God and eventually resurrected

▶ the human race is close to the 'End time', when those who have been anointed by God will go to heaven and rule the Earth with Christ.

The religious practices of Jehovah's Witnesses include:

▶ carrying out missionary work to promote God's word and recruit people to the Jehovah's Witness faith

▶ avoiding eating bloodied animal flesh, alcohol, gambling, drug misuse, homosexuality, masturbation and sex outside marriage

▶ a degree of separation from modern-day life – being in but not of the world – so that they don't vote, don't work in the military or take part in religious or secular festivals (e.g. they don't celebrate birthdays).

Jehovah's Witnesses celebrate the Memorial of Christ's Death (on the anniversary of the Last Supper) but, unlike most other Christians, don't celebrate Easter or Christmas, as they believe them to be based on pagan customs or religions. Jehovah's Witnesses refuse blood transfusions and believe it is wrong to terminate a pregnancy except to save the mother's life.

Over to you!

If a group of Jehovah's Witnesses called at your home, what questions could you ask them about their health beliefs or lifestyle?

Judaism

Judaism is the religion of Jewish people. It originated in the Middle East about 3800 years ago. The fundamental belief of people who practise Judaism is that God created the world and everything in it. They also believe that God spoke to Moses through a 'burning bush', telling him to save the Jewish people from slavery in Egypt.

The religious writings of Judaism are contained in the Torah, the books of the prophets and other holy writings. Altogether these scriptures are known as the Tenakh. However, it is the Torah which tells religious Jews how to live and fulfil God's will. Central to this are the Ten Commandments, which define right and wrong and provide important guidance on how to live.

The religious practices of Judaism include detailed food rules. These specify foods that are 'kosher' (acceptable) and those that are prohibited, as well as ways of preparing and serving food (see Unit 11 for more details). For some Jewish people:

▶ medication also has to be kosher

▶ separate towels must be used to clean and dry different parts of the body

▶ women are spiritually unclean during their period, labour and shortly after childbirth and cannot have contact with their husbands at these times

▶ termination of pregnancy is only permitted for medical purposes.

Jewish people celebrate a number of different festivals and holy days including Passover, Rosh Hashannah, Jewish New Year, the Day of Atonement and Hannukah, the Jewish festival of lights. Shabbat or Sabbath, from nightfall on Friday until nightfall on Saturday, is the Jewish holy day. This is observed by sharing a meal with family or other Jewish people, resting from all work and going to the synagogue to worship.

 Case study

Edith Goldmann, aged 83, is no longer able to live independently. Her son has reluctantly decided that Edith needs to move to live in a care home. He has tried to talk to Edith about her needs and what she would like, but is unsure how much Edith is able to understand. Edith has a diagnosis of dementia and has been supported at home by two home care workers for the last year. Both of the day care workers were Jewish and understand Edith's religious and cultural needs. Edith had very strong connections with the Jewish community in her local area and was a regular visitor to her local synagogue before she became too unwell to attend. Edith's son is now looking for a Jewish nursing home, as he knows that Edith's faith and Jewish customs and traditions have been important to her throughout her life.

1. Identify two aspects of care provision that would need to take Edith's religious beliefs into account.

2. How might the care staff at a Jewish care home help Edith to express her religious faith?

3. Explain why it would be better for Edith to live in a Jewish care home rather than a secular (non-religious) home.

Islam

Islam is the religion of Muslim (or Moslem) people. It originated in the Middle East 1400 years ago when the Prophet Muhammad heard the word of God (Allah). Islam is based on the teachings of Allah, who is believed to be the one and only God, that are contained in the Qur'an. The Prophet Muhammad is believed to be the last messenger from God, sent to guide humanity until the Day of Judgement. Religious practices include:

▶ the Five Pillars of Islam (Shahada – profession of faith; Salah – prayers; Zakeh – giving of alms; Saum – fasting during Ramadam; Hajj – pilgrimage to Mecca) which all Muslims should perform

▶ worshipping at a Mosque at midday on Friday

▶ eating food that is halal (permitted), with meat killed according to Islamic law

▶ wearing clothes that cover the body – men from waist to knees, women from head to toe

▶ women avoiding contact with unrelated males

▶ celebrating Eid-ul-Fitr to mark the end of the holy month of Ramadan and Eid-ul-Adha to mark the end of Hajj (pilgrimage to Mecca)

▶ fasting during daylight hours for the holy month of Ramadan.

The religious beliefs of many Muslims have a profound effect on the way they live their lives and deal with issues relating to health and illness. For example, some Muslims:

▶ avoid pain relief as they believe that suffering is Allah's will

▶ avoid medicines containing pork, blood or alcohol products

▶ may want a same-sex care worker or chaperone when being physically examined

▶ avoid using contraception unless pregnancy would put the woman's health at risk

▶ will not terminate a pregnancy except to save the mother's life.

Activity

Imagine that you are caring for a Muslim woman who has been admitted to a ward of your local hospital. Describe the issues that you would have to think about and deal with in order to provide appropriate care for her. The care that you provide and the way that you meet her everyday needs must respect her religious beliefs.

Hinduism

The Hindu religion is most common in Nepal and India, but followers live throughout the world. It is thought to have originated over 3000 years ago. There is a wide variety of different beliefs and practices within Hinduism, with no single source of scripture and no single founder. However, Hindus believe:

▶ in one God, Brahma, who is said to have created the universe

▶ that human beings experience a cycle of birth, death and rebirth governed by **Karma**

▶ that a person's next reincarnation is dependent on how their previous life was lived.

Hindu religious practices include:

▶ worshipping in a temple or at a shrine

▶ celebrating religious festivals including Diwali (Festival of Lights), where the triumph of good over evil, light over darkness and knowledge over ignorance is celebrated (this five-day festival involves fireworks, lights, sharing of special meals, exchanging gifts and redecorating the home)

▶ eating a vegetarian diet and other food restrictions (see Unit 11 for more details)

▶ treating the cow as a sacred animal and avoiding medications that include animal products

▶ avoiding alcohol and tobacco

▶ using traditional foods and **ayurvedic medicine** (exercise, meditation and herbal remedies) to heal some illnesses

▶ not terminating a pregnancy except to save the mother's life.

Sikhism

Sikhism was founded in the Punjab by Guru Nanak in the 15th century. Sikhs believe in one God who can be accessed by everyone. Sikhism encourages followers to live a good life by living as part of a community, being honest and caring for others. Sikhs believe in a cycle of birth, life, death and rebirth in which the quality of a person's life depends on Karma. Sikhs have three main religious duties:

▶ Nam japna – keeping God in mind at all times

▶ Kirt Karna – earning an honest living (avoiding gambling, begging or working in harmful industries)

▶ Vand Chhakna – giving to charity and caring for others.

Sikh religious practices include:

▶ the 5Ks of Sikhism as devotion to the Guru:

   Kesh – not cutting body hair and men tying hair up in a turban

   Kangha – wearing a small wooden comb

   Kara – wearing a steel bracelet on the wrist

   Kaccha – wearing a cotton undergarment

   Kirpan – carrying a ceremonial steel sword

▶ worshipping on Sunday

▶ celebrating many festivals including Diwali, Guru Nanak's birthday and Vaishkh (Sikh New Year in April)

▶ avoiding alcohol and tobacco consumption and other things that can damage the body

▶ avoiding medication that contains animal products

▶ wanting a same-sex care worker or chaperone when being physically examined

▶ needing to bathe in running water and wash hair frequently

▶ not terminating a pregnancy except to save the mother's life.

Rastafarianism

Rastafarianism is a movement of black people that originated in Jamaica in the 1930s. Rastafarians believe that:

▶ Haile Selassie (Ethiopian Emperor) was the living God who revealed himself through his humanity

▶ black people have been chosen by God but are suppressed through slavery and corporate greed

▶ Africa, specifically Ethiopia, is the homeland of God's chosen people and the place to which they will return.

Rastafarian religious practices include:

▶ covering hair with a scarf or hat

▶ not cutting or combing hair, typically wearing it in 'dreadlocks'

▶ worshipping in people's homes or community centres, chanting, praying and singing

▶ sometimes smoking marijuana (known as the 'wisdom weed') to produce religious visions and a sense of calm

▶ eating a vegetarian diet as a way of respecting nature

▶ not drinking tea, coffee, milk or alcohol

▶ not using contraception or terminating a pregnancy.

Paganism

Paganism is a general term for ancient religions such as Witchcraft, Druids and Wiccans that were popular in pre-Christian times. People who follow pagan religions have strong beliefs about the power and sacredness of nature and tend to be very eco-friendly. Some also believe in spirits, and contact spirits for guidance and advice. Most pagans worship outdoors, celebrating gods and goddesses often linked to the seasons and changes in nature. Pagan worship involves singing, chanting and dancing and is an attempt to contact the 'divine world' that is seen to exist all around. There are no special forms of dress, dietary or medical beliefs associated with paganism. However, because of their strong focus on the divine power of nature, some pagans are vegetarian and use herbal medicines to treat illness.

 Over to you!

Do you know what a Druid is? Use the internet or other sources to find out about this type of Pagan and their beliefs.

Atheism

Atheists don't believe in any gods. They believe in rational thought and reject the idea of God and religious faith as supernatural beliefs. Atheists argue that God doesn't, and logically can't, exist. This is more than not believing – it is also a rejection of the possibility that God can exist. Atheists sometimes celebrate weddings, births and death in a non-religious way by focusing on the people involved rather than the spirituality of the occasion.

Humanism

Humanists believe that each individual should make the best of their life. Like atheists, they also see rational, logical and ethical thinking as the basis of a good life. Humanists are non-religious, believing that there is no afterlife, and accepting the theory of evolution. As they don't believe in God, humanists can also be classed as atheists. However, humanists tend to have strong anti-discriminatory principles and don't wish to argue against other people's beliefs. Both atheists and humanists tend to believe that individuals should take personal responsibility for ensuring that they look after their own health and wellbeing.

 Case study

Three people have been admitted to D1 Ward at the local hospital this evening. They are:

- Darvesh Singh, aged 46, who has been involved in a car accident. He told the nurse admitting him that he is a practising Sikh.

- Salifah Khan, aged 32, who was knocked over in the street by a cyclist. She told the doctor who examined her that she is a practising Muslim.

- Trevor Tyndale, aged 62, who has fallen off a ladder and sustained a head injury which has left

him unconscious. His wife has informed the hospital that Trevor is a Jehovah's Witness.

The nursing staff on duty are aware that they should respect each individual's religious beliefs and provide them with appropriate care.

1. Create a table or diagram that summarises the main religious beliefs of each patient.

2. Identify how the religious beliefs of each person may affect the way they want to be cared for.

 Topic check

1 Identify four different religious faiths that are practised in the UK.

2 What are the main religious beliefs of Buddhists?

3 Describe how people who have Christian religious beliefs practise their religion.

4 Identify one health belief associated with Jehovah's Witnesses.

5 What do people who follow the Sikh religion avoid that helps to promote their health and wellbeing?

6 Explain how the concept of 'Karma' is sometimes used by Hindus to explain suffering and ill health.

Factors influencing equality of opportunity

Getting started

This topic focuses on forms of discriminatory practice that can affect an individual's health, wellbeing and equality of opportunity. When you have completed this topic, you should:

- know about different forms of discriminatory practice
- be able to describe the effects of discriminatory practice
- understand how care workers can practise in a non-discriminatory way.

Key terms

Labelling: defining or describing a person in terms of a label, such as a diagnosis (e.g. 'the depressed man')

Mass media: the main means of communicating with a large population (e.g. TV, radio, newspapers)

Prejudice: a biased, unfounded and usually negative belief about a group of people

Stereotyping: having a simplified, over-generalised view or description of a person that doesn't take into account their individual characteristics or differences (e.g. 'all young women are...')

Equality, discrimination and difference

People in the UK are different in a variety of respects (see Topic 6.1). However, despite social and cultural differences between people, each individual is entitled to be treated fairly and equally. Sometimes this doesn't happen and people are discriminated against because of their differences. Understanding that other people can be different but equal is particularly important when our own culture and beliefs are challenged. Care workers need to have a good understanding of diversity and difference so they can avoid discriminatory practice.

Discrimination and discriminatory practices

Unfair discrimination can result from the way people respond to social differences. All people are different, but sometimes some people are treated less favourably or with hostility, e.g. because they are members of minority groups.

Discrimination can be:

▶ direct, when a person is treated less favourably, e.g. because they are a woman, black or disabled

▶ indirect, when everyone is treated in a similar way but this disadvantages or works against certain people or groups (e.g. insisting that employees should not wear any headwear would indirectly discriminate against Sikh men).

Treating black people differently when they apply for jobs, or not appointing a woman to a post because she may become pregnant are examples of unfair discrimination. Common forms of discrimination are based on:

ethnicity – racism

gender – sexism

disability – disablism

sexuality – homophobia

religion – sectarianism.

People are discriminated against because of **stereotyping**, **labelling** and **prejudice**. Discrimination occurs when a person favours 'people like us' and feels threatened by 'people like them' who are different from 'us' in some way. Care workers must not discriminate, should avoid an 'us and them' mentality and must be accepting of social differences.

Stereotyping

Stereotyping involves making assumptions about 'types' of people and applying them to individuals. Stereotypes don't take into account individual differences and can be crude, hostile caricatures of people (e.g. male nurse = gay, feminist = man-hater). When people make stereotypical assumptions about others, inappropriate and discriminatory treatment can occur.

Care workers need to acknowledge individuals' differences because these are important to our identity and who we believe we are. However, it is also important to avoid clumsy and insensitive stereotyping. People are not 'all the same'.

Labelling

Labelling involves summing up a person in one label or term, such as 'schizophrenic' or 'aggressive' or 'stupid'. Labels are usually negative and damaging to the person. They stop us from seeing the person to whom they are applied as a person. They can also be very 'sticky' and difficult to get rid of. No other information about the person seems to matter when a strong label is applied to them. This is damaging because it strips away the person's individuality and dignity and exposes them to insensitivity and unfair discrimination. Labelling can also lead to a self-fulfilling prophecy occurring if the person who is labelled conforms to the expectations or predictions of the label.

Activity

1. Complete the stereotype:
   All men are…
   All teenagers are…
   All gay people are…
   All black people are…
   All single mothers are…
2. Can you think of reasons why each of the stereotypes you have produced is not actually true?

Prejudice

Prejudices are sets of negative, critical or hostile ideas about a person or group of people. They are prejudgements that are usually based on false or inadequate information and which are damaging to the person or group to whom they are applied. Prejudices can become fixed or very difficult to change. They are closely connected to stereotypes. When people act on their prejudices, they discriminate unfairly against people.

An individual might show a lack of respect for others by:

▶ using hostile language

▶ not sitting by certain people

▶ avoiding working with another individual

▶ not touching another person

▶ having negative body language towards certain people.

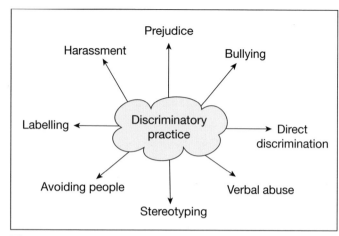

Figure 6.2 Forms of discriminatory practice

These discriminatory behaviours devalue and disrespect those whom they are aimed at. They can also lead to unfair and unequal treatment or discrimination. Sometimes discriminatory behaviours are unthinking and thoughtless rather than deliberate and calculated. However, there are times when care workers do deliberately discriminate against others, though this is always unacceptable and should be reported when it occurs. Forms of discriminatory practice include physical abuse, neglect, avoidance and exclusion of certain people, verbal abuse and devaluing or unjustified criticism.

Case study

In January 2009, a reporter from the BBC programme *Inside Out West*, carried out an investigation into racial discrimination by lettings and employment agencies. Thirty agencies that supplied temporary workers were contacted by the programme. Each was asked whether they could provide candidates for a receptionist post. The researcher telephoned each agency to ask whether they could advertise the post to 'white only' workers. These are a selection of the replies:

Agency: 'That's fine. You are not allowed to say it but, no, we certainly hear what you say. That's not a problem.'

Agency: 'We'll ignore it and pretend you didn't say it but listen to what you said, if you see what I mean.'

Agency: 'It's difficult with the accent over the phone isn't it? I understand that, yeah, shouldn't really say that but taken on board.'

Agency: 'OK. You are not supposed to tell me that but I will forget you did (laughter) but bear it in mind.'

Researcher: 'Just send through white.'

Agency: 'Yep. Normal people.'

Twenty-five of the 30 agencies telephoned agreed to provide 'white only' candidates, even though this is unlawful.

1. What kind of prejudice is being expressed by the researcher?

2. How should the agency staff who are talking with the researcher respond to his request for 'white only' job candidates?

3. Why is it wrong to favour one ethnic group over another when trying to fill a job vacancy?

Effects of discrimination

Unfair discrimination can be seen as a form of abuse. It can have a number of permanent and damaging physical, intellectual, emotional and social effects on an individual.

Role of the media

'The media' is a term given to forms of mass communication such as newspapers, television, magazines, the internet and radio. Ideas and images communicated through the media can have a powerful effect on those who receive them. The ideas and beliefs we have about different groups in society are formed and shaped by what we see, hear and read in the **mass media**. People can be portrayed in both positive and negative ways.

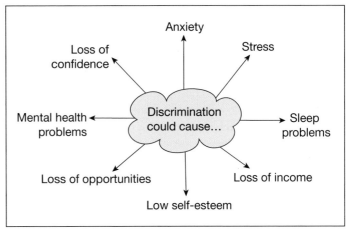

Figure 6.3 Discrimination could cause...

 Activity

Investigate how people classified as 'refugees' or 'immigrants' are portrayed by the mass media. You could do this by watching television news and entertainment programmes and noting how members of these groups are portrayed in any stories or shows where they appear. Alternatively, review the stories that appear about refugees or immigrants in a national newspaper over a period of about a week. When you have obtained some background information:

1. Identify any stereotypes being used to describe members of these groups.

2. Describe the kinds of issues or stories members of these groups are associated with.

3. Summarise your findings by explaining how the media plays a role in creating ideas and beliefs about refugees and immigrants in the United Kingdom.

 Over to you!

How are young people (particularly teenagers) portrayed in the media? Are young people like yourself stereotyped in any particular way? How accurate are these stereotypes and what impact do you think they have on the feelings, self-image and behaviour of teenagers? Discuss your ideas with a class colleague.

Non-discriminatory practice

Care organisations try to promote equality of opportunity. This prevents discriminatory practice. Care organisations need to have relevant policies and procedures in place to achieve this. Care workers also need to be aware of the ways in which discrimination occurs and what their responsibilities are in challenging it and preventing it from occurring. Other ways of promoting non-discriminatory practice include:

▶ using varied materials to portray positive images of diversity, e.g. visual displays should avoid stereotypes and celebrate diversity and difference

▶ organising diverse activities that celebrate different religious festivals and promote understanding of different religious beliefs and cultures

▶ using books and toys that avoid stereotypical images of men and women, ethnic groups and other social differences.

Individual workers' responsibilities

Induction training and policies usually tell workers what their equal opportunities responsibilities are. Basically, care workers need to respect and meet the individual needs of each service user. They need to:

▶ think about how best to communicate to meet each individual's language needs

▶ consider how they can avoid and challenge prejudice

▶ avoid stereotyping and labelling others

▶ challenge incidents of unfair discrimination.

Institutional responsibilities

Care organisations, or institutions, need to have equal opportunities policies, training and supervision of staff. They must ensure that their policies, procedures and codes of practice are strong enough to protect individual rights.

Working with colleagues

Working with colleagues in a care setting should be a supportive and enjoyable experience. However, this is not always the case as tensions can arise over the best or most appropriate ways of doing things. Direct and indirect discrimination can occur and should always be challenged. This is difficult to do, but a care worker who witnesses discrimination by a colleague should report this to their employer or manager.

Working with service users

Care workers need to find ways of promoting positive, non-discriminatory practice. Strategies for doing so include:

▶ encouraging people who use care services to make choices, and accepting their decisions, wishes and preferences

▶ finding out about the preferences of service users when providing care

▶ facilitating religious worship and the expression of personal identity and beliefs

▶ ensuring that the food offered to an individual meets their religious and dietary needs

▶ finding out about and meeting the individual's particular needs when providing care or support.

Assessment activity 6.2 (P3, M2, D1)

As a student representative on the Equal Opportunities Committee at your school or college, you have been asked to make a presentation to the teaching staff at their next training day. Your presentation should cover:

• factors that influence equality of opportunity for individuals in society

• discriminatory practice and how this can be avoided

• the impact of discriminatory practice on individuals.

You may want to use information technology to create your presentation materials. Your materials should focus on the key points relating to each of the three issues identified above.

Topic check

1 Identify four different forms of unfair discrimination.
2 Give an example of a stereotype based on negative assumptions about people.
3 Describe three ways in which people express their prejudices towards others.
4 Explain why it is wrong for care workers to be prejudiced.
5 What impact can unfair discrimination have on people who experience it?
6 Explain how care workers can practise in positive, non-discriminatory ways.

Promoting and protecting individual's rights

▶ Getting started

Legislation, codes of practice and charters promote diversity and protect the rights of individuals. When you have completed this topic, you should:

■ be able to identify examples of legislation, codes of practice and charters that promote diversity and protect rights

■ know the responsibilities care employers and employees have for promoting diversity and rights.

Key terms

Charter: a document granting certain rights

Code of practice: a document setting out standards for practice

Independent Safeguarding Authority: an organisation created to prevent unsuitable people from working with children and vulnerable adults (www.isa-gov.org.uk)

Legislation: written laws, also known as statutes and Acts of Parliament

Paramount: most important

Policy: a plan of action

Procedure: a way of doing something

Role of legislation, codes of practice and charters

People in the UK are free to live their lives in the way they wish – provided they don't break the law. **Legislation** protects individuals' rights and imposes responsibilities to promote equal opportunities on employers and employees in care settings.

Legislation

The main statutes protecting people against discrimination are:

▶ The European Convention on Human Rights and Fundamental Freedoms

▶ The Mental Health Act

▶ The Convention on the Rights of the Child

▶ The Children Act

▶ The Race Relations (Amendment) Act

▶ The Disability Discrimination Act

▶ The Human Rights Act

▶ The Data Protection Act

▶ The Nursing and Residential Care Homes Regulations.

These laws influence the rights of individuals and standards of quality in care provision. Every health and social care organisation needs to have policies and practices that put these laws into action.

The European Convention on Human Rights and Fundamental Freedoms

This Convention established the European Court of Human Rights and provides the basis for the Human Rights Act 1998. It protects every individual's right:

▶ to life

▶ not to be tortured, punished or receive degrading treatment

▶ not to be enslaved

▶ to freedom and a fair trial

▶ to freedom of thought, religion and expression

▶ to marry and join organisations

▶ not to be discriminated against.

The Mental Health Acts 1983 and 2007

This piece of legislation updated the Mental Health Act 1983, which was the main piece of law affecting the treatment of adults experiencing serious mental disorders in England and Wales. The Mental Health Act 2007 seeks to safeguard the interests of adults who are vulnerable because of their mental health problems, by ensuring that they can be monitored in the community by care practitioners and admitted to hospital if they don't comply with treatment. The Mental Health Acts 1983 and 2007 also protect the rights of people who use mental health services in a number of ways. They give individuals the right to appeal against their detention in hospital and give them some rights to refuse treatment. The 2007 Act also gives individuals detained in hospital the right to refuse certain treatments, such as electroconvulsive therapy, and ensures that a person can only be detained in hospital if appropriate treatment is available for them.

Over to you!

What are the pros and cons of people having a right to refuse treatment for 'mental illness'? Would you want to be able to say 'no' to medication or other forms of treatment if you became mentally unwell?

The Convention on the Rights of the Child (1989)

This introduced rights for children and young people under the age of 18. It is based around the principles that:

▶ decisions about a child should be based on what is in the child's best interests

▶ children should not be discriminated against

▶ children should be free to express themselves

▶ children have the right to survive and develop.

The Children Act 1989 and 2004

The 2004 legislation updated the Children Act 1989 following an inquiry into the death of Victoria Climbié in 2000. The Children Act 1989 established that care workers should see the needs of the child as **paramount** when making any decisions that affect a child's welfare. Under the 1989 Act local authorities are required to provide services that meet the needs of children identified as being 'at risk'. The goal of the Children Act 2004 is to improve the lives of all children who receive informal or professional care. It covers all services that children might use, such as schools, day care and children's homes as well as health care services. The Children Act 2004 now requires care services to work collaboratively so that they form a protective team around the child.

The Children Act 2004 resulted from a report called *Every Child Matters*, which led to significant changes in the way services for children and young people are provided in the UK. The aims of *Every Child Matters* (www.everychildmatters.gov.uk) are that all children should:

- be healthy
- stay safe
- enjoy and achieve
- make a positive contribution
- achieve economic wellbeing.

The ongoing *Every Child Matters* programme of children's service development ensures that safeguarding remains the key priority for everyone who is part of the children's workforce. People who work with children, young people and vulnerable adults now have to have their background checked by the Criminal Records Bureau (CRB) to ensure that they are a suitable person to be working with vulnerable people. In 2009, a Vetting and Barring Scheme administered by the **Independent Safeguarding Authority** and the Criminal Records Bureau required all adults who work with children to register with them. Equivalent agencies called Disclosure Scotland and Access Northern Ireland operate in other parts of the UK.

Activity

Using the internet, investigate the case of Victoria Climbié and try to identify why her death led to changes in the way that services for children operate and are organised in the UK. Produce a short summary or magazine article of your findings.

 Case study

Beverley, aged 15, suffered neglect and abuse at the hands of her mother and stepfather for 6 years before the local authority and police became aware of the situation. From the age of 9, when her mother remarried, Beverley was forbidden to play with her two half-brothers. She was also locked in her room at night, given too little to eat and made to do all the household chores for her family. Beverley was deliberately excluded from family life by her parents. They made her use an outside toilet, stopped her having any books in her room and starved her of love and affection, even though she could see her siblings being hugged and cuddled. Because she was shabbily dressed, underweight and often unkempt, Beverley was bullied at school. Beverley was frightened of her mother who didn't want to be near her, shouted at and hit her and always made her stay at home on family days out. Beverley eventually told a teacher at school what her life was like at home. A doctor who examined her said that she was underweight, had eyesight and teeth problems and had suffered emotional abuse and neglect. Beverley and her half-brothers were removed from the family home by social workers. Her parents admitted charges of cruelty and neglect and were given community sentences.

1. In what ways was Beverley subjected to ill treatment?

2. Identify examples of legislation that could be used to protect Beverley and promote her rights.

3. How did care practitioners intervene to safeguard Beverley's interests and wellbeing?

The Race Relations (Amendment) Act 2000

The Race Relations Act 1976 made racial discrimination unlawful. The Act defined racial discrimination as 'less favourable treatment on racial grounds'. The Race Relations (Amendment) Act 2000 extended and strengthened the 1976 law by making racial discrimination by public authorities, such as the Police, NHS and local authorities unlawful. The Race Relations Acts of 1976 and 2000 aim to eradicate racial discrimination and to promote equal opportunities for members of all ethnic groups.

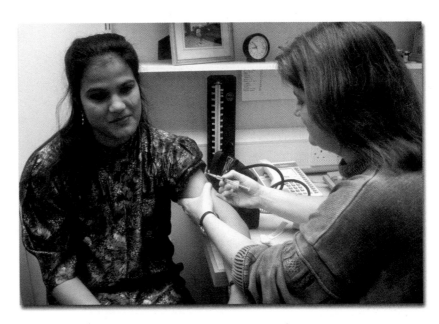

The Disability Discrimination Act

This Act safeguards the rights of disabled people by making 'less favourable treatment' of disabled people in employment, the provision of goods and services, education and transport unlawful. The aim of the Act is to ensure that disabled people receive equal opportunities and that employers, traders, transport and education providers make 'reasonable adjustments' to their premises and services to allow access.

 Activity

Use the Equality and Human Rights Commission website (www.equalityhumanrights.com) to find out about the rights of disabled people and those with mental health problems.

 Case study

Alex, aged 42, signed on with a recruitment agency to do temporary work. When he applied, Alex made it clear to the agency that he has an hearing impairment and uses a number of technological devices to communicate face-to-face and on the telephone. Alex's previous experience as both a sales consultant and a diversity trainer seemed to make him suitable for the type of work being advertised by the recruitment agency. After he completed an application form and sent in various documents, the agency replied to Alex, asking him to take part in a telephone interview. Alex did this using *TypeTalk* (a telephone service for hearing-impaired people).

Despite a good interview performance, the recruitment agency said that Alex was unsuitable for the work they had because of his hearing impairment. Alex reported the agency to the Equalities Commission and took them to court on the grounds of 'disability discrimination'.

1. What kind of disability does Alex have?

2. How has Alex experienced disability discrimination in this situation?

3. What rights does Alex have under the Disability Discrimination Act?

The Human Rights Act

The Human Rights Act 1998 is the most recent addition to equality law in the UK. It is important in relation to care environments because it entitles people resident in the UK to seek redress for infringements of their human rights by a 'public authority'. A 'public authority' is an organisation that has a public function or which operates in a public sphere. As such the legislation covers all kinds of care homes, hospitals and social services departments.

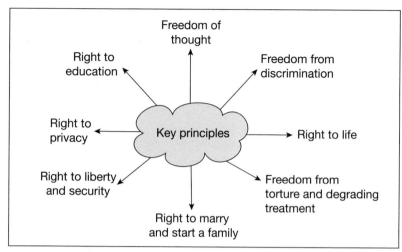

Figure 6.4 Principles of the Human Rights Act 1998

The Data Protection Act (1998)

The most important law on confidentiality of information is the Data Protection Act (1998). This sets out rules for the processing of personal information. The eight main principles of the Act are illustrated in Figure 6.5.

The Data Protection Act (1998) says that information which can be used to identify a particular patient or service user must be protected, and should not be revealed to people who don't actually need to know about it. This can mean that certain people in a care organisation need to know about some of the information held on a particular person but don't need to know all of the details. In such cases they should only be provided with access to the part of the information relevant to their work or particular needs.

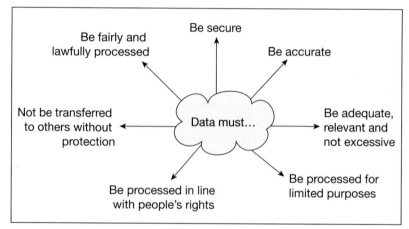

Figure 6.5 Principles of the Data Protection Act 1998

The Nursing and Residential Care Homes Regulations

The Nursing and Residential Care Homes Regulations 1984 (amended 2002) affect the setting up and running of care homes. The regulations ensure that people who live in care homes have the right to be protected from danger and harm. Residential homes are also inspected and must keep detailed information on residents and staff who work at the home. The 2002 amendments to these regulations set a range of legally enforceable minimum standards, such as room sizes and access to bathroom facilities.

Codes of practice and charters

The standards of practice care workers have to meet are set by their regulatory bodies, by the government and by their employer's policies and procedures. Care workers and their employers have a variety of responsibilities to meet the law and national minimum standards of care provision.

Codes of practice provide guidance and rules on ways of behaving and standards of practice. They identify what a care worker should do in specific situations. Codes of practice reflect standards of good practice in care settings. The Nursing and Midwifery Council produces a code of practice for nurses and midwives, while the General Social Care Council produces a code of practice for social workers.

Charters are government publications that set out service users' rights and say what can be expected from statutory services. *Your Guide to the NHS* is an NHS charter that explains rights to treatment, referral, complaints etc. Local health centres may also produce charters.

Policies and procedures

A **policy** is a set of guidelines or rules that tell care workers how to do things in a certain way in a particular care setting. Policies usually include a range of procedures that are designed to put the policy into practice.

Procedures set out how tasks, such as giving an injection or medication, should be performed. The aim of procedures is to ensure consistent, safe and effective standards of care practice.

Assessment activity 6.3 (P4, M3, D2)

Following your presentation to the teaching staff at their recent training day, you have been asked to contribute to a booklet that can be used by all staff to update their knowledge and understanding of equal opportunities law and guidelines.

Your section of the booklet should highlight how one piece of legislation and a code of practice or charter aim to promote diversity.

Topic check

1 Identify five examples of legislation that promotes and protects individuals' rights in the UK.
2 Describe how the Mental Health Acts protect the rights of people who are mentally unwell.
3 Explain how legislation protects and promotes the rights of children.
4 What rights do disabled people have as a result of the Disability Discrimination Act 1995?
5 Explain how an individual's rights are protected and promoted by the codes of practice that apply to registered care workers.

Assessment summary

The overall grade you achieve for this unit depends on how well you meet the grading criteria set out at the start of the chapter (see page **119**). You must complete:

■ all of the P criteria to achieve a **pass** grade
■ all of the P and the M criteria to achieve a **merit** grade
■ all of the P, M and D criteria to achieve a **distinction** grade.

Your tutor will assess the assessment activities that you complete for this unit. The work you produce should provide evidence which demonstrates that you have achieved each of the assessment criteria. The table below identifies what you need to demonstrate to meet each of the pass, merit and distinction criteria for this unit. You should always check and self-assess your work before you submit your assignments for marking.

Remember that you MUST provide evidence for all of the P criteria to pass the unit.

Grading criteria	You need to demonstrate that you can:	Have you got the evidence?
P1	Identify social, cultural and political factors that create diversity within society	
P2	Explain the beliefs and practices of individuals from two contrasting religious groups/secular groups	
M1	Compare the similarities and differences in the practices and beliefs of individuals from two contrasting religious or secular groups	
P3	Explain factors that may influence the equality of opportunities for individuals	
M2	Discuss how discriminatory practice can be avoided	
D1	Assess the possible effects of discrimination on the physical, intellectual, emotional and social health/wellbeing of individuals	
P4	Outline one piece of relevant legislation and one code of practice or charter for a chosen health or social care environment that aims to promote diversity	
M3	Describe how the legislation and code of practice or charter promotes diversity	
D2	Assess the effectiveness of the chosen legislation and code of practice or charter in promoting diversity	

Always ask your tutor to explain any assignment tasks or assessment criteria that you don't understand fully. Being clear about the task before you begin gives you the best chance of succeeding. Good luck with your Unit 6 assessment work!

7 Anatomy and physiology for health and social care

Unit outline

This unit introduces you to the organisation of the human body and the major body systems. You will need to investigate the structure and function of two of them in detail. You will learn how and why routine measurements and observations are made on people who use health and social care services. You will also learn about potential malfunctions of body systems and the care people require when something goes wrong with the functioning of their body.

Learning outcomes

1 **Know the organisation of the human body.**
2 **Understand the structure, function and interrelationship of major body systems.**
3 **Be able to carry out routine measurements and observations of body systems.**
4 **Know the effects of malfunctions on body systems.**
5 **Know routine care given to individuals with body malfunctions.**

Grading guide

To achieve a **pass**, your evidence must show that you are able to:	To achieve a **merit**, your evidence must show that you are able to:	To achieve a **distinction**, your evidence must show that you are able to:
P1 Identify the organisation of the human body and the position of the main body organs		
P2 Illustrate the structure and function of two major body systems and how they interrelate	**M1** Discuss, for each system, how its structure helps it to carry out its functions	**D1** Explain how systems interrelate to maintain homeostasis
P3 Carry out routine measurements and observations used to monitor the two body systems		
P4 Outline a common malfunction in each of the two body systems	**M2** Describe how the presence of the malfunction might affect routine measurements and observations of each body system	
P5 Identify potential risk factors for each of the two malfunctions		
P6 Identify the routine care given for each malfunction	**M3** Describe the routine care for each malfunction	**D2** Explain how the routine care given for each malfunction affects the body systems

Organisation of the human body

This topic introduces you to the organisation of the human body. When you have completed this topic, you should:

- know how the human body is organised into cells, tissues, organs and body systems
- be able locate the main organs in the human body.

Key terms

Anatomy: the study of how the human body is structured and organised

Cells: the basic 'building blocks' of the human body

Enzymes: naturally occurring chemical substances that help chemical reactions to take place in the human body

Hormones: substances released into the blood that affect the way the body works

Neurons: cells in the nervous system that process and transmit information

Organs: tissues that perform specific functions in the body

Physiology: the study of how the body works

Tissues: groups of specialised cells with a common structure and function

The human body

In terms of its **anatomy** and **physiology**, the human body consists of cells, tissues, organs and body systems.

Cells

Cells are the smallest, microscopic elements of the body. The human body consists of many millions of cells that vary in size, shape and function. Each cell has three parts:

- ▶ a nucleus that controls the way the cells works, e.g. as a nerve cell, a muscle cell or a blood cell
- ▶ cytoplasm, a jelly-like substance containing the structures that enable the cell to function
- ▶ a membrane surrounding and protecting the cell.

Each of the cells in the human body has a specific function, such as being a brain cell (making the brain work) or a red blood cell (delivering oxygen to tissues).

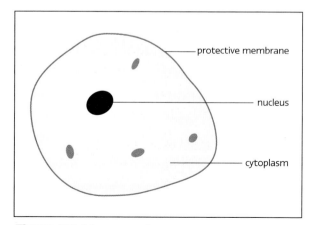

Figure 7.1 A human cell

Tissues

Tissues are made up of groups of cells that have the same structure and function, e.g. bone tissue consists of bone cells, muscle tissue consists of muscle cells and blood tissues consist of blood cells. There are four main types of human tissue:

▶ epithelial tissue covers internal and external surfaces of the body

▶ connective tissue has a supporting role and includes blood, bone and cartilage tissues

▶ muscle tissue is present in all muscles, including the heart

▶ nervous tissue consists of **neurons** that make up the nervous system.

Organs

Organs consist of different types of tissues that are grouped together in order to perform one or more specific function in the human body. Organs are located throughout the human body (see Figure 7.2).

The skin

The function of the skin is to protect the body, maintain body temperature, receive and communicate information from the person's environment (e.g. through touch, pain and pressure) and to produce sweat that carries waste products out of the body.

The heart

The heart's vital function is to pump blood to the lungs and around the body. Blood delivers oxygen, nutrients, **hormones** and antibodies to the areas of the body that need them.

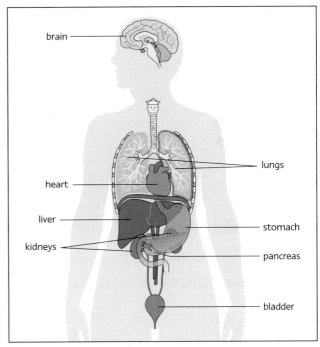

Figure 7.2 Location of organs in the body

Case study

In 1995 Hannah Clark, then a 2-year-old girl from Wales, had a heart transplant because of cardiomyopathy. This condition made her heart double in size and likely to fail within a year. She underwent a pioneering heart transplant in which a second donor heart was inserted into her body. Hannah's new heart took on the task of pumping blood around her body allowing her own, still beating heart, to rest. Following complications, Hannah's donor heart had to be removed 10 years later. When surgeons operated to remove the donor heart, they discovered that her own heart had recovered enough to function normally.

1. What would have happened if Hannah's heart had failed before she had a transplant?

2. What vital role did the transplanted heart perform in Hannah's body?

3. Describe what a person's heart does when it functions normally.

The lungs

The two main functions of the lungs are to:

▶ transport oxygen from the atmosphere into the bloodstream

▶ remove carbon dioxide from the bloodstream and release it into the atmosphere.

A person's lungs are located in the chest, on either side of their heart.

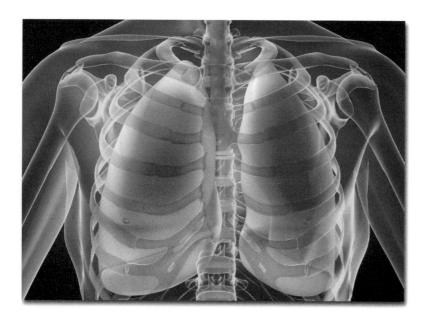

The brain

The three main functions of the brain are to:

▶ receive and respond to information about the person's environment

▶ coordinate and control physical functions such as breathing, heart rate, balance and movement

▶ make the individual self-aware and able to think about themselves and others.

A person's brain is located in their skull. It is a very complex organ that is the control centre for the nervous system and the body as a whole.

Eyes and ears

The eyes and ears are sensory organs that receive information that is sent to the brain for interpretation. The eyes are connected to muscles that allow them to move. The ears channel sound waves onto the eardrum. This vibrates and transmits the sound waves further into the body until they become nerve impulses that can be interpreted by the brain. The inner parts of the ear also play an important role in a person's sense of balance.

The stomach

The main role of the stomach is to digest food. It is basically a bag that stores and digests food. Digestive **enzymes** are released in the stomach to help this

Activity

Television presenter Fern Britton caused controversy in 2008 when she revealed that her substantial weight loss was partly the result of having a 'gastric band' operation on her stomach. This type of surgery is based on a simple principle – when a person's stomach feels full they will stop eating.

The gastric band operation involves a silicone loop being placed and tightened near the top of the person's stomach. When food enters the pouch that is created, the person has the feeling of being full. The 'pouch' then slowly empties through the gap into the rest of the stomach, and appetite returns.

1. Create a diagram to show how a gastric band works.

2. Why should a person who has a gastric band fitted lose weight?

3. Investigate the risks and drawbacks of having a gastric band fitted.

vital process. Solids are broken down into fluids. Partly digested food moves from the stomach into the small intestine where further enzymes are released to complete the digestion process.

The pancreas

The function of the pancreas is to produce hormones that control glucose levels in the blood and to secrete enzymes into the small intestine that help the body to break down and digest food.

The liver

The liver is the largest internal organ in the human body. It is on the right side of the abdominal cavity, just below the diaphragm. The liver performs a number of functions including:

▶ storing iron and some vitamins

▶ removing drugs and alcohol from the blood

▶ helping to control levels of glucose in the blood

▶ producing heat that keeps the body warm

▶ producing bile salts that break down fat in the small intestine.

Case study

Diane Hughes, aged 62, has a long history of alcohol misuse. She has been drinking excessive amounts of alcohol since her early forties when one of her children died in a boating accident. Diane has managed to stop drinking for up to a year at a time but always relapsed and resumed drinking again. Diane has been diagnosed with alcoholic hepatitis and also suffers from diabetes. Diane's GP and hospital consultant have both advised her to stop drinking as she is now at risk of developing cirrhosis of the liver. One of the reasons that Diane hasn't stopped misusing alcohol is that she doesn't understand the functions of the liver or the reasons why alcohol can cause liver disease.

1. How would you explain the main functions of the liver to Diane?

2. What happens to the liver when alcoholic hepatitis develops?

3. What happens to the liver when cirrhosis develops?

The intestines

The intestines are part of the alimentary canal, extending from the stomach to the anus. The human intestine consists of two segments, the large and small intestine. The small intestine is a greyish purple colour, 35 mm in diameter and about 6-7 m (20-23 feet) long in an average adult. The main function of the small intestine is to break down and digest food. The large intestine is dark red in colour and about 1.5 m long. It stores undigested food as faeces until it is passed out of the body through the anus.

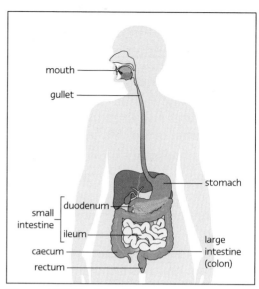

Figure 7.3 The intestines

Activity

Investigate the causes, symptoms and effects on the intestines of gasteroenteritis, Coeliac disease or irritable bowel syndrome. Produce a diagram or poster to explain how one of these health problems affects the normal functioning of the intestines.

The kidneys

The kidneys filter out and remove excess salt, water and waste products from the blood. The kidneys keep the composition of the blood balanced by maintaining correct levels of minerals, salts and fluids. Their main function is to produce urine. The kidneys are located behind the abdominal cavity, one on each side of the spine just below the level of the diaphragm. The kidneys are bean shaped, weigh between 115 g and 170 g in adults, with the left kidney slightly larger than the right.

Case study

Sam Jacobs was 30 years of age when he went to see his GP, complaining of severely blurred vision in both eyes and weight loss. The GP examined Sam and found he had high blood pressure and some other worrying symptoms of kidney disease. Sam was referred to a consultant at his local hospital. Following several more tests, the consultant diagnosed the early stages of kidney failure. Sam was shocked and didn't want to accept that the diagnosis was true. However, Sam returned to see the consultant a year later as he was still having trouble with blurred vision and was now feeling very tired and nauseous. He was also feeling quite depressed about his condition. Within 2 years Sam's condition had deteriorated to the point where he needed to start kidney dialysis or have a transplant. Sam's brother Phil volunteered to donate one of his own kidneys. Following medical assessment, Phil was found to be a suitable donor because he had two healthy kidneys and was the same blood type as Sam. The transplant was carried out successfully and both Sam and Phil are now in good health.

1. What symptoms of kidney disease did Sam have?

2. What does kidney dialysis remove from the patient's blood?

3. Why do potential kidney donors have to undergo a detailed medical assessment before they can donate a kidney?

The bladder

The bladder's function is to store urine until it is excreted (removed) from the body. The bladder stretches when it fills and contracts when it is emptied.

The testes and ovaries

The testes are the male reproductive organs that produce and store sperm cells and the hormone testosterone. The ovaries are the female reproductive organs that produce and store egg cells and the hormones oestrogen and progesterone.

The uterus

The uterus, or womb, is a muscular structure that protects and feeds the baby as it is developing. During labour, it contracts and pushes the baby down the birth canal.

Case study

Two women living in Florida suffered organ failure and severe health problems after receiving cosmetic injections, which they thought would enhance their appearance, from a fake doctor. One of the women received 40 injections of silicon and the other 20, at the 'doctor's' home, in the belief they would give them 'J.Lo' style bottoms. Both became seriously ill with internal organ failure and ended up in intensive care with damage to their livers, kidneys and lungs.

1. Where in the human body is the liver located?

2. What are the main functions of the lungs?

3. Identify two possible consequences of kidney damage.

Assessment activity 7.1 (P1)

You have been asked to help produce materials on the human body for a training day for new health care assistants at a local hospital. Your task is to produce a poster or a leaflet that identifies the position of the main organs in the human body.

Topic check

1 Name the three parts that make up every human cell.
2 List four different types of body tissue.
3 Where is the heart located and what is its main function in the human body?
4 Outline the main functions of the brain.
5 What is the largest internal organ in the human body and where is it located?
6 Identify the main functions of the kidneys.

What do the major body systems do?

Getting started

This topic is about the main functions of the human body's organs. When you have completed this topic, you should:

- be able to name the main body systems
- know the main functions of the body organs.

Key terms

Arteries: blood vessels that carry blood away from the heart

Capillaries: small blood vessels composed of a single layer of cells that connect arteries to veins

Cardiovascular: related to the heart and circulatory system

Digestive: related to the breaking down of food into forms that the body can use

Endocrine: related to hormones and the glands that

make and secrete them into the bloodstream

Musculoskeletal: related to muscles and the skeleton

Peristalsis: the rippling or contraction of muscles in the intestines

Respiratory: related to the process of breathing

Ureter: a tube that carries urine from the kidneys to the bladder

Veins: blood vessels that carry blood towards the heart

Major body systems

The human body consists of a number of major systems (see Figure 7.4) that are connected. A body system is simply a group of organs that work together for a particular purpose.

The cardiovascular system

The **cardiovascular** system consists of the heart, the blood and blood vessels. In basic terms, it is a pumping system. The heart is the pump and **arteries**, **veins** and **capillaries** are the tubes that carry blood around the body. The function of the cardiovascular system is to supply body tissues with oxygen and essential nutrients and to remove waste products such as carbon dioxide.

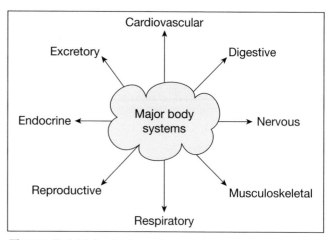

Figure 7.4 Major body systems

Figure 7.5 shows the structure of the heart. This is based around four chambers and a number of tubes (arteries and veins) that allow blood to be brought into and then pumped out of the heart. The right side of the heart pumps blood to the lungs to pick up oxygen. The left side of the heart then pumps the oxygenated blood through the arteries to tissues around the body. Deoxygenated blood is then returned to the heart through the body's network of veins.

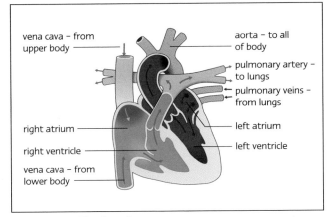

Figure 7.5 The heart

Figure 7.6 The respiratory system

The respiratory system

The **respiratory** system brings oxygen into, and takes carbon dioxide out of, the human body.

The respiratory system looks like a tree upside down (see Figure 7.6). Oxygen enters the mouth and nose and is then drawn down the trachea and into the bronchus and bronchioles of each lung. It is then transferred into the blood through the alveoli sacs. Carbon dioxide flows the other way through the respiratory system. It passes out of the blood into the alveoli, back down the bronchioles, through the bronchus and trachea and out through the mouth and nose.

The nervous system

The nervous system covers the whole of the human body. It consists of a network of specialised cells that receives, interprets and then responds to information about a person's internal and external environment.

There are two main parts to the nervous system. The central nervous system consists of the spine and brain. This part of the nervous system interprets information sent from the peripheral nervous system, which consists of nerves throughout the body. Sensory nerves respond to internal and external stimuli by producing and passing on signals to the brain. The brain then processes and sends signals back to the muscles and glands of the body. A person's nervous system enables them to be physically active (e.g. walking, running, jumping) and also controls the way their body functions (e.g. reducing temperature, speeding up heart beat, blinking).

The endocrine system

The **endocrine** system consists of glands that produce and release hormones into the body via the blood. The endocrine system controls metabolism, growth, development, puberty, tissue function and also plays a part in controlling mood. It works by releasing hormones in response to a change in the structure or function of the body. This is known as negative feedback because an endocrine gland will produce hormones when it receives a signal that the body needs them, but will stop producing them when there is enough of a particular hormone in the body.

Activity

Using textbooks and the internet, investigate the role of the pituitary gland. Produce a brief summary of your findings, explaining why the pituitary gland plays such an important role in the human body.

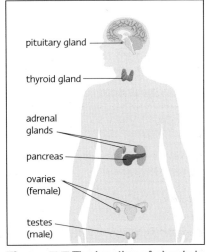

Figure 7.7 The location of glands in the endocrine system

The digestive system

The **digestive** system is responsible for the physical and chemical digestion, absorption and elimination of food materials. Food is first ingested, or taken into, the mouth. It is chewed and softened by saliva. This starts to break down the food. When a ball of food is swallowed it goes down the oesophagus, partly through gravity and partly through a process called **peristalsis**, to the stomach. When the food reaches the stomach, chemical digestion takes place, and nutrients are absorbed as it broken down further by enzymes and gastric juices. This partly digested food stays in the stomach for about 5 hours. It is then pushed into the small intestine for further chemical digestion. More enzymes and pancreatic juices break the food down into the components that the body needs and can absorb. This process takes about 4 hours. Between 7 and 9 hours after food has first been eaten, it will have reached a stage where the nutrients have been extracted. The remaining undigested mass is moved into the large intestine as faeces to be eliminated via the anus.

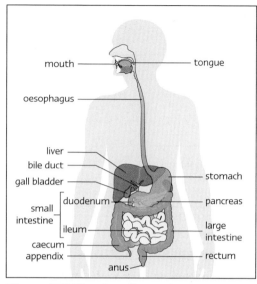

Figure 7.8 The digestive system

The excretory system

The excretory system consists of the skin, the lungs, the kidneys, the bladder and bowel and the various tubes that connect them up.

The purpose of the excretory system is to remove or eliminate waste products from the body. The main waste products that have to be removed are:

▶ carbon dioxide, a by-product of respiration

▶ water, mainly from the digestive system

▶ urea, from the liver

▶ mineral salts, such as excess sodium chloride.

The kidneys filter waste products and excess water from the blood and pass this through the **ureters** into the bladder. It is excreted as urine from here. The skin eliminates excess water, salt and urea in sweat. The lungs eliminate carbon dioxide when air is exhaled.

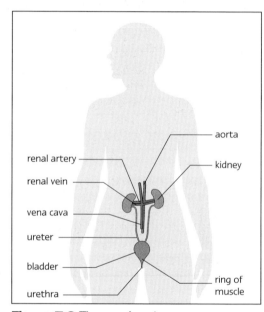

Figure 7.9 The renal system

The reproductive system

The male and female reproductive systems produce sperm and egg (ova) cells that, when combined, have the capacity to produce a child. The male reproductive system consists of:

▶ two testicles (testes) that produce and store sperm and produce male hormones

▶ the sperm tubes (vas deferens) that carry sperm from the testes to the penis

▶ the prostate gland and seminal vesicle that produce fluid which, when mixed with sperm, results in semen

▶ a penis that places sperm inside the female vagina during sexual intercourse.

 Activity

People who have serious kidney problems may have to have dialysis to clean their blood. Go to the NHS Choices website below to listen to an explanation of this from Francesca Crozier, a dialysis patient. http://www.nhs.uk/conditions/dialysis/Pages/Introduction.aspx

The female reproductive system consists of:

 two ovaries that produce and store eggs (ova) and produce female hormones

 two fallopian tubes that transport the egg to the uterus

 the uterus and cervix, where fertilisation takes place and in which the foetus develops

 the vagina, where sperm is transferred into the female reproductive system.

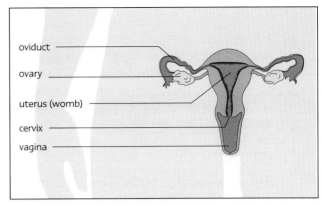

oviduct

ovary

uterus (womb)

cervix

vagina

Figure 7.10 The female reproductive system

 Case study

Stacy was diagnosed with premature ovarian failure (early menopause) at the age of 25. This was very upsetting for her as she wanted to start a family. Using in-vitro fertilisation techniques, she was implanted with eggs donated by her twin sister that had been fertilised by her husband's sperm. When this procedure failed, Stacy's twin sister agreed to have one of her own ovary's removed and transplanted into Stacy. The surgery was successful and Stacy had her first menstrual cycle three weeks after the operation. She is now hopeful of being able to conceive a child.

1. Why is it now possible that Stacy might become pregnant?

2. Describe what happens when an ovary releases an egg during ovulation.

3. Where in the female body are the ovaries located?

The musculoskeletal system

The **musculoskeletal** system consists of the bones of the human skeleton and the muscles that are attached to these bones. The function of this body system is to control movement. The bones of the skeleton also protect organs such as the lungs, heart and brain.

Topic check

1 Can you name five different human body systems?

2 Which parts of the body make up the cardiovascular system and how do they work together?

3 What is the function of the respiratory system?

4 What happens to food once it has entered the human digestive system? Describe the structure of the digestive system and the processes that occur within it.

5 Which parts of the human body make up the excretory system and what do they excrete?

6 How does the musculoskeletal system enable the human body to move?

Interrelationships between body systems

Topic 7.3 focuses on how the different systems in the human body are connected and work together. When you have completed this topic, you should:

- be able to describe examples of interrelated human body systems
- know what homeostasis is
- understand how the body maintains homeostasis.

Key terms

Homeostasis: the process by which internal systems of the body maintain a balance or a stable state

Interrelationship: a connection between two or more things

Negative feedback system: a process the body uses to counter changes (e.g. a rise in temperature) that might threaten its stable internal environment

Parasympathetic nervous system: part of the nervous system that slows heart rate and breathing and lowers blood pressure

Sympathetic nervous system: part of the nervous system that raises blood pressure and heart rate and narrows the arteries when the body is under stress

Vasoconstriction: narrowing of the blood vessels so that less heat is lost

Vasodilation: widening of the blood vessels so that more heat is lost

Interrelationship of body systems

The systems of the human body which you have learnt about are linked. They support each other and share the goal of maintaining life in an individual's body. The **interrelationships** between body systems are quite complex but include, for example:

- ▶ the respiratory system supplying oxygen to the cardiovascular system, which then pumps oxygenated blood around the body to keep cells alive
- ▶ the musculoskeletal system working closely with the nervous system to enable physical movement and coordination of limbs
- ▶ the digestive system working closely with the endocrine system to ensure that digestive hormones are secreted to allow the digestion of food and absorption of nutrients.

Homeostasis

The human body has the ability to regulate and maintain a stable internal (physiological) environment. This is known as **homeostasis**. This ability enables the body to respond to changes in the external environment. For example, when the weather is very hot or very cold, homeostatic mechanisms in the body notice and make adjustments to the way the body functions. The liver, kidneys and brain are the main organs involved in homeostasis:

▶ The liver breaks down toxic substances and carbohydrates.

▶ The kidneys regulate water levels, excrete waste products and clean the blood.

▶ The hypothalamus in the brain is the control centre responding to changes that occur in the environment.

Homeostasis works through a **negative feedback system**. This means that when changes are noticed in the body's external environment, the body takes action to correct any deficits or deficiencies in order to maintain a constant internal environment.

A range of physiological processes in the body is controlled through homeostasis. These include:

▶ body temperature

▶ blood pressure

▶ breathing

▶ blood glucose levels.

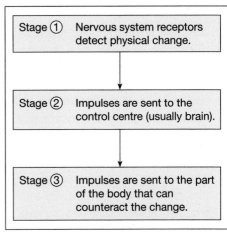

Stage ①	Nervous system receptors detect physical change.
Stage ②	Impulses are sent to the control centre (usually brain).
Stage ③	Impulses are sent to the part of the body that can counteract the change.

Figure 7.11 A negative feedback system

Maintenance of body temperature

Body temperature is controlled through a negative feedback system in which changes in temperature are detected and corrective action is taken to keep core body temperature constant. This is vital to prevent the body's internal organs from overheating. The body will respond to:

▶ hot conditions by losing heat to keep the core cool

▶ cold conditions by retaining heat to keep the core warm.

Temperature receptors in the skin and around internal organs pick up changes in temperature and report them to the brain. The brain then switches on either the body's heat loss or heat retention mechanisms in response to this.

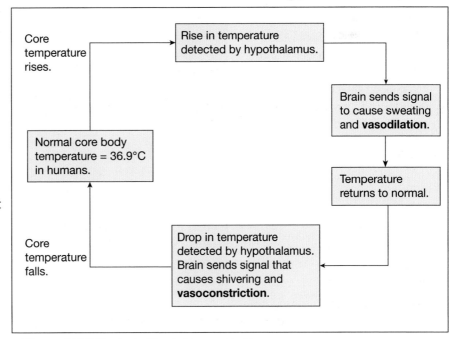

Figure 7.12 Control of body temperature

Maintenance of blood pressure

Control of a person's heart rate and blood pressure are linked. A person's heartbeat is automatically controlled by the cardiovascular centre in the brain. The pumping action of the heart creates and maintains pressure in the person's arteries.

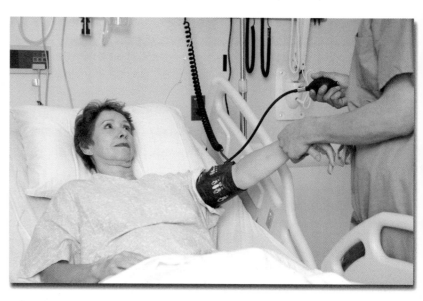

The rate at which a person's heart beats is affected by a number of factors including weight, fitness and whether they smoke. Rapid changes in the rate at which the heart beats are caused by excitement, fear and physical exertion. Receptors in the individual's **sympathetic nervous system** send messages to the brain to increase heart rate in these circumstances. Receptors in the **parasympathetic nervous system** send messages to the brain to decrease heart rate when the excitement, fear or physical exertion stops. In both cases, messages are sent to the brain because these receptors have picked up changes in the levels of carbon dioxide and oxygen in the blood. A person's arteries will widen to slow down the rate of blood flow in the body – lowering blood pressure – and narrow to increase blood pressure.

Maintenance of oxygen supply

A person's breathing is controlled by nerve impulses in their brain. It uses a negative feedback system to adjust the rhythm, depth and rate of breathing when receptors in the blood detect either a decrease or an increase in the amount of carbon dioxide in the body:

- During exercise or exertion a person will have a high level of carbon dioxide in their bloodstream.

- When resting and relaxed they will have a low carbon dioxide level.

When carbon dioxide levels are high, receptors report this to the brain, which quickens and deepens the person's breathing rate so that they breath out more carbon dioxide and obtain more oxygen.

Maintenance of blood glucose levels

Blood glucose (a type of sugar) is the body's main source of energy. Its levels are controlled by a negative feedback system. The pancreas is the control centre. It monitors how much glucose is in the bloodstream and whether there is sufficient insulin and glucagon (types of blood sugar) to maintain a correct blood sugar level. A person's blood glucose level, and their negative feedback system, is affected by food:

▶ Shortly after eating a meal a person will have a high blood sugar level.

▶ When they are hungry they will have a low blood sugar level.

Case study

Andrew hadn't eaten for over 10 hours. He was determined to complete his drive to a holiday cottage in France with as few stops as possible. When he got on the ferry he felt weak, tired and had poor concentration. He almost hit a post as he drove onto the ship! Andrew thought he'd better have something to eat as he had another long drive ahead of him when the ferry reached France. After eating a meal and drinking a cup of coffee Andrew felt much less tired and much more alert. He also bought a sandwich and some chocolate to eat on the next leg of his journey.

1. Give a biological explanation for the way Andrew felt when he arrived at the ferry.

2. How would eating a meal boost Andrew's blood glucose levels?

Assessment activity 7.2 (P2, M1, D1)

As part of your work producing training materials for the care assistant training day at a local hospital, you have also been asked to:

• Produce a poster or leaflet that illustrates the structure and function of two major body systems and how they interrelate. The material you produce should include annotated diagrams and a brief explanation of the role each body system plays.

• Discuss and explain how the two systems interrelate to maintain homeostasis.

Topic check

1   What does the term 'homeostasis' refer to?
2   Identify three physiological processes that are maintained through homeostasis.
3   Explain how 'negative feedback' systems work to correct changes in the human body.
4   How does the body ensure that a stable internal temperature is maintained during very hot weather?
5   Explain how the body responds to excess carbon dioxide in the bloodstream.
6   Describe how optimum blood glucose levels are maintained in the body.

Getting started

This topic focuses on ways of carrying out routine measurements and observations of body systems. When you have completed this topic, you should:

- know about a range of routine physiological measurements

- be aware of considerations that influence the taking and interpretation of routine measurements

- be able to describe ways of observing abnormalities in body systems.

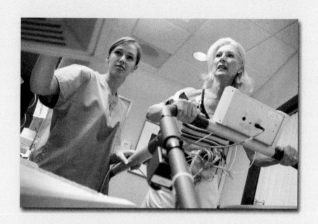

 Key terms

Carotid artery: an artery located in the neck

Core temperature: the temperature at which the body's organs and internal structures are operating

Ovulation: the part of a woman's menstrual cycle when an egg (ovum) is released

Radial artery: an artery located in the forearm and wrist

Sphygmomanometer: an instrument for measuring blood pressure

Measuring health indicators

There are many different ways of measuring physical health. They are all based on the same basic idea – the health care practitioner measures and records something and then compares the individual's 'score' against a standard scale. In order to interpret the results of any physical measurement procedure, a health care practitioner has to take into account the individual's age, sex and lifestyle. This is important because a pulse rate of 100 beats per minute would be fast for an adult but normal for a baby, for example.

Health, safety and accuracy issues

Health practitioners who measure and observe patients for signs of illness are trained to carry out procedures safely and accurately. Most observations require knowledge and experience rather than equipment, and are straightforward and non-hazardous to carry out. Where equipment is used to measure a patient's health, the health care practitioner has a responsibility to:

▶ Ensure the safety and wellbeing of the individual during measurement.

▶ Only use equipment they have been trained to use.

▶ Check that equipment is in a safe, clean condition before using it with a patient.

▶ Ensure that they minimise the risk of cross-infection by washing their hands before and after touching the measuring equipment.

▶ Carry out the measurement procedures according to local policies and by following the equipment manufacturer's instructions. This can mean duplicating or repeating measurements to get an accurate impression of the person's state of health.

▶ Safely dispose of any equipment that may be hazardous because it is broken, inaccurate or has become infected.

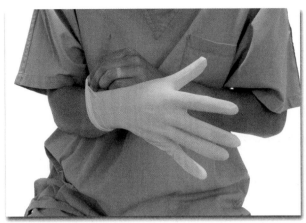

Measuring pulse rate

A person's pulse rate indicates how fast their heart is beating. It is a wave of pressure caused by blood being pumped through the arteries by the heart – it can be felt in any artery. For adults, the average (or normal) resting rate is usually between 70 and 80 beats per minute. Babies and young children normally have a faster pulse rate than adults.

In conscious people, it is usual to take a person's pulse at the **radial artery**, which can be found in the wrist. In unconscious people, the **carotid artery**, which can be felt at the neck, may be used. A person's pulse rate increases when they exercise, when they are emotionally upset, or if they develop a form of heart or respiratory disease. Unfit people, smokers and overweight people have a faster resting pulse rate than normal.

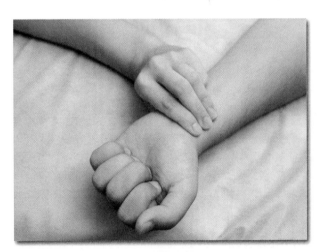

Measuring blood pressure

Health care professionals routinely measure blood pressure as well as pulse rate. Blood pressure measurement is a direct way of checking heart function, and an indirect way of checking physical fitness.

Blood pressure is measured with an instrument called a **sphygmomanometer** or 'sphyg' for short. Some health care professionals use electronic sphygs which measure automatically and display the results on a screen. Blood pressure can be measured using a manual sphyg, but this is less accurate.

 Activity

Measure your own, or another person's, pulse rate (using the radial pulse) for one minute. Compare the resting pulse rate with the pulse rate taken after some brief exercise.

 Over to you!

How might each of the following factors have an impact on an individual's pulse rate?

- stress
- blood loss
- drugs
- strenuous exercise
- age
- infection
- sleep

When a person's blood pressure is checked, two measurements are taken by the sphyg:

▶ systolic blood pressure – the maximum pressure of the blood in the arteries when the heart beats

▶ diastolic blood pressure – the continuous pressure that the person's blood puts on the arteries between heart beats.

A person's blood pressure is then recorded and written as two numbers. The systolic measure comes first, followed by the diastolic measure. An average, healthy young adult will have a blood pressure reading of 120/80 mm Hg (millimetres of mercury), though BP rises with age and body weight.

A person's blood pressure fluctuates throughout the day and night. It increases when the person is active and decreases when they are inactive, resting or sleeping. Consistently high blood pressure (hypertension) is linked to a higher risk of heart attacks and strokes. Low blood pressure (hypotension) may be an indicator of heart failure, dehydration or other underlying health problems.

Measuring body temperature

Normal body temperature is between 36.5 °C and 37.2 °C. A person's temperature will vary throughout the day and is responsive to their activity levels, clothing, **ovulation** and the weather, for example. Regardless of conditions, a thermometer is needed to measure body temperature accurately. A health practitioner would usually place a thermometer under a person's armpit or in their mouth to record their temperature. **Core temperature** is measured by placing a thermometer in the person's anus. Specialist equipment such as ear thermometers and thermometer strips placed on the forehead can also be used to measure body temperature where an individual is too young, too unwell or is unable to manage to hold a thermometer in their mouth or under their arm for some other reason.

Measuring blood glucose levels

Blood glucose is a sugar found in the blood. It is the body's main source of energy. A healthy adult should have between 4 and 8 mmol/l of blood glucose. Blood glucose levels can be measured in several ways:

▶ *Random glucose tests* are carried out on two separate occasions. The person's finger is pricked to draw blood, which is then wiped onto a special strip and inserted in a machine that identifies the blood glucose level. A reading above 11.1 mmol/l usually indicates diabetes.

▶ *Fasting glucose tests* are carried out in the same way as the random glucose test, again on two separate occasions. However, the person is tested after fasting (not eating and drinking only water) overnight. A reading above 7.0 mmol/l usually indicates diabetes.

▶ *Glucose tolerance tests* are also carried out after a person has fasted, usually overnight, for between 8 and 14 hours. The person's blood glucose levels are measured and then they are given a special drink that contains glucose. The person's blood glucose levels are measured again after 30, 60, 90 and 120 minutes. A reading above 11.1 mmol/l after 2 hours is an indication of diabetes. A reading below 7.8 mmol/l is normal.

Activity

Find out what effect each of the following can have on a person's blood pressure:

- a diet high in fat and salt
- regular exercise
- stress
- cigarette smoking
- malnutrition (lack of food).

Over to you!

Observe a friend or relative for a few minutes as a way of measuring their breathing rate. It's probably best to do this by watching their chest rise and fall rather than feeling their breath on your cheek!

Measuring breathing rate

A person's breathing rate is simply the number of times they take a breath per minute. A healthy adult would be expected to have a breathing rate of 16–18 breaths per minute. Babies and children have a faster breathing rate, which slows as their lungs grow and develop to maturity. Breathing rate can be measured by:

▶ observing and counting the number of times a person's chest rises and falls in a minute

▶ putting your cheek close to the person's nose and mouth and counting the number of breaths you feel on your cheek.

Peak flow measurement

A peak flow meter measures the maximum rate at which air is expelled (pushed out) from the lungs when a person breathes out as hard as they can. A healthy adult should record a peak flow result of 400–600 litres of air per minute. Peak flow tests are used to monitor several aspects of respiratory function. For example, the peak flow meter can be used to diagnose whether a person has a problem with the use of their lungs, because there is a standard scale of expected scores against which the results can be compared. People with chronic (long-term) asthma usually record a measurement that is lower than 350 on the peak flow scale when they breathe out as hard as they can.

Case study

Mia was only 18 months old when she was diagnosed with diabetes. Mia's mum had to inject, feed and care for her throughout her childhood and had many sleepless nights worrying about Mia becoming hypoglycaemic. Mia is now 43 years of age but grew up thinking that she would die young because of her diabetes. When she was at primary school, some of the other pupils thought that they might 'catch' diabetes from her if they played with her too much! This caused Mia lots of unhappiness. Despite being told by a family planning nurse that she was 'probably sterile' because of her diabetes, Mia gave birth to a daughter when she was 24 and a son when she was 26 years old. Mia's pregnancies were very carefully monitored but passed without incident. Neither of her children have diabetes. Mia has now been taking insulin to control her diabetes for over 40 years and remains in good health.

1. How are a person's glucose levels linked to diabetes?

2. What happens to a person's blood glucose levels when they become hypoglycaemic?

3. What testing method would Mia be able to use to check her blood glucose levels quickly?

Observing physical signs of illness

Some physical signs of health and illness cannot be directly measured using devices such as blood pressure machines or thermometers. Instead, health practitioners observe their patients and then use their knowledge and experience to make a judgement about the person's health.

Skin colour and texture

Healthy young skin is firm, smooth and has an even tone. As people age their skin loses elasticity and becomes more lined and wrinkled. Signs of ill health that can be seen in a person's skin colour and texture include:

▶ dry, flaky, itchy or clammy skin

▶ changes in colour, such as blueness around the lips or finger nails, flushed red or very pink

▶ congested skin pores with spots and blackheads

▶ tenderness, sensitivity and pain on touching

▶ puffy, swollen skin

▶ broken skin, rashes, blisters.

Breathing rate and rhythm

A healthy adult has a breathing rate of about 16–18 breaths per minute. A health care practitioner should notice if a patient has an abnormal breathing rate or rhythm. They would look for:

▶ breathlessness, particularly where the person is struggling or making more effort to breath

▶ shallowness of breathing

▶ an increased rate of breathing

▶ abnormal (louder, gasping or wheezing) breathing sounds.

Abnormal breathing rates and rhythms can be caused by a number of conditions, including asthma, heart problems and pneumonia, and should always be reported immediately.

Sweating, temperature and thirst

Everybody sweats as a way of cooling down their body's temperature. This is a normal, natural response to heat. However, some medical conditions and acute health problems can cause excessive sweating to occur. A care worker who notices that a person is sweating is likely to assess whether there are any environmental reasons for this (hot day, inappropriate clothing) before considering whether it might be caused by exertion or anxiety. If this isn't the case, they would then have to consider whether the person's sweating and high temperature is caused by an

 Activity

Using health care, medical or biology books and the internet, investigate a skin problem such as eczema, psoriasis or dermatitis. Produce a summary of the main causes and symptoms of your chosen skin condition.

underlying health problem, such as an infection. In a similar way, a person might complain of feeling thirsty because they have become too hot or have not consumed sufficient fluid during the day. If this isn't the case and the thirst persists, the care worker should consider whether the person's thirst is a symptom of an underlying health problem, such as diabetes.

Case study

Edwin recently turned 50 years of age. He was concerned about this birthday because he's always believed that people over the age of 50 suffer from ill health. His own parents died when they were in their late fifties of heart and lung diseases. Edwin tries to live a healthy life. He doesn't smoke, drinks in moderation and exercises regularly. However, he was worried enough about his health to go to a private clinic to have a range of health checks carried out. These revealed that his:

- blood pressure is 120/80 mm Hg

- blood glucose levels are 4 mmol/l
- breathing rate is 18 respirations per minute
- peak flow result was 600 litres of air per minute.

1. Should Edwin be pleased or worried about the results of his health checks?

2. Describe how Edwin's peak flow result would have been obtained.

3. What kind of blood glucose level should be a cause for concern for someone like Edwin?

Assessment activity 7.3 (P3)

Health care workers need to have a range of practical skills. They need to be able to carry out routine measurements or observations to monitor an individual's state of health. In this activity you are required to:

- Identify ways of carrying out routine

measurements or observations of the two body systems you described in Assessment activity 7.2 (Topic 7.3).

- Demonstrate that you are competent at carrying out these routine measurements or observations yourself.

Topic check

1. Can you name five different ways of measuring physical health?
2. Identify and describe two methods of measuring a person's cardiac (heart) health.
3. Using your own words, explain what the systolic and diastolic numbers in a blood pressure reading are measuring.
4. What is the purpose and use of a peak flow meter?
5. How can a person's breathing rate be observed?
6. Describe how a person's pulse can be taken.
7. Why do people sweat?

How can body systems malfunction?

 Getting started

This topic identifies a range of illnesses and diseases that can cause human body systems to malfunction. When you have completed this topic, you should:

- know how major body systems can malfunction
- understand the potential risk factors that can lead to body systems malfunctioning.

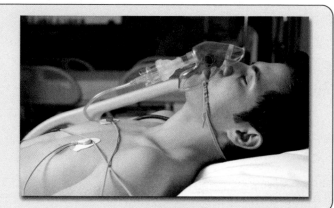

 Key terms

Allergen: any substance that causes an allergic reaction

Cyanosis: lack of oxygen in the blood, which makes the skin, lips and nails appear 'blue'

Atheroma plaques: abnormal fatty deposits that develop within the walls of the arteries

Steroid drugs: medicines that reduce swelling or inflammation

Disease, illness and malfunctioning body systems

The human body is often likened to a machine. When all of the parts are in good condition and working properly, the machine performs well. However, parts of the machine can break, be damaged or deteriorate. When this happens the machine malfunctions. In medical terms, illnesses and diseases are the main causes of malfunctioning body systems. Different illnesses and diseases affect different body systems. Some are temporary and can be treated and even cured, others have more long-term effects and can cause death.

High blood pressure

Blood pressure is the force of the blood on the walls of the arteries as the blood moves through them. A person with high blood pressure may not have any obvious physical symptoms. However, their heart is working harder than it should. Being overweight, not exercising, eating a diet high in salt and fat and drinking excess alcohol all increase the risk of high blood pressure. High blood pressure can lead to cardiovascular disease such as stroke and heart attack. It can be reduced through lifestyle changes and medication.

Heart attack

A heart attack occurs when part of the heart muscle dies because it has been starved of oxygen. Typically a person has a heart attack when a blood clot forms in one of their coronary arteries, blocking the oxygen-carrying blood supply to the heart.

 Activity

Using the British Heart Foundation website (www.bhf.org.uk), investigate the factors that lead to coronary heart disease (CHD) and ways of preventing this. Produce a leaflet or poster about CHD, summarising your findings.

Symptoms include:

▶ crushing pain in the middle of the chest, spreading to the neck, jaw, arms and wrists

▶ cold, clammy skin

▶ a loss of normal skin colour, replaced by a pale, grey colouring

A heart attack can be fatal if it leads to cardiac arrest (the heart stops completely), though many people also make a full recovery.

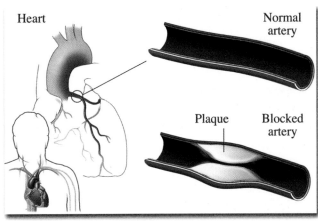

Atheroma plaques can cause blockages in arteries

Stroke

Like a heart attack, a stroke is a malfunction of the cardiovascular system. A stroke occurs when a blood vessel in the brain becomes blocked or bursts, depriving the brain of sufficient oxygen. The effects of a stroke depend on which parts of the brain are affected by the loss of oxygen. These often include loss of speech (sometimes temporarily), loss of movement on one or both sides of the body, confusion and memory loss.

High blood pressure, smoking, heart disease, obesity and diabetes are all risk factors associated with stroke. Lifestyle changes such as reducing salt levels in the diet, stopping smoking, and taking regular exercise can reduce the risk of having a stroke.

Asthma

Asthma is a condition that affects the respiratory system. It is an allergic response to **allergens** that cause irritation and inflammation in the bronchi or large air passages in the lungs. The bronchi become obstructed with mucous and an inflammatory response occurs, making the air passages narrow. This results in the person wheezing, coughing and struggling for breath.

Asthma is a condition that can be inherited, may be triggered by childhood infections and is associated with environmental factors such as cigarette smoke, animal hair, dust mites and air pollution. A person may be prescribed a bronchial inhaler (usually brown, red or orange in colour) which they use regularly to prevent the swelling and inflammation that can trigger an asthma attack. Alternatively, some people carry inhalers (usually blue) which can be used during an attack to relieve swelling and relax the muscles that are needed for breathing.

 Case study

Rachel, aged 22, was diagnosed with asthma after experiencing coughing, wheezing and sudden, unexpected breathlessness while out shopping. She was taken to hospital by ambulance. During the short trip a worried paramedic gave her oxygen to help her breathing. Rachel found this very helpful. On admission to the accident and emergency department Rachel produced a peak flow score of 70. This improved after she was given some medication but was still only 300 when she was discharged later in the morning. Rachel's GP has now prescribed preventer and reliever inhalers to help her cope with her asthma symptoms.

1. Identify three symptoms of asthma.

2. Explain why people who have asthma become breathless.

3. Describe the biological reasons why Rachel's peak flow score improved.

Emphysema

Emphysema is a chronic, irreversible condition of the lungs that results in breathing problems. It is often caused by long-term exposure to toxic chemicals, including tobacco smoke. Emphysema occurs when the alveoli in the lungs are damaged. This reduces the amount of oxygen that can be absorbed by the blood and traps air in the lungs because the person has difficulty breathing out carbon dioxide. Symptoms of emphysema include breathlessness, **cyanosis** and tiredness. Smoking, exposure to chemicals or dust and air pollution are the main risk factors. Individuals with emphysema may be given **steroid drugs** or use oxygen therapy machines to help them to breathe more easily.

Chronic bronchitis

Like emphysema, chronic bronchitis is a disease that causes irreversible damage to part of the respiratory system. Bronchitis is caused by inflammation of the bronchioles of the lungs. These are the tubes that link the larger bronchus to the alveoli where oxygen and carbon dioxide are transferred into and out of the blood.

Inflammation of bronchioles can be caused by exposure to smoke, dust, air pollution or chemicals. Mucus is produced in response to this inflammation and gradually blocks the bronchioles. This causes a tightness in the chest, breathlessness and wheezing and coughing that is often painful. Repeated, hard coughing to remove the mucus can further damage the bronchioles by scarring and making them narrower. People who suffer from chronic bronchitis often develop chest infections and go on to develop emphysema too. Weight loss, drug therapies, exercise and stopping smoking may all help to relieve the symptoms of chronic bronchitis.

Multiple sclerosis

Multiple sclerosis (MS) is a neurological condition that can affect people at any age. It is caused by damage to a protective substance called myelin that surrounds the nerve fibres of the central nervous system. Myelin helps messages travel quickly and smoothly from the brain to other parts of the body. When it is damaged the messages get disrupted and mobility, balance and muscle problems occur. The precise cause of MS is not known and there is no cure at present. There are many treatments that can ease symptoms and the condition is not fatal, but can reduce a person's quality of life.

Hypothermia

Hypothermia refers to a drop in the body's core temperature below 35.5°C as a result of exposure to the cold. The human body tries to retain heat by shivering and restricting blood flow to the skin when it is exposed to cold temperatures. However, when a person is exposed to very cold conditions, such as freezing air or water, this is sometimes not enough. An individual who is suffering from hypothermia will lose muscular and brain functions, lose consciousness and may die if their core temperature drops too low.

 Activity

Multiple Sclerosis (MS) is not infectious or contagious. However, some people are more at risk of developing this disease than others. Using the Multiple Sclerosis Society website (www.mssociety.org.uk), investigate the risk factors for MS. Produce a brief summary of your findings.

Older people, babies, young children and people who take part in outdoor activities that expose them to extreme weather conditions or the cold waters of the sea, lakes or rivers are most at risk of experiencing hypothermia. An older person may experience hypothermia because they cannot afford to heat their home. Babies and young children may not be able to respond appropriately to cold conditions and are unlikely to understand the consequences of not doing so.

Case study

When Lianne, aged 18, left home to go to a birthday party, the weather was dry but a little windy. Lianne was wearing a short-sleeved top and jeans. She decided not to take a coat or a sweater, even though her mum warned her she would catch cold. Lianne had a great time at the party and was almost the last to leave at 2.30 a.m. As there were no buses, she decided to walk home with a friend. She began feeling cold as soon as she began the 3-mile walk home. At first she rubbed her arms but then noticed she was shivering and that her hands and feet were getting colder and colder. After about

20 minutes Lianne was so cold she had to stop walking. Her friend phoned an ambulance. The ambulance crew suspected that Lianne had hypothermia and took her straight to hospital.

1. How did Lianne's body react to the change in temperature when she left the warmth of the party?

2. What happens when a person develops hypothermia?

3. Why is hypothermia a dangerous condition that requires immediate treatment?

Diabetes

Diabetes is a condition that occurs when a person's blood glucose (sugar) levels are too high. A person's blood glucose levels can be too high because:

▶ their pancreas produces little or no insulin (Type 1 diabetes)
▶ their pancreas doesn't produce enough insulin for the body's needs (Type 2 diabetes)
▶ pregnancy is affecting the way their body functions (Gestational diabetes)
▶ illness or medication is affecting the way their body functions (Secondary diabetes).

Insulin is a hormone produced by the pancreas to enable glucose to enter the cells and be used as energy. A sufficient supply of insulin is needed to control blood glucose levels. Symptoms of diabetes include:

▶ increased thirst
▶ frequent urination
▶ weight loss
▶ itchiness around the genitals
▶ recurrent skin infections.

Diabetes can be an inherited condition, though lifestyle and viruses also play a part in its development. Approximately 2.3 million people have diabetes in the UK. Poor diet, obesity and other lifestyle problems have resulted in an increase in Type 2 diabetes over the last 20 years. Most people can manage their diabetes and stay healthy by limiting the sugar and fat content of their diet and taking regular exercise. In some cases people also need to monitor their blood glucose levels and take insulin.

Crohn's disease

Crohn's disease is a chronic form of inflammatory bowel disease that usually affects the lower part of the small intestine but can affect the whole of the digestive tract. It causes thickening of the intestinal wall and inflammation of the mucous membrane that lines it. Symptoms include:

- abdominal pain
- diarrhoea
- rectal bleeding
- anal abscesses
- fever
- weight loss.

The cause of Crohn's disease is unknown, but it does appear to run in families. There is currently no cure for the disease. However, suffers can be symptom-free for long periods and can use drugs and make dietary choices that prevent flare-ups. In more severe cases people have surgery to remove the affected parts of the their digestive system.

Activity

Go to the website of the National Association for Colitis and Crohn's (www.nacc.org.uk) and find the information sheet about *Children with IBD*. Use this to build up your knowledge about the causes, effects and treatment of Crohn's disease and ulcerative colitis.

Renal failure

One of the main functions of the kidneys is to remove waste from the body. Urea is a waste product that is extracted from the blood and sent along the ureter to the bladder for elimination in urine. However, if kidney function is impaired or fails, waste products like urea build up in the blood.

Acute renal (kidney) failure can occur if the blood supply to the kidneys is insufficient, if there is a fall in blood pressure, severe dehydration or a lack of salt, or if drainage of urine from the kidneys is blocked. Chronic renal failure can occur if urine doesn't drain from the kidneys properly, if the kidney tissue becomes inflamed or because of complications associated with diabetes. Symptoms include:

- nausea, vomiting and diarrhoea
- high blood pressure
- sudden inability to drain urine
- fluid retention, such as swollen ankles
- tiredness
- loss of appetite
- weakness.

Acute renal failure can usually be treated by drugs and short-term dialysis (cleaning) of the blood. Chronic renal failure generally requires long-term dialysis, drug treatment and eventually a kidney transplant.

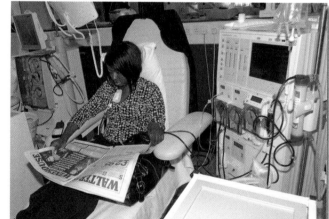

Dialysis treatment

Osteoarthritis

Arthritis is a disease of the musculoskeletal system that causes pain in the joints. There are two main types of arthritis – osteoarthritis caused by wear and tear, and rheumatoid arthritis caused by inflammation. Osteoarthritis usually develops in people over the age of 50, but can result from physical injury in younger people too. It can cause damage to the cartilage that enables the joints to move easily, cause inflammation around the joints and result in bony growths around the joints. Osteoarthritis usually affects the hips, knees and hands and can cause considerable pain and disability. Exercise, physiotherapy, medication and surgery can all be used to ease symptoms, but the condition cannot be cured.

Parkinson's disease

Parkinson's disease is a chronic neurological condition that affects the way the brain coordinates body movements. It can affect walking, talking and a person's ability to hold and use objects (e.g. cutlery). Parkinson's disease results from the loss of nerve cells in the brain. Without these cells, movement becomes progressively difficult. People with Parkinson's disease typically have a tremor, difficulty moving even slowly and stiff or rigid muscles. Parkinson's disease is not fatal but can cause significant disability.

Assessment activity 7.4 (P4, P5, M2)

You have been asked to write a case study that could be used during a training session with a group of new care assistants and students on work placement. Your case study should:

- Describe a person with health problems related to the two body systems you described in Assessment activity 7.2.

- Identify potential risk factors that can lead to each of the two malfunctions developing.

- Outline a common malfunction in each of the two body systems.

- Describe how the presence of the malfunction might have an impact on routine measurements and observations of each body system.

Topic check

1. Can you name three diseases or conditions that are the result of the respiratory system malfunctioning?
2. Describe what happens to a person's cardiovascular system when they have a heart attack.
3. What are the main symptoms of diabetes?
4. Explain why a person who has emphysema may struggle for breath.
5. Identify two groups of people who may be more at risk of developing hypothermia and explain why.
6. Explain the causes and effects on the body of multiple sclerosis.

Routine care for body malfunctions

This topic focuses on the care needs of people who have bodily malfunctions. It outlines routine care procedures that are used to monitor and support people who have particular body malfunctions. When you have completed this topic, you should:

■ know about the care needs of people with bodily malfunctions

■ be able to describe routine care for a range of body malfunctions

■ be able to identify a range of risk factors affecting care needs.

Care needs

 Key terms

Anti-coagulants: drugs used to prevent the blood from clotting

Thrombosis: a blood clot that forms within an artery

People who develop physical health problems because one of their body systems malfunctions in some way may require care and treatment at home or in hospital. A person's care needs may include:

▶ monitoring of their physical condition for signs of change (deterioration or improvement)

▶ pressure area care to prevent ulcers and other skin problems from developing

▶ ensuring that they are warm and comfortable

▶ lifestyle changes, e.g. to eat a healthy diet, take exercise, stop smoking and take any medication prescribed for them

▶ monitoring of their blood pressure, blood glucose levels or peak flow readings, depending on their condition

▶ ensuring that they are as physically active as they can be to minimise the risk of **thrombosis**

▶ protection from infection and any health and safety hazards within the home or care setting

▶ provision of self-care aids and adaptations such as mobility equipment, inhalers or adapted cutlery.

A person's need for care will be affected by:

▶ lifestyle factors such as whether they smoke, exercise, misuse drugs or alcohol and consume a balanced diet

▶ environmental factors such as their housing conditions, the type of area they live in and whether they have support from other people

▶ inherited factors such as their family history of a particular illness or genetic disorder

▶ exposure to infections, which may affect their ability to recover from physical health problems or which they may develop when they are unwell.

Active support in care settings

Health care workers who provide active support for service users deliver care in a way that assists an individual to meet their needs without reducing their independence. Wherever possible, care workers should ask the individuals they work with to participate in their own care routines. This can be achieved:

▶ through using verbal and non-verbal communication

▶ by developing an awareness and understanding of how the individual can best function in their home environment or in a care setting.

A balance has to be found between enabling an individual to care for themselves and providing sufficient care for them. However, the importance of encouraging individuals to do as much as possible for themselves to maintain their independence, self-care skills and physical abilities should not be underestimated. It is helpful to ask the individual what they can do for themselves first, and then to provide assistance where they clearly cannot carry out self-care tasks independently.

Meeting individual needs

Health care practitioners should aim to provide individualised care that meets each person's particular needs, as shown in the examples in Figure 7.13.

Figure 7.13 Ways of meeting individual needs

Area of care need	Examples of assistance required
Dietary needs	• Choosing and consuming a healthy, balanced diet • Assistance with eating and drinking (being fed) • Assistance with cutting their food up • Monitoring in case they choke on their food
Monitoring of condition	• Regular measurement of blood pressure and pulse • Examination and observation of physical condition • Specific tests or scans to check on response to treatment
Pressure area care	• Monitoring and examination of skin condition • Regular movement or turning to ensure skin doesn't break down • Treatment and monitoring of any areas of dry or broken skin to minimise and cure problems
Prevention of hypothermia	• Monitoring of temperature to ensure that it's within normal range • Management of environment to ensure adequate warmth • Ensuring appropriate clothing is available and worn inside and outside of care setting
Maintenance of blood glucose levels	• Regular blood tests to check blood glucose levels • Monitoring of diet to ensure healthy, low sugar intake • Treatment of diabetes using insulin if prescribed
Reduction of thrombosis risk	• Regular exercising of limbs to ensure adequate blood flow • Raising of limb (e.g. leg) if person is unable to mobilise to prevent blood clots forming • Treatment using **anti-coagulant** drugs to prevent blood clots forming

Cardiovascular system malfunctions

High blood pressure, heart attack and stroke are conditions that result from malfunctions in the cardiovascular system.

High blood pressure

Hypertension, or high blood pressure, is usually defined as having a sustained blood pressure of 140/90 hg or higher. Over time this can weaken the heart and damage the walls of the arteries. This can lead to blockages or to the arteries splitting and haemorrhaging. There are no obvious symptoms of high blood pressure. It is diagnosed by a health care practitioner, such as a doctor or nurse, using a sphygmomanometer to measure the individual's blood pressure.

Risk factors for high blood pressure include:

▶ age

▶ obesity

▶ poor diet

▶ lack of exercise

▶ excessive alcohol consumption.

Routine care for people who have high blood pressure includes:

▶ regular monitoring of blood pressure

▶ dietary education and changes to reduce salt intake and levels of saturated fat in the diet

▶ increasing exercise levels to lose weight and improve cardiovascular and respiratory function

▶ reducing and controlling alcohol and caffeine intake

▶ relaxation therapies, such as meditation, craft or art activities

▶ medication prescribed by a GP or hospital specialist in cases of severely high blood pressure.

Heart attack

A heart attack occurs when part of the heart muscle dies because it is starved of oxygen. This is usually the result of a blood clot or narrowing of the arteries that carry oxygenated blood to the heart. The main symptom of a heart attack is a crushing chest pain. A person who is suspected of having a heart attack should be taken to hospital. A number of tests may then be carried out, including:

▶ an ECG (electrocardiogram) to detect problems with the electrical activity in the heart

▶ a blood test to test for heart enzymes which may indicate that a heart attack has occurred

▶ a chest X-ray to look for enlargement of the heart.

A person having a heart attack will probably be given clot-busting drugs and pain relief. Following the heart attack, the person may also be prescribed different types of medication which prevent clots from forming in the blood, help the heart to beat more slowly and open up the arteries to allow blood to flow more freely. Some people who have experienced serious damage to their heart or arteries may also require surgery. This is usually to open up the arteries or to by-pass a blocked blood vessel.

Routine care for a person who has experienced a heart attack includes:

▶ an activity and exercise programme to improve and maintain physical health and fitness

▶ blood pressure and symptom monitoring, and medication to reduce the risk of further heart attacks

▶ education about cardiovascular health and its links to lifestyle

▶ lifestyle changes, such as giving up smoking, eating a low-fat, low-salt balanced diet

▶ relaxation and support to cope with the emotional difficulties and shock of having a serious health problem.

Stroke

A stroke occurs when blood vessels in the brain become blocked or burst, depriving part of the brain of oxygen. The symptoms of a stroke include:

▶ numbness and weakness or paralysis on one side of the face or body

▶ slurred speech or difficulties understanding or finding words

▶ confusion and unsteadiness

▶ severe headache

▶ sudden loss of sight or blurred vision.

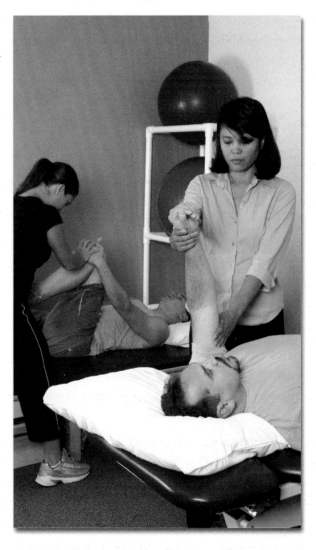

Some people recover fully from a stroke. Other people experience permanent brain damage and long-term disability. The routine care that people who have had a stroke receive depends on the severity and impact of the stroke. This can include:

▶ physiotherapy to help with balance problems, paralysis or muscle weakness and to maintain mobility

▶ speech and language therapy to help with using and understanding language

▶ dietary advice and assistance to ensure a balanced and easy-to-swallow diet

▶ occupational therapy and rehabilitation to redevelop or maximise everyday, independent living skills

▶ support for emotional problems like mood swings, anxiety and depression

▶ monitoring of blood pressure and medication to reduce risk of further strokes.

Respiratory system malfunctions

Asthma, emphysema and chronic bronchitis are all conditions that result from some part of the respiratory system malfunctioning.

Asthma

Asthma causes the small airways in the lungs to narrow when they become irritated and inflamed by allergens such as smoke, dust mites or pollen. Narrowing of the bronchi and tightening of the muscles around them causes sticky phlegm to be produced. This makes breathing more difficult and causes the person to cough and wheeze. Routine care for asthma sufferers includes:

- education about the causes, effects and ways of managing asthma
- regular use of a peak flow meter to monitor symptoms and the effect of medication
- a reliever inhaler which prevents symptoms such as muscle tightening from occurring
- a preventer inhaler to reduce inflammation if symptoms become more frequent
- advice and guidance on lifestyle changes such as stopping smoking, healthy eating, exercising and reducing alcohol intake.

Emphysema

Emphysema is a lung disease that damages the small air sacs (alveoli) where oxygen passes into the blood and carbon dioxide passes out of it. Damage to the alveoli, usually from cigarette smoke, means that less oxygen can enter and less carbon dioxide can be removed from the blood. As a result, the person has great difficulty breathing and is prone to infections, is at risk of respiratory failure and is likely to be very disabled by the condition. Emphysema is often present at the same time as chronic bronchitis, and is irreversible. Routine care is similar to that provided for chronic bronchitis, though emphysema suffers usually require more practical help and assistance with everyday living and may require home oxygen therapy to enable them to breathe.

Chronic bronchitis

Chronic bronchitis is an inflammatory disease affecting the lungs, usually caused by smoking. Inflammation causes the respiratory passages to become swollen, irritated and partly blocked by increased mucus production. This makes breathing more difficult and causes the sufferer to cough and gasp for breath. It is a very uncomfortable, sometimes frightening and often disabling condition. Routine care for chronic bronchitis and emphysema sufferers includes:

- support and encouragement to stop smoking
- avoidance of air pollution and sudden changes in temperature
- being as active as possible, ideally doing some regular exercise
- monitoring lung function through peak flow tests
- using inhalers to reduce inflammation in the air passages
- drinking lots of fluid to help thin the mucus lining the air passages, making it easier to cough up.

Case study

Albert 'Dick' Whittamore, aged 85, died in February 2010 as a result of emphysema. In his will Mr Wittamore requested that the undertakers who buried him display signs on the side of his hearse and on his grave saying 'Smoking killed me – please give up!' The undertakers agreed to carry out Mr Whittamore's dying wishes.

1. What physical changes are likely to have occurred in Mr Whittamore's lungs as a result of his lifelong smoking habit?

2. What are the main symptoms of emphysema?

3. Why does emphysema lead to significant disability and often prove fatal for sufferers?

 Activity

Investigate one of the conditions listed below and produce a 'Routine care' leaflet or poster that identifies the body system(s) affected by the condition and describes the:

- main causes of the condition
- symptoms and effects on the body of the condition
- forms of treatment and routine care provided for a person with the condition

- the effects of routine care on the body systems.

Conditions:

- diabetes
- Crohn's disease
- Parkinson's disease
- multiple sclerosis
- renal failure
- osteoporosis

 Assessment activity 7.5 (P6, M3, D2)

Using the case study you developed for Assessment activity 7.4, write a report that:

- identifies forms of care that are routinely given to people experiencing each malfunction you've described

- describes the type of routine care for each malfunction
- explains how the routine care you describe for each malfunction affects the body systems.

 Topic check

1 Identify three reasons why an individual with physical health problems may require care.

2 What does providing 'active support' for someone in hospital involve?

3 Describe three ways in which a care worker might help a person who has had a stroke to meet their dietary needs.

4 What kind of care and treatment can be used to help asthma sufferers?

5 Why are people who smoke more at risk of developing chronic bronchitis and emphysema than non-smokers?

6 What kind of lung damage does an emphysema sufferer have and how does this affect their respiratory system?

Assessment summary

The overall grade you achieve for this unit depends on how well you meet the grading criteria set out at the start of the chapter (see page 145). You must complete:

- all of the P criteria to achieve a **pass** grade
- all of the P and the M criteria to achieve a **merit** grade
- all of the P, M and D criteria to achieve a **distinction** grade.

Your tutor will assess the assessment activities that you complete for this unit. The work you produce should provide evidence which demonstrates that you have achieved each of the assessment criteria. The table below identifies what you need to demonstrate to meet each of the pass, merit and distinction criteria for this unit. You should always check and self-assess your work before you submit your assignments for marking.

Remember that you MUST provide evidence for all of the P criteria to pass the unit.

Grading criteria	You need to demonstrate that you can:	Have you got the evidence?
P1	Identify the organisation of the human body and the position of the main body organs	
P2	Illustrate the structure and function of two major body systems and how they interrelate	
M1	Discuss, for each system, how its structure helps it to carry out its functions	
D1	Explain how systems interrelate to maintain homeostasis	
P3	Carry out routine measurements and observations used to monitor the two body systems	
P4	Outline a common malfunction in each of the two body systems	
M2	Describe how the presence of the malfunction might affect routine measurements and observations of each body system	
P5	Identify potential risk factors for each of the two malfunctions	
P6	Identify the routine care given for each malfunction	
M3	Describe the routine care for each malfunction	
D2	Explain how the routine care given for each malfunction affects the body systems	

Always ask your tutor to explain any assignment tasks or assessment criteria that you don't understand fully. Being clear about the task before you begin gives you the best chance of succeeding. Good luck with your Unit 7 assessment work!

8 Human lifespan development

Unit outline

Human beings grow and develop through a number of different life stages. Health and social care professionals require a good understanding of human growth and development as this is closely linked to the differing care needs that people have.

This unit gives you a broad introduction to human growth and development in each of the main life stages. You will also learn about the ways that individuals' care needs change in different life stages, as well as about the positive and negative influences on human growth and development, including self-concept.

Learning outcomes

1 **Know developmental changes that occur at different life stages.**
2 **Know positive and negative influences on individuals at different life stages.**
3 **Know factors that can influence an individual's self-concept.**
4 **Understand the different care needs of individuals at different life stages.**

Grading guide

To achieve a **pass**, your evidence must show that you are able to:	To achieve a **merit**, your evidence must show that you are able to:	To achieve a **distinction**, your evidence must show that you are able to:
P1 Identify key aspects of physical, intellectual, emotional and social development at each of the life stages	**M1** Outline key aspects of physical, intellectual, emotional and social development at each of the life stages	
P2 State the positive and negative influences on growth and development		
P3 State factors that influence an individual's self-concept	**M2** Outline how factors can influence the development of an individual's self-concept	**D1** Describe how factors can influence the development of an individual's self-concept
P4 Explain potential differences in the care needs of individuals at different life stages	**M3** Discuss potential differences in the care needs of individuals at different life stages	**D2** Justify care provided to an individual at their different lifestages

Human growth and development

 Getting started

This topic is about the main patterns of human growth and development across a person's **lifespan**. When you have completed this topic, you should:

- know about the five main life stages
- be able to describe patterns of physical growth in each life stage
- be able to describe features of physical development in each life stage.

Key terms

Development: this occurs when skills, abilities and emotions become more sophisticated and complex

Fine motor skills: manipulative movements of the fingers that rely on control over smaller muscles and fine movement

Foetus: an unborn human baby from about 8 weeks until it is born

Gross motor skills: whole body movements that depend on a person being able to control the large muscles in their arms and legs

Growth: an increase in size or mass

Growth spurt: a rapid increase in physical size

Hormones: chemical secretions that pass directly into the blood from the endocrine glands

Lifespan: the time between conception and death

Maturation: the process of becoming mature

Menopause: this usually occurs between the ages of 45 and 50 when a woman's menstrual cycle gradually stops because their ovaries no longer produce eggs

Lifespan development

Human beings experience **growth** and physical, intellectual, emotional and social **development** in each of the main stages of their life. These stages are:

- conception
- birth and infancy (0–3 years)
- childhood (4–10 years)
- adolescence (11–18 years)
- adulthood (19–65 years)
- old age (65+).

Patterns of human growth and development

During infancy, childhood and adolescence, most individuals experience predictable growth and developmental norms, or 'milestones'. These are points where particular changes happen, such as when a child first sits up unaided, begins to walk or says their first words.

Figure 8.1 Examples of developmental norms

Age	Ability
3–4 months	Infants start on solid foods, develop better head control, can roll from side to side, reach for objects
6–9 months	Teething begins, infants learn to sit unaided, lift their heads and look around, use thumb and index finger to grasp objects
9–12 months	Infants can crawl, chew food, use their hands to explore, walk holding onto parent or furniture ('cruising'), may say a few words, know their name and start to understand their parents' words
12–18 months	Toddlers learn to feed themselves, walk unaided, can understand simple requests ('give it to me'), develop better memory and concentration
18–24 months	Toddlers can run, turn the pages of a book, use simple sentences, have temper outbursts and know their own name
10 years (girls) 12 years (boys)	Puberty begins
45–55 years (women)	**Menopause** occurs

Physical growth and development

Physical growth and development refer to the way in which a person's body changes throughout their life. It is a process that continuous from birth until death.

Physical growth from conception to birth

Human growth begins when a woman's egg meets up with a man's healthy sperm and is fertilised. The genetic material from the sperm combines with the genetic material in the egg to create a new cell. The new cell divides rapidly and repeatedly to create an embryo. The embryo grows and develops into a **foetus** with human organs and tissues over about a 9-month period until it is mature enough to be born.

 Activity

Go to www.babycenter.com/pregnancy-fetal-development-index. This website explains how growth occurs in the womb during pregnancy. In small groups, choose one trimester of pregnancy and investigate what is happening to both the mother and the baby. Summarise your findings in the form of a poster or leaflet.

Physical growth and development in infancy

Infants experience rapid physical growth, quickly changing from being small, very dependent babies into much larger, stronger and more capable 'toddlers'. Infants gradually develop **gross motor skills** (e.g. sitting up, crawling and walking) and some **fine motor skills**. The physical changes that infants experience transform their appearance as well as their movement abilities. They are also needed for other forms of intellectual, social and emotional development to occur.

Over to you!

Ask your parents about your own early growth and development. Try to find out whether you followed the expected pattern of development, when you reached different 'milestones' and what their memories are of you as a baby and infant.

Physical growth and development in childhood

Young children gain greater control over their bodies and develop a range of complex physical skills during childhood. Improvements in balance, control and coordination allow children to develop more complex physical skills, such as skipping, catching a ball and riding a bicycle. A child loses their baby shape in early childhood and gradually develops the body shape and proportions of a small adult. Most children will experience a **growth spurt** in the middle part of childhood.

Over to you!

Compare pictures of yourself as a baby and as a young child. Can you see how your body shape changed between infancy and childhood?

Puberty and adolescence

The process of physical **maturation** that happens in adolescence is called puberty. The growth spurt and physical changes that occur in puberty are caused by **hormones**. During puberty, the testes in boys produce the hormone testosterone and the ovaries in girls produce oestrogen and progesterone. These hormones control the development and function of the reproductive organs and secondary sexual characteristics that enable most males and females to produce children, and which give them their adult body shape.

Physical change during adulthood

Physical changes in adulthood are not always about growth. A lot of physical development occurs in early adulthood as people apply their physical potential and abilities. Most individuals are capable of achieving their maximum physical performance during early adulthood, though physical change is an ongoing process. From about 30 years to 45 years, adults develop more fatty tissue, start to move more slowly and take longer to recover from their efforts. From about 45 to 65 years of age, a person may experience hair loss, slower movement, reduced stamina and muscle power, reduced hand–eye coordination, deteriorating eyesight, wrinkles as the skin loses elasticity, and a decline in fertility.

Physical change in old age

During old age, individuals experience a gradual physical decline in both the structure and functioning of their body. These changes are part of the normal ageing process and affect:

▶ heart and lung function

▶ mobility

▶ hair colour (grey then white) and texture (finer and thinner)

▶ sense of taste and smell, hearing ability and eyesight

▶ physical strength and stamina.

The final stages of life

An individual can die at any age. However, most people expect to die at some point after they reach old age. An individual will die when their body stops working biologically. Accidents, short-term but fatal illnesses, infections or chronic diseases can all cause death. The main causes of death in developed countries such as the UK are heart disease and strokes. These causes lead to cardiac arrest, lack of oxygen and irreversible damage to the brain and other body tissues.

 Case study

Sylvia Scott (aged 75) lives alone. She has an active social life and keeps herself busy looking after her garden. Neil is Sylvia's only son. He is 50 years old today and has invited his mum to a celebration lunch at a local restaurant. Neil's wife Sara (aged 48), their daughter Linda (aged 27) and her son Steven (aged 3) are all getting ready to go out for the meal. Steven is struggling to button up his shirt but can now put most of his clothes on by himself. Linda is sitting in the kitchen with her parents waiting for Steven to get ready. She is explaining that she has been to some antenatal classes to prepare for the birth of her second child in about 12 weeks' time. Sylvia, Neil and Sara are all excited and looking forward to this moment.

1. Which life stage is each member of the Scott family in at the moment?

2. Give two examples of ways in which members of the Scott family are experiencing physical growth.

3. What kinds of physical skills does Steven need to have to be able to get himself dressed?

Topic check

1 Identify six different life stages in which human growth and development occur.

2 Identify the four different ways that human beings grow and develop.

3 What does the term 'growth' refer to?

4 Identify two physical milestones that occur during infancy.

5 Explain what gross motor skills are, giving examples.

6 Describe how people change physically during adulthood and old age.

Intellectual, emotional and social development

This topic focuses on the way human beings develop intellectual, social and emotional skills and abilities in each life stage. When you have completed this topic, you should:

- know what intellectual, emotional and social development involves
- be able to describe features of intellectual, emotional and social development in each life stage
- understand how individuals develop a self-concept.

 Key terms

Abstract thinking: the ability to think about and apply complex ideas

Attachment relationship: an emotionally close, secure relationship with a parent or carer

Bonding: having a very close emotional link between two people

Cohabitation: 'living together' without being married

Communication skills: abilities and behaviours that allow people to interact with each other

Concepts: another term for 'ideas'

Dementia-related illnesses: a group of diseases that result in gradual loss of brain function

Self-concept: another term for personal identity

Socialisation: the process of learning the attitudes, values and culture, or way of life, of a society

Using the PIES approach

Human growth and development affects every person in a range of ways. As well as growing and changing physically, each person experiences intellectual, emotional and social development throughout their life. The so-called PIES approach to development focuses on each of these areas of development.

Figure 8.2 PIES

Intellectual development

Intellectual development changes a person's thinking, memory, problem-solving and language skills and occurs in every life stage.

Birth and infancy

Infants begin learning about themselves and the world through their senses (touch, hearing, sight, smell and taste) and through physical activity. An infant handles, listens to and looks at things and will often put new objects into their mouth as a way of learning about them. By 2 years of age, most infants point at and can name familiar objects when they see them (e.g. 'dog' or 'bus') and can join a few simple words together (e.g. 'go park' or 'shoes on').

 Case study

Lucas is 18 months old. His mum, Cheryl, spends most of her time with Luke, looking after him at home while his dad, Simon, is out at work. Cheryl has recently started taking Luke to a playgroup one day a week. Lucas really enjoys this. He likes running around, using the toys and playing alongside other children. Lucas likes toys that he can pick up and hold, like teddies and small building blocks, as well as toys that he can push and move about, like toy cars and trains. Lucas

also likes dogs. He will point and say 'dog' whenever he sees a dog on the television or while he is outside at the park or in his pram.

1. Who is Lucas likely to have formed the strongest **attachment relationship** with?
2. How will going to playgroup help Lucas's social development?
3. Is Lucas's language development appropriate for his age? Give reasons for your answer.

Childhood

Children develop the ability to think about objects and **concepts** that are not actually there in front of them. This allows them to learn numbers, letters of the alphabet and colours, for example. As a result, most people first learn to read, write and tell the time during childhood. In early childhood, children ask lots of questions about their environment and the society in which they live. By the end of childhood, a child will be able to use adult speech easily and will have vastly improved their knowledge and thinking skills.

Adolescence

Abstract thinking skills develop during adolescence. These allow a person to think about things in a theoretical or hypothetical way. For example, mathematical equations involve abstract thinking, as does thinking about what you would like to do in the future. Children do not have abstract thinking skills so they can't plan ahead in the same way as adolescents.

Adulthood

People use experience to develop their thinking and problem-solving skills during adulthood. Most adults use abstract thinking, have a good memory and can think very quickly. An adult's intellectual skills and abilities can be developed further through education and training and by problem solving at work and in everyday life situations. Acquiring new knowledge and skills is necessary during adulthood to cope with the changes that frequently occur in an adult's personal life (e.g. having children) or at work.

 Over to you!

How have your memory and problem-solving skills developed since childhood? What kinds of intellectual skills do you have now that you didn't have in childhood?

Old age

Older people maintain and use their intellectual abilities in much the same ways as adults because they need and enjoy intellectually stimulating activities. Thinking speed and response declines in old age, but mental capacity and intelligence are not lost. The experience of life that comes with old age can, in fact, improve a person's thinking and problem solving. An older person may become wiser and make better judgements as a result of their experiences. In general, older people do not become any less intelligent as a result of ageing! Only the minority of older people, who develop **dementia-related illnesses**, tend to lose their intellectual abilities. People with these conditions develop memory problems, especially in recalling recent information, and become confused more easily. These types of illnesses also result in sufferers gradually losing speech and other abilities that are controlled by the brain.

 Activity

In pairs or as part of a small group, carry out an investigation into the kinds of social and educational opportunities that are provided for older people in your local area. Further education colleges, community education services and the University of the Third Age, as well as private sector providers, may all offer courses and other learning activities for older people. Summarise your findings by suggesting how an older person may benefit from using each of the services you find out about.

Emotional development

Emotional development is concerned with a person's feelings. Love, happiness, disappointment and anger are examples of emotions that we gradually learn to recognise, understand and take into account in our relationships with others. Emotional development is a lifelong process that involves:

- ▶ becoming aware of your 'self'
- ▶ developing feelings about your 'self'
- ▶ working out your feelings towards other people
- ▶ developing a self-image and personal identity.

Infancy

A child should develop feelings of trust and security during infancy. A secure and consistent attachment relationship with their parents or main caregivers in the first year of life is needed for this to happen. The parental response to this emotional linking is known as **bonding**. Newborn infants cry when they are frustrated or uncomfortable and make cooing noises when they are happy. As they develop, infants learn to express their feelings through facial expressions, body movements and, eventually, through speech.

Childhood

Learning to control feelings like anger, jealousy and frustration and dealing with disapproval and criticism of 'naughty' behaviour is part of emotional development during this life stage. Nurturing a child's emotional development by offering love, acceptance and respect is also important. Parents, siblings, teachers and friends all play a part in this process. Most children gradually increase their self-confidence, make friendships and become a little more independent at primary school. Children learn to co-operate and can appreciate the viewpoints and feelings of others in ways that infants cannot. This enables children to play together and to join in groups and team games.

Adolescence

Adolescence can be an emotionally difficult but eventful time. Hormonal changes can cause mood swings and intense emotions that may be difficult to cope with. Developing a personal identity, making friendships and experiencing emotional support from peers and family members are important concerns in adolescence. Adolescents often experiment with intimate personal relationships with members of the opposite sex, and sometimes the same sex, as they explore their sexuality and the positive and negative emotions that result from close relationships. Adolescence is a period when individuals develop greater understanding of their own emotions as well as the thoughts, feelings and motives of others.

 Over to you!

When was the last time you felt an emotion really strongly? Which emotion (e.g. anger, happiness, anxiety) was this? Did you learn anything about yourself or other people as a result of this experience?

Adulthood

Adults are expected to be emotionally mature and to have more self-control and self-awareness than adolescents. Despite this, adulthood can still be emotionally challenging and eventful. Marriage, divorce, parenthood and increasing work responsibility, and the loss of elderly parents, are life events that may affect emotional development during adulthood. For some people, middle age is a period of contentment and satisfaction, whereas for others it is a period of crisis and concern about what will happen in old age.

 Activity

Produce a diagram or a poster that identifies events within adulthood that can be emotionally challenging. You should indicate which emotions may result from each of the key events you identify.

Old age

Older people often reflect on their achievements and past experiences as a way of making sense of their life. This can involve coming to terms with changing family relationships as children move into early and middle adulthood, with the death of partners or friends and with the ending of previous life roles (work and personal). Older people do continue to develop and change emotionally as they experience new life events and transitions, such as becoming grandparents and retiring from work. An older person may also have more leisure time to build relationships with friends and family members. Despite this, insecurity and loneliness can occur if an individual's social contacts are reduced and they become isolated.

Social development

Social development is concerned with the relationships we create with others, the social skills we develop and with **socialisation**.

Infancy

Attachment to and bonding with a parent or carer are needed for a first social relationship to occur. A person's ability to form satisfying friendships and romantic attachments later in their life is strongly influenced by the quality of their very first relationships in infancy. An infant will gradually expand their social circle by forming relationships with other family members and perhaps with neighbours' children. The development of social skills and relationships is strongly influenced by the infant's emerging **communication skills**.

Childhood

Children need to make relationships with people from outside of their own family to develop socially. A child will develop social skills by learning to co-operate, through communicating and by spending time with new people. As a child grows older they are able to choose their own friends and will want their peers to like and approve of them. Parents and teachers also promote social development by teaching children about acceptable ways of behaving, how to relate to others in everyday situations and why it is important to make and keep good relationships with others.

Adolescence

Adolescents strive to achieve a personal identity that distinguishes them from their parents. Relationships with peer groups, close friends and other people outside the person's immediate family become more important during adolescence. Wearing the right clothes, listening to the right music and being seen in the right places with the right people become important issues for many

adolescents. Because of their need to fit in and belong, adolescents can be vulnerable to peer group pressure. This can lead some adolescents into activities and situations (such as experimenting with alcohol, drugs and sex) they are uncomfortable with but find difficult to resist or challenge.

Adulthood

Social development in early adulthood is stimulated by leaving home. This usually results in an individual making new relationships through their work and social life. Adulthood is also the life stage when people focus quite strongly on finding a partner and sustaining an intimate relationship. New responsibilities and an extension of the person's social circle may also result from marriage or **cohabitation**. Much of adulthood is concerned with trying to find a balance between the competing demands of work, family and friends.

Social development during middle age often revolves around an adult trying to achieve their position in society and making adjustments to some of their existing relationships. In the later stages of adulthood, people often review and adjust their social relationships as children leave home (the 'empty-nest syndrome'), ageing parents become unwell or infirm and they retire from work. These changes in social relationships can result in changes to an adult's **self-concept**.

Old age

Many older people are very good at maintaining their friendships and other social relationships. However, loss of health, retirement from work or the death of a partner or close friends can make this difficult and sometimes leads to social isolation. Social development does occur in old age where people have opportunities to participate in social activities and meet others in social situations.

Over to you!

How do young people in your local area dress and style their hair to fit in with their peers (and differentiate themselves from their parents)?

Assessment activity 8.1 (P1, P2, M1)

You have been asked by a local health promotion team to prepare a series of articles for a magazine they produce for secondary school pupils aged 12–16.
- The articles should identify and describe key aspects of physical, intellectual, emotional and social development at each life stage.
- You should word process your magazine pages and present them in a way that will appeal to the target group of readers.

Topic check

1 What is meant by 'development'?
2 What are developmental norms?
3 Which four aspects of growth and development are referred to as PIES?
4 What kinds of skills and abilities improve as a result of intellectual development?
5 Describe the kinds of factors that influence social development during early adulthood.
6 Do all people over the age of 70 suffer from dementia-type illnesses?

Factors influencing human growth and development

Getting started

This topic is about the factors that influence human growth and development throughout a person's lifespan. When you have completed this topic, you should:

- know about a range of positive and negative influences on growth and development
- be able to describe how a range of factors can affect physical, intellectual, emotional and social development throughout life.

Key terms

Ageism: prejudice and discrimination against people because of their age

Chronic: another term for 'ongoing' or 'long-term'

Culture: the shared beliefs, values, language, customs and way of life of a group of people

Disablism: prejudice, discriminatory or abusive behaviour towards people with disabilities

Homophobia: prejudice and hostility towards people who are lesbian, gay or bisexual

Postcode lottery: a term used to describe unequal access to services in different parts of the country

Poverty: the condition of having insufficient money to afford everyday items such as food, heating and housing costs

Prejudice: a negative, hostile belief about an individual, group or issue that is based on a lack of knowledge and wrong or distorted facts

Primary socialisation: the process through which children learn the 'norms' or expectations of society, usually from their family

Racism: discriminatory or abusive behaviour towards members of another racial or ethnic group

Secondary socialisation: the process of learning skills and attitudes outside of the family, usually through education, work and friendship experiences

Sexism: discriminatory or abusive behaviour towards members of the opposite sex

Socio-economic: this refers to the combined influence of social (relationship-based) and economic (money-based) factors on an individual's personal development

Social skills: the talking, listening and relationship skills a person needs to communicate and interact with others

Stereotype: an over-generalised and over-simplified view of an individual or group of people

Socialisation

Socialisation is the process of learning the values, ideas, practices and roles of a society. It is about becoming a socially aware and socially skilled member of society. **Primary socialisation** is largely carried out within the family during early childhood. A child's family will usually teach them:

- the 'norms' or expectations of society
- attitudes and values about what is 'right' and 'wrong'
- basic **social skills**, like the importance of saying 'please' and 'thank you'.

Young children are taught how to behave 'normally' so that they can fit in and become accepted members of the social groups and broader society they are a part of. Primary socialisation also has an important influence on a child's ways of thinking and their expectations of people outside of their family.

Secondary socialisation
occurs from later childhood onwards and continues to the end of an individual's life. It involves people learning a range of new skills and attitudes, and also modifying their existing attitudes, values and behaviours, as a result of going to school, getting a job and spending time with non-family members. Schools, the mass media, workplaces, friends and peer groups all play an important part in an individual's secondary socialisation.

Over to you!

Can you think of an example of how your parents carried out primary socialisation when you were growing up?

Activity

How might the media (TV programmes and advertisements, radio and children's comics or books) and other young children (at playgroup or nursery, perhaps) also play a part in the primary socialisation of young children? Give an example of how each of these factors might influence a child's early development.

Over to you!

How might a person's work role and experiences influence their social development? Give a couple of examples to show how work roles and experiences could affect an individual's social skills and relationships.

Socio-economic factors

A range of **socio-economic** factors can influence an individual's physical, intellectual, emotional and social development in each life stage.

Income and expenditure

Income refers to the money that a family or individual receives. Expenditure is the term for all of the expenses or bills that an individual or family has to pay. People receive money through working, pension payments, welfare benefits and other sources such as investments. An individual or family's expenditure depends partly on their lifestyle but can also be affected by the number of people in a household and the particular needs of those people.

The amount of income that an individual and their family have, and the things they spend it on, can affect their quality of life. People with plenty of income and manageable expenditure are likely to have better educational and leisure opportunities and will live in better circumstances than people living in **poverty**. As a result, people from high-income families can have more opportunities to make the most of their abilities and potential than people from low-income families.

Housing and environment

A person's housing provides them with physical shelter and protection. This is important for physical health and development. For example, lack of adequate heating, dampness and overcrowding can lead to people of all ages developing respiratory disorders, stress and mental health problems. Children who live in overcrowded homes are more likely to be victims of accidents. Older people with low incomes sometimes have to choose between buying food and heating their homes. The consequence of not having enough heating can be hypothermia (a fall in body temperature to below 35°C – normal body temperature is 37°C). It is also important to note that a person's home provides them with a sense of emotional wellbeing and psychological security, so housing can affect an individual's emotional development too.

Over to you!

Identify the features you feel are important in making a person's housing 'healthy'.

Family, friends and peer groups

The family is often seen as the foundation of society because of the key role it plays in human development. The relationships we have with parents, brothers and sisters ensure that we are provided for, supported and protected as we grow and develop. For example, an individual's family:

▶ *provides* them with informal education and socialisation during infancy and childhood

▶ *supports* them emotionally, socially and financially from infancy through to adulthood

▶ *protects* their health and wellbeing by giving informal care, advice and guidance in every life stage.

Friendships also play an important role in a person's social and emotional development. As we move into early childhood, we begin meeting other children and increase our range of friendships. Friendships can feel especially important during adolescence when young people are trying to forge an identity separate from their parents'. During this life stage peer groups become influential in a person's social and emotional development. Adolescents often want to belong to a group of like-minded friends and have a strong need to be liked, respected and accepted by their peers. In adulthood, friendships remain important because they usually form the basis of an individual's social life outside the family. Friendships in later adulthood can be a vital source of companionship and connection to a person's past.

Throughout life, an individual's personality, social skills and emotional development are all shaped by their friendships. Friendship enables people to feel they belong, are wanted and liked by others and that there are people they can turn to for support. However, if an individual is bullied or rejected by their friends or peer group, they can lose self-confidence and suffer low self-esteem.

 Over to you!

Make a list of all the current and past friendships that have influenced your personal development. Try to identify how each friend has influenced you – positively or negatively.

Media and culture

The media, including newspapers, television, radio and the internet, can have a powerful effect on the ideas and images that people develop about themselves and each other. Parents are often concerned about television programmes and cartoon characters that involve violence or the kinds of behaviour that they feel might have a negative effect on their children's development. The use of gender, racial and ageist **stereotypes** is also a concern for people who see the media as having an influence on ideas about how members of different groups should look or be treated by others. At the same time as having a potentially negative influence on an individual's development, the media can also be used positively to deliver health education and promote healthy living.

Culture is also a very powerful influence on an individual's development. Cultural influences, such as the way an individual dresses, their diet and the types of relationships they form, are often unnoticed because we take them for granted as being the 'normal' or right way of doing things. However, in a multicultural society like the UK, cultural differences do result in people developing in different ways.

Activity

Use the internet, the library or other sources of information to investigate how cultural differences might influence an individual's development. You should identify a cultural group different from your own and find out about the type of diet, family relationships or religious beliefs associated with this group. Describe how these things might influence the development of a person who belongs to the cultural group you have chosen.

Gender

A person's sex refers to whether they are biologically male or female. Gender refers to the behaviour society expects from men and women. In Western societies girls are socialised to express 'feminine' qualities such as being kind, caring and gentle. This leads to assumptions that women should look after children, cook and do non-manual work. In contrast, boys are socialised to express 'masculine' characteristics such as being boisterous, aggressive and tough. This leads to assumptions that men should go out to work, do physical, manual jobs and be decision-makers. Parents, schools, friends and the media all play a part in gender socialisation.

The gender expectations that an individual experiences influence the way their identity develops, how they relate to others and the opportunities that may be open to them. The idea that boys and men should experience better opportunities than girls and women – especially in education and employment – because they are the 'superior sex' is not as powerful as it once was. However, gender does still play an important part in an individual's intellectual, social and emotional development because ideas about socially acceptable ways for men or women to behave remain very powerful in society.

Discrimination

Unfair discrimination involves treating an individual or group less favourably or unfairly in comparison to another individual or group. There are a number of different forms of discrimination, including **sexism**, **racism**, **homophobia**, **disablism** and **ageism**. Unfair discrimination is usually based on **prejudice** and not really knowing enough about the person or group concerned.

Discrimination can affect an individual's development in a number of ways. For example, it can:

▶ damage a person's self-image and self-esteem

▶ undermine a person's self-confidence and inhibit them from achieving their potential in life

▶ cause emotional distress and fear

▶ result in physical assault and injury

▶ prevent a person from having equal opportunities in education, work or other areas of their social life

▶ act as a barrier to an individual getting the care services, social support or treatment they need.

> ⚙ **Activity**
>
> In pairs or a small group, identify two forms of discrimination that affect some students who attend your school or college. Identify the reasons for this discrimination, make a list of the possible effects it has on the people who are discriminated against and suggest how it could be challenged or tackled in a positive way.

Education

Intellectual development happens when a person increases their knowledge and thinking skills. This is the aim, and often the result, of education. However, education also has a powerful effect on a person's social and emotional development. Educational experiences are part of secondary socialisation. Friends, peers and teachers at school or college all influence an individual's attitudes, values and behaviour and play a part in their intellectual, social and emotional development.

Some people learn a lot at school, succeed at exams, make good friends and see education as a positive influence on their personal development. Educational success and strong friendships are very good for the self-esteem and self-image of these people. However, not everybody enjoys school and not everybody succeeds. Failure and bad experiences in education can lead some people to develop a negative self-image and low self-esteem.

Figure 8.3 The benefits of a good education

Access to services

Good access to health and welfare services is likely to improve a person's health and development, as they will be able to obtain services that meet their needs. Access to services is especially important for people who have **chronic** health problems, for pregnant women and young children and for older people who make more use of health and welfare services as they age. However, the '**postcode lottery**' means that some people may not have an equal and fair chance of accessing services when they require them. Specialist care for children or for people with cancer, for example, is not equally available throughout the UK. People living in more remote rural areas may also find they have to travel long distances to access both general health care and more specialist services.

Case study

April is 3 years of age. She lives with her mum in a small cottage 3 miles from the nearest town. April is a friendly child. Her mum reads stories to her every day, they go out walking in the countryside whenever they can and also do art activities at home. April's mum has been encouraging her to be polite and to develop 'good manners'.

Despite being a talented artist, April's mum earns very little money and relies on child benefit and income support to pay the bills. The cottage where they live is damp and isolated. April gets colds and chest infections a lot, is underweight

and has no friends of her own age. April's mum is worried about her daughter's health and has started looking for somewhere new to live.

1. Identify two aspects of April's life that may have a positive effect on her personal development.

2. Explain why the housing conditions April lives in may have a negative effect on her health and development.

3. How is April's mum trying to influence the way in which she develops?

Assessment activity 8. 2 (P2)

As a follow-up to your articles on different aspects of human growth and development, the health promotion team have asked you to produce some 'Life Stage Guides' that state the positive and negative factors that may influence an

individual's growth and development during their lifespan.

You should produce your life stage guides in a format, such as a poster, leaflet or booklet, suitable for 12–16 year olds.

Topic check

1 In which life stage(s) does primary socialisation occur?

2 Identify four socio-economic factors that influence personal development.

3 Explain how a family's income might affect the personal development of its members.

4 Describe two ways in which housing conditions can influence a person's health and development.

5 What is a peer group and how can it influence an individual's development during adolescence?

6 Explain the term 'discrimination' and describe how experiencing discrimination might affect an individual's social or emotional development.

7 Describe how living in a rural environment may affect an individual's ability to access health and welfare services.

Getting started

This topic focuses on the positive and negative influence that life events can have on an individual's personal development. When you have completed this topic, you should:

- know about a range of predictable and unpredictable life events that affect personal development
- be able to describe how life events can influence an individual's development at different stages in their life.

Key terms

Acute: sudden and usually short term

Bereavement: the deep feelings of loss that people experience when someone to whom they are emotionally attached, such as a partner, relative or friend, dies

Life event: an important, significant change that affects the course of a person's development

Redundancy: when an employer decides that a job is no longer required and ends the employment of the person who does that job

Retirement: the point at which people end their working career.

Sibling: a brother or sister

Understanding life events

Life events are turning points in a person's life that affect their personal development. Some life events, such as starting school, getting a job and getting married, occur in a predictable way. Other life events, such as serious illness, divorce and redundancy, occur in a more unpredictable way. Every individual's development is affected by the life events they experience. The impact of life events can be:

▶ positive, such as when a person gets married, starts school or succeeds in getting the job that they want – in situations like this, a person's self-confidence and emotional wellbeing may be boosted

▶ negative, such as when a partner, relative or close friend dies – in a situation like this, a person's emotional wellbeing may decline due to the sadness and grief they feel as a result of their loss.

Life events can result in significant change in a person's life because of the need to adapt to or overcome them.

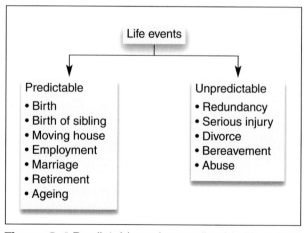

Figure 8.4 Predictable and unpredictable life events

Birth and parenthood

The birth of a child is a life event for both the parents and the brothers and sisters of the baby. New relationships are formed and existing relationships, between parents and older brothers and sisters, change as a result of the birth. For many children, the birth of a **sibling** is an exciting and happy event. However, some children later become jealous and feel a need to compete for their parents' affection.

For many people becoming a parent is a very emotional moment that motivates them to be the best possible mum or dad they can be. However, for others, parenthood can be an unwelcome burden that causes them stress and mental health difficulties, or can lead them to neglect or abuse their child because they cannot cope with the pressures and demands of parenthood. New parents also have to adapt their own roles and relationship to cope with the needs of a dependant child. Some people are able to offer their partner practical and emotional support and strengthen their relationship when they become parents. Other people find that they are unable or unwilling to do this and suffer relationship difficulties and even the breakdown of their marriage as a result. Parenthood can result in a major change in a person's identity as they adapt to their new 'mum' or dad' role.

Going to nursery/school

Starting school or nursery is one of the first expected life events that a child experiences and is very significant for personal development. Beginning nursery or primary school:

▶ promotes physical and intellectual development through learning and play

▶ provides opportunities for social and emotional development through friendships and regular contact with other children and adults.

A child's self-confidence, relationships, communication skills and knowledge and understanding of the world around them will all change as a result of going to nursery and starting school. However, some children see this as a negative life event because they are anxious about leaving the security of their parents. Despite some tears and tantrums, most children do adjust and come to see going to nursery and school in a positive way.

Over to you!

Can you remember what your first day at primary school was like? If not, ask one of your parents how you reacted on your first day and how you changed as a person during your first year at school.

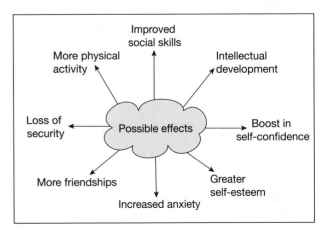

Figure 8.5 Possible effects on a child of starting school

Moving house and leaving home

Moving house is a stressful life event for many people. It can mean a break with the past and perhaps with friends, neighbours and the security of familiar surroundings. Home is usually a place that people associate with safety, security and stability in their lives. The practical demands of organising the removal of possessions, arranging finance to cover the cost of moving, and perhaps buying a house or flat, add to the emotional strain associated with this life event.

 Over to you!

Make a list of the reasons why a person may move house. Think about reasons why people choose to move as well as reasons why people are forced to move. In each case, describe the possible impact that moving might have on an individual who has to move house for the reason you have identified.

Employment, redundancy and retirement

Everybody finishes studying at school, college or university at some point in their life. Most people then enter employment. Starting work affects personal development because it:

▶ requires people to behave more independently, without the support of parents or teachers

▶ can involve training and the development of work-related skills that promote intellectual development

▶ can lead to new social relationships and social skills through time spent with work colleagues

▶ leads to changes in self-confidence and identity as an individual gains experience, is promoted and achieves higher status positions in their field of work.

Work can also affect personal development when a person loses their job because they are made redundant. **Redundancy** can lead to:

▶ loss of self-confidence and self-respect

▶ loss of status and identity

▶ increased stress levels

▶ problems with sleeping, eating and mood

▶ loss of social relationships with work colleagues

▶ increased strain in personal and family relationships.

Losing a valued job can take away a person's usual routine and the structure of their day, and can leave them wondering about their own worth and abilities. However, even though the loss of a job may be unexpected, some people find that it is a positive turning point in their life, where they are able to identify a new direction and pursue new opportunities.

Retirement is a third life event linked to a person's working life. For people who have been very committed to their work, and whose work provided their social life, retirement can result in too much time to fill and the loss of contact with work friends. Retirement can also cause financial problems. State and occupational pensions usually provide less money than a salary. For many older people retirement can be the beginning of financial hardship. For other people who have planned for their retirement and who have other interests and friendships, retirement can offer new opportunities, provide more time to enjoy hobbies and more time to enjoy the company of friends and family. For these people retirement is welcomed as a positive life event.

Serious injury

An unexpected serious injury can have a dramatic effect on a person's health, development and lifestyle. Serious injury can affect:

▶ physical development and wellbeing, particularly where the injury or illness affects a person's ability to look after themselves or live independently

▶ intellectual development, where the injury or illness affects a person's ability to learn or use their existing skills

▶ emotional development if the person is traumatised by the injury or illness, or experiences problems in adapting to the effects the injury or illness has on their life

▶ social development if the individual finds that their relationships with others change because they need practical help or care because of their illness.

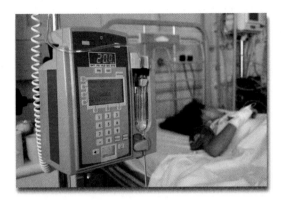

Accidents that cause serious injury can affect a person's development at any stage of their life. Where an injury is serious it may either have a temporary effect, which the person can recover fully from, or have a permanent effect on the person. Some serious injuries can result in a disability, such as the loss of a person's sight or hearing or the loss of a limb. This may mean that the person will need to adapt their skills and lifestyle if, for example, they are no longer able to move, pick up and hold things or manage personal hygiene and toilet needs without assistance. Friends, family and colleagues will also need to adjust their relationship with the person to take account of the disabled person's new situation.

Activity

Use the internet or library resources to investigate the impact that a spinal injury can have on an individual's health and wellbeing. Use your findings to produce a short leaflet or poster that describes the physical, intellectual, emotional and social effects that this kind of serious injury can have.

Case study

Leah Mukherjee is 21 years of age. She lost an arm in a car accident six months ago. Luckily she and her boyfriend both survived the accident, but Leah has been left with a permanent disability. Leah has spent most of the last 6 months in hospital. She is now coming to terms with the loss of her arm and is learning to adapt. Leah says that she sometimes forgets that her arm has gone and this is upsetting – because reality kicks in very quickly! Leah's home has been adapted so that she can use the bathroom and open doors and cupboards without needing both hands. She has also had an occupational therapy assessment to assess her everyday living skills and to provide her with guidance and tips on living without her arm. Leah is about to start counselling as she thinks this will help her to understand what has happened to her.

• Which areas of Leah's development are likely to be affected by the injury she has suffered?

• How might counselling help Leah's emotional development?

• What impact might Leah's injury have on her social and personal relationships?

Marriage and divorce

Marriage is a life event that generally occurs in early adulthood. Couples are usually very positive about their future together when they first get married. However, both individuals have to adapt to their new relationship and marital roles and may find that their relationships with friends and family members change as a result of their marriage.

Divorce statistics in the UK indicate that many people don't adjust well to married life or experience problems at some stage in their marriage. Divorce can lead to:

▶ poor sleep, loss of appetite, weight gain

▶ emotional distress due to the loss of a close bond

▶ loss of self-confidence

▶ disruption to social relationships if friends and relatives 'take sides'.

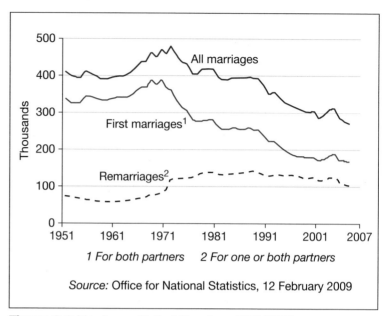

1 For both partners   2 For one or both partners

Source: Office for National Statistics, 12 February 2009

Figure 8.6 Marriages, United Kingdom, 1951–2007

Ageing

Ageing is an expected life event. The ageing process results in a gradual decline in a person's physical abilities. This can cause problems where an individual finds it difficult to adapt to the loss of their independence or previous skills. An individual's personal and social relationships can also be affected by ageing as partners, friends and relatives grow old and die. Ageing can cause some people to feel anxious about their ability to cope with everyday life and about what will happen to them in the future.

Bereavement

Feelings of **bereavement** usually accompany the death of a partner, relative or friend and can affect a person's social and emotional development. Sometimes a person's death may be anticipated and prepared for because of their old age or because they have a terminal illness. In other cases, however, a person's death can be sudden and unexpected. Bereavement can result in:

▶ **acute** emotional distress (confusion, crying, anger)

▶ loss of self-confidence and emotional insecurity as the person adjusts to life without their partner, friend or relative

▶ the loss of friendships and other social contacts if the person who died played a significant part in the individual's social life.

 Over to you!

Can you think of any benefits of growing old? Is ageing always a negative life event that should be dreaded?

Abuse

Abuse, neglect and ill treatment can damage a person's development as well as their physical and mental health in any life stage. Abuse and neglect are most commonly perpetrated by parents on children, by one partner on another and by carers on vulnerable people who are unwell, frail or who have developmental problems.

The effects of abuse can be short term or long lasting. For example, a person who experiences physical abuse may suffer temporary or permanent injuries as a result of being hit, slapped or treated roughly.

Abuse can also lead to self-harm if the person turns their anger about it against themselves. Some people also misuse alcohol and drugs as a way of coping with the distressing feelings they are left with. A person who is abused is also likely to lack confidence, may find it difficult to trust other people and may be more aggressive towards others as a way of protecting themselves and expressing their anger and upset about the abuse.

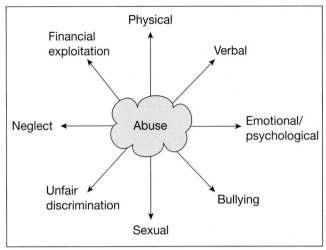

Figure 8.7 Forms of abuse

 Case study

Sinead and Ian decided to go on holiday to Costa Rica as a way of celebrating their first wedding anniversary. At the beginning of their second week, Ian and Sinead went out for a meal to a beachside restaurant. Both had some wine to drink. On the walk back to their hotel, they decided to go for a quick swim in the sea. Ian quickly got into trouble. Sinead lost sight of him in the waves but managed to get herself back to the beach. Ian's body was washed up on another beach the next morning. Sinead says that she still thinks about the incident every day and is still grieving for Ian. She hasn't returned to work since the incident six months ago, takes anti-depressant tablets to help with her mood and is beginning to lose touch with friends who have tried hard to support her.

1. What kind of life event has Sinead experienced?

2. Describe the impact of Ian's death on Sinead's emotional wellbeing.

3. Which care practitioners might be able to provide help and support for Sinead?

 Topic check

1 Identify three expected life events that can affect human growth and development.

2 What impact might marriage have on an adult's social and emotional development?

3 Identify three unexpected life events that can affect human growth or development.

4 Explain how losing a job might affect an individual's social development and emotional wellbeing.

5 Describe how becoming a parent can affect an individual's development.

6 Explain the term 'bereavement' and describe the impact this can have on an individual's development and wellbeing.

Getting started

This topic focuses on the factors that influence the development of an individual's self-concept. When you have completed this topic, you should:

■ know what a self-concept is

■ be able to identify a range of factors that influence an individual's self-concept

■ be able to describe how self-concept is affected by a range of different factors.

Key terms

Gender stereotypes: conventional, over-simplified ideas about men and women based on general assumptions

Self-concept: a person's view of 'who' they are

Self-esteem: the way a person values themselves

Self-image: the way a person views themselves

Self-concept

A person's **self-concept** is continually developing during each life stage and is closely linked to their emotional and social development. It expresses what we think and feel about ourselves as individuals and gives us our sense of identity.

An individual's self-concept is a combination of their **self-image** and their **self-esteem**. Self-image is a kind of mental picture that a person has of themselves. It gradually develops as the person becomes aware of their physical, intellectual, emotional and social abilities, qualities and attributes. This awareness is developed through interacting with others. When a person talks about their self-image, they will often compare themselves with others.

Self-esteem also results from the way we compare ourselves with other people. People who compare themselves negatively with others,

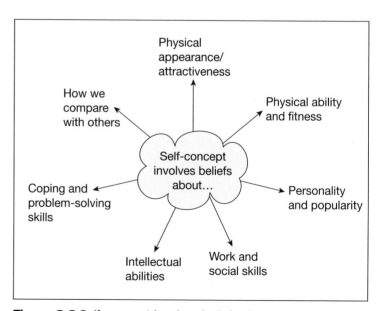

Figure 8.8 Self-concept involves beliefs about...

Over to you!

How would you sum up your view of the 'essential you' at this point in your life? Using both words and pictures, describe your self-concept. Think about your main features and characteristics. Consider things like your appearance, your gender, where you live, your personality and what you think others think about you as a person.

thinking they are not as good, not as attractive or not as capable as others, for example, are more likely to have low self-esteem. People who are confident but not arrogant, who accept that they have both strengths and weaknesses, and who feel encouraged, loved and wanted, tend not to undervalue themselves so much, and usually have higher self-esteem as a result.

Factors influencing self-concept

Having a clear, positive picture of who we are and how we feel about ourselves helps to make us feel secure and affects the way that we relate to other people. Figure 8.9 identifies a number of factors that influence the way an individual's self-concept develops and changes.

Age

The image that you have of yourself today will not be the same self-image that you reflect on when you are 40, 60 or 80 years old. The physical, intellectual, emotional and social changes that occur as you age and mature will affect your self-concept over time. For example, your physical capabilities will change as you experience health, fitness, illness and disability at different points in your life. The value that society attaches to you as an individual will also alter as you grow older. In Western societies old age is generally viewed negatively and older people seem to be less valued than younger people. This is sometimes different for members of minority ethnic groups who may value old age more. The way people of different ages are portrayed in the media confirms this and inevitably affects the self-concepts of many older people.

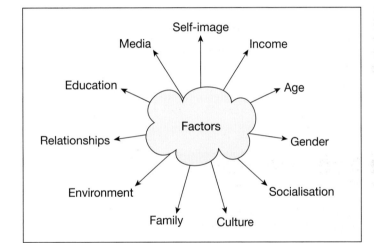

Figure 8.9 Factors affecting self-concept across the lifespan

Over to you!

Make a list of words or phrases that you associate with 'old woman'. Make a second list of words and phrases that you associate with 'young woman'. Is one list more positive or more negative than the other? How might you be affected if these words and phrases were applied to you at some point in your life?

Appearance

A person's physical features, their clothes and their non-verbal behaviour, all influence and express aspects of their self-concept. How we present ourselves and how we believe others see us are particularly important influences on self-concept when we are adolescents and young adults. As we get older, physical appearance and the way we present ourselves tend to have less impact on our self-concept.

Gender

Gender refers to the way ideas about masculinity and femininity are applied to men and women in our society. Wider social attitudes towards gender can shape a person's self-concept. In Western societies there are a number of **gender stereotypes** associated with male and female roles and behaviour. The images of men and women presented in the media express these stereotypes and the general social expectations of men and women.

Even though gender stereotypes do not reflect the reality of most people's lives in British society, they can still shape self-image and self-esteem. This can be positive where an individual is able and wishes to conform to the role, appearance and ways behaving that the stereotype suggests. However, gender stereotypes can also have a negative effect on self-concept. They can induce guilt, a sense of inadequacy and lack of self-confidence, especially where the person is unable or unwilling to match up to the stereotype of men or women in a particular situation.

 Activity

Use your knowledge and understanding of the influences on self-concept to write some survey questions about the way male and female teenagers think about themselves and develop their self-concepts. Conduct your survey by asking the questions to an equal number of boys and girls. Write a brief summary of your findings.

Culture

Ethnicity affects self-concept by influencing people's feelings of belonging to a particular cultural or social group. Culture and ethnic identity can, for example, give people a sense of shared values. However, it can also lead to people being treated differently, perhaps in an unfair and discriminatory way, and thereby affects their sense of self-worth and self-esteem.

Relationships

People form different types of relationship at different stages of their life. Family relationships tend to be most important during infancy and childhood. There is then a gradual shift in adolescence as friendships become more important, though emotional support from within family is also essential for adolescent development.

A whole range of new personal and working relationships are formed as the individual progresses into adulthood.

Friends are people whom we generally see as likeable, dependable and whom we can communicate easily with. People form friendships for a variety of reasons, such as common attitudes, values and interests, a need for emotional support and companionship. Friendships tend to boost a person's self-esteem and self-confidence, and help people to develop social skills. Overall, friendships make an important contribution to an individual's emotional and social development and the formation of their self-concept.

 Case study

Ffion, Nia and Eleri are all 30 years of age. They have known each other since primary school. All three women are now married, have two children each and live in different parts of the UK. They communicate regularly, sending each other text messages a couple of times a week and speaking frequently on the phone. Ffion still lives in the part of Wales where the three friends grew up. When Nia and Eleri visit their families at Christmas and in the summer, the three women arrange to meet up and go out for a meal together. They discuss their lives and seek advice from each other. Each of the women trusts the other a great deal and believes that they can rely on each other for support.

1. What kind of relationship do the three women have with each other?

2. Which aspects of the women's personal development might have been affected by their relationships with each other?

3. What impact do you think the women's relationships with each other have on their self-concept?

Abuse

Physical, emotional and sexual abuse has a damaging effect on an individual's self-concept, particularly their self-esteem. A person who experiences abuse is likely to develop a negative self-image and lower self-esteem. Lack of self-confidence and self-worth may make the person vulnerable to further abuse or to self-harm.

Family and socialisation

The relationships that an individual develops within their family, at school or college and at work will have a powerful effect on their self-concept. Family relationships play a critical role in shaping our self-concept. Early relationships are built on effective attachments to parents and close family members. The sense of security and feelings of being loved that can develop from these bonds are key ingredients in a positive self-concept. Poor family relationships, however, can also do lasting damage to a person's self-concept.

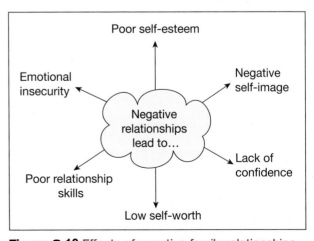

Figure 8.10 Effects of negative family relationships

Over to you!

Identify one way in which the following individuals have influenced your personal development:

- your mum or dad
- your brother(s) or sister(s)
- another relative in your family.

Analyse which aspects of your development each person influenced and then explain who has had the most significant effect on the development of your self-concept.

Income

Income in itself may not have a direct effect on an individual's self-concept. However, when people who live on a low income compare their lifestyle and opportunities with those on higher incomes they may feel they are somehow also less valued or less capable as people. This is not the case, but people on higher incomes are in a better position to afford goods and services that are highly valued and sought after and which people sometimes purchase to boost their self-esteem.

Media

Television and magazines are often criticised for presenting inappropriate, stereotyped images of men and women that some viewers and readers identify with and try to copy. Unattainable body images, wealthy lifestyles and perfectly happy lives often feature in films, soap operas and television advertisements. These media images can affect an individual's body image and self-concept if they believe them to be true or very desirable. However, the unrealistic, sometimes false images and stereotypes presented in the media can lead to people being unhappy and dissatisfied with their life and self-critical of the perfectly normal body they have.

Over to you!

Review a selection of TV or magazine advertisements that are selling products to young women. Identify how young women are portrayed in the adverts. Are the actresses a variety of different sizes, shapes and ethnicities or are they stereotypically similar in some way? What messages are the adverts sending about body shape and physical appearance? How might these affect a young woman's self-concept?

Education

Educational experiences can have a major impact on a person's self-concept. The things that teachers and fellow students say, and the way they treat us, can affect our self-image and self-esteem during childhood and adolescence. Children and young people are very open to suggestions about who and what they are like during these life stages. For some people, educational success helps to form a positive self-image and promotes high self-esteem. For others, school can be a more negative experience that leaves them feeling less capable than others, or with a negative view of themselves, their skills and their self-worth.

Emotional health and wellbeing

An individual will generally become more emotionally mature as they age. Growing maturity allows a person to become more reflective and accepting of themselves. This can mean that as people age they come to recognise both their personal strengths and limitations. Emotional maturity and self-knowledge play an important part in an individual's ability to establish and maintain close personal relationships as well as working relationships with others.

Assessment activity 8.3 (P3, M2, D1)

Use your knowledge of the way self-concept develops and is influenced to interview an adolescent, adult or older person about their self-concept. You will need to ensure that your interviewee is a willing volunteer and is happy for you to write about the things they tell you.

Produce a profile describing five factors that have influenced the person's self-concept.

Topic check

1. What does the term 'self-concept' mean?
2. Why might a person have low self-esteem?
3. What are the characteristics of high self-esteem?
4. How can a person's educational experiences affect their self-concept?
5. What impact can family relationships have on an individual's self-concept?
6. During which life stage does physical appearance seem to have a strong influence on an individual's self-concept?
7. Explain how a person's ethnicity may have a positive effect on their self-concept.
8. Explain how being uncomfortable with their gender may affect a person's self-concept.
9. Describe how a person's self-concept changes as they get older.

Care needs in different life stages

This topic is about the way care needs change and differ in different life stages. When you have completed this topic, you should:

- know how an individual's care needs can be identified and planned for
- understand how individual's care needs change and vary in different life stages
- know how care is provided to meet individuals' diverse care needs.

Key terms

Assessment: a process of identifying, assessing or measuring a person's care needs

Care planning: developing a plan of action to meet an individual's care needs

Formal care provision: services provided by paid, usually trained, care practitioners on behalf of a care organisation

Holistic: concerned with the 'whole' person

Informal care provision: services provided on a voluntary, unpaid basis by partners, relatives and friends

Multidisciplinary: involving more than one type of care practitioner

Safeguarding: another term for 'protecting'

Specific care needs: the additional requirements of some form of specialist care or treatment for an individual

Care needs

In each life stage, an individual should:

▶ be physically healthy (physical needs)

▶ develop their knowledge, skills and abilities (intellectual needs)

▶ develop their communication skills and personal relationships (social needs)

▶ feel secure and have good mental health (emotional needs).

Because an individual grows, develops and changes physically, intellectually, emotionally and socially in each life stage, their care needs also change as they progress through life. The care needs of an infant will be different from those of an adolescent or an older person, for example.

Assessing needs and planning care

People who use care services should have their individual care needs identified and assessed. A care practitioner should undertake a **holistic assessment** that covers the person's physical, intellectual, emotional and social care needs. Once these needs have been identified, the care practitioner will then plan forms of care that will meet the person's general and **specific care needs**. Care practitioners follow the **care planning** cycle to assess needs and plan care provision.

The care planning cycle is a way of ensuring that each individual's particular care needs are assessed and identified so that appropriate care can be provided for them whichever life stage they are in.

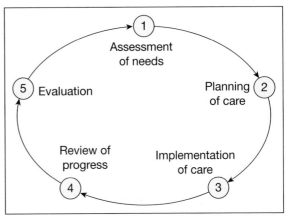

Figure 8.11 Care planning cycle

Infants' care needs

An infant has a variety of care needs because they are vulnerable and dependent on others for their survival and development. These include basic care needs such as washing, dressing and **safeguarding**.

An infant who has physical health or developmental problems is likely to require specialist assistance from health and early years practitioners to meet their specific care needs.

Children's care needs

Children are more physically robust and independent than infants. For example, most 3-year-old children can safely walk up and down stairs without assistance, can use a spoon to feed themselves and can occupy themselves with toys and other play activities. However, a child's care needs change throughout childhood because of continuous physical, intellectual, emotional and social development. As a result, the care needs of a 5-year-old child are likely to be different from those of a 9-year-old child. Care in childhood focuses on encouraging development and increasing an individual's capabilities.

A child may have additional or specific care needs because they experience:

▶ problems with their physical or mental health

▶ difficulties with learning, behaviour or relationships with others

▶ social or financial problems affecting their family.

Adolescents' care needs

Adolescents are moving towards independent adulthood but still require help, support and guidance from adults around them to feel safe, secure and cared for. Many adolescents benefit from the emotional support that their parents and other relatives provide as a kind of 'safety net' while they seek out and experiment with new friendships and more personal and intimate relationships with partners. Care in adolescence focuses less on directly meeting basic needs and more on providing opportunities, encouragement and support so that the individual can gradually take on the responsibility of meeting their needs independently.

As in childhood, an adolescent may develop additional or specific care needs because they experience:

▶ problems with their physical or mental health

▶ difficulties with their learning, behaviour or relationships with others

▶ social or financial problems affecting their family.

Over to you!

How do you think the parents of an older adolescent (16–17 years old) could encourage and enable them to be more independent while also providing an appropriate level of support and assistance?

Adults' care needs

Adulthood is often seen as the life stage where a person is able to meet their needs independently. This is true to some extent, but nobody is truly independent – we all need other people and tend to live in ways in which we both support others and are supported by them in adulthood. Adults have largely completed their physical growth and have developed many of the skills, abilities and attributes that they will make use of throughout the rest of their life. As a result, an adult's care needs tend to be linked to maintaining their health and wellbeing.

An adult may develop additional or specific care needs because they experience:

▶ problems with their physical or mental health

▶ difficulties in their personal or work relationships

▶ social or financial problems.

Over to you!

How might financial problems affect an adult's ability to meet their basic physical care needs?

Older peoples' care needs

Later adulthood is the final stage in an individual's life. It is also a stage in which an individual's care needs are likely to increase. Many older people are very healthy and live active, enjoyable lives. However, the loss of physical and sensory abilities in particular is a common feature of ageing, as is the reduction in a person's social network as they retire from work and see less of old friends. As a result, the care needs of older people tend to focus on using support services and adaptations to maximise independence, maintain an active lifestyle and minimise the effects of illness and ageing.

Providing care

Care practitioners assess each individual's care needs and try to develop individualised care plans setting out how these needs can be met most appropriately. When care plans are being devised and delivered, the care practitioner must:

▶ recognise that people who use care services have diverse needs

▶ treat all individuals with respect and dignity

▶ collaborate with the person who requires care to find out what their wishes and preferences are regarding how they would like their care to be provided

▶ ensure that the person who requires care is adequately safeguarded if they are vulnerable in any way

▶ provide active support for the individual by encouraging them to maintain their independence, while also providing sufficient assistance where the person is unable to meet their own needs.

Individuals who have care needs may receive **formal care provision** from health, social care or early years practitioners or may receive informal support from family, friends or neighbours. In many cases an individual's care needs are met through a combination of formal and **informal care provision**. Where this happens, a **multidisciplinary** team of care practitioners will assess the individual's care needs, devise a care plan for them and use the specialist skills of team members to deliver appropriate care. Informal carers often play an important supporting role in providing forms of care and giving emotional support to the person with care needs.

Activity

Using the internet, find the website of Helen and Douglas House (www.helenanddouglas.org.uk), a hospice service for children and young people in Oxford. Select 'About us' and then 'Types of care'.

1. Read about and summarise the different types of care that are provided for the children and young people who use Helen and Douglas House.

2. What kinds of care are provided as 'respite care'?

3. Explain the purpose of 'palliative care'.

Assessment activity 8.4 (P4, M3, D2)

This activity requires you to use your knowledge of human growth and development to find out about the changing care needs of an older person. You should:

- Identify an older person who is willing to talk to you about their life and their changing care needs.

- Design a set of questions that you could use to interview the person about the way their care needs have changed throughout life.

- Use your questions to obtain information about the person's changing care needs.

- Produce a timeline and a profile describing the main differences in the person's care needs at different life stages.

- Write and justify a care plan that shows how the person's care needs could best be met in their current life stage.

Topic check

1. Identify three examples of basic physical needs that all service users have.
2. What type of need do relationships with others meet?
3. Describe two ways of meeting the physical care needs of an infant.
4. Describe two ways of meeting the intellectual needs of a child.
5. Explain how an adolescent's emotional care needs are different from those of a child.
6. What type of need does stimulating work and access to leisure opportunities meet for an adult?
7. Describe two ways of meeting the emotional care needs of an older person.
8. Identify three reasons why individuals may have specific care needs in addition to their basic care needs.

Assessment summary

The overall grade you achieve for this unit depends on how well you meet the grading criteria set out at the start of the chapter (see page 179). You must complete:

- all of the P criteria to achieve a **pass** grade
- all of the P and the M criteria to achieve a **merit** grade
- all of the P, M and D criteria to achieve a **distinction** grade.

Your tutor will assess the assessment activities that you complete for this unit. The work you produce should provide evidence which demonstrates that you have achieved each of the assessment criteria. The table below identifies what you need to demonstrate to meet each of the pass, merit and distinction criteria for this unit. You should always check and self-assess your work before you submit your assignments for marking.

Remember that you MUST provide evidence for all of the P criteria to pass the unit.

Grading criteria	You need to demonstrate that you can:	Have you got the evidence?
P1	Identify key aspects of physical, intellectual, emotional and social development at each of the life stages	
M1	Outline key aspects of physical, intellectual, emotional and social development at each of the life stages	
P2	State the positive and negative influences on growth and development	
P3	State factors that influence an individual's self-concept	
M2	Outline how factors can influence the development of an individual's self-concept	
D1	Describe how factors can influence the development of an individual's self-concept	
P4	Explain potential differences in the care needs of individuals at different life stages	
M3	Discuss potential differences in the care needs of individuals at different life stages	
D2	Justify care provided to an individual at their different stages	

Always ask your tutor to explain any assignment tasks or assessment criteria that you don't understand fully. Being clear about the task before you begin gives you the best chance of succeeding. Good luck with your Unit 8 assessment work!

9 Creative and therapeutic activities in health and social care

Unit outline

Creative and therapeutic activities are a common feature of treatment plans in health and social care settings. They are used by a variety of different care practitioners to meet the physical, intellectual, emotional and social needs of people who use care services. A care practitioner needs to have a good understanding of the benefits of different activities, as well as the legislation and regulations relevant to them, in order to use creative and therapeutic activities safely and effectively.

Learning outcomes

1. **Know different creative and therapeutic activities and their benefits.**
2. **Know legislation and regulations relevant to the implementation of creative and therapeutic activities.**
3. **Understand the role of the professional in supporting individuals who undertake creative and therapeutic activities.**
4. **Be able to implement appropriate creative and therapeutic activities.**

Grading guide

To achieve a **pass**, your evidence must show you are able to:	To achieve a **merit**, your evidence must show you are able to:	To achieve a **distinction**, your evidence must show you are able to:
P1 Identify creative and therapeutic activities for people using health and social care services		
P2 Identify the benefits of creative and therapeutic activities for individuals using health and social care services	**M1** Outline the benefits of creative and therapeutic activities for individuals using health and social care services	
P3 Identify legislation, guidelines and policies relevant to the implementation of creative and therapeutic activities	**M2** Outline legislation, guidelines and policies relevant to the implementation of creative and therapeutic activities	**D1** Describe the importance of relevant legislation, guidelines and policies relevant to the implementation of creative and therapeutic activities
P4 Explain the role of the professional when planning creative and therapeutic activities in a health and social care environment		
P5 Plan a creative or therapeutic activity for an individual using health or social care services	**M3** Carry out a planned creative or therapeutic activity in a health or social care environment	**D2** Present an evaluation of the effectiveness of your planned activity to meet the holistic needs of an individual

Creative and therapeutic activities

Getting started

This topic introduces you to a range of creative and therapeutic activities used in the health and social care sector. When you have completed this topic, you should:

- be able to identify and describe a range of creative and therapeutic activities
- understand how different creative and therapeutic activities are used in care settings.

 Key terms

Art therapy: the use of art techniques to improve physical, mental, emotional or spiritual wellbeing

Drama therapy: the use of theatre techniques to help people to achieve personal growth and promote health

Expressive: communicating (expressing) thoughts or feelings

Horticultural therapy: the use of gardening to improve health and wellbeing

Massage: physical manipulation of someone's body for medical or relaxation purposes

Movement therapy: the therapeutic use of movement (often dance) to support and help people who have emotional, social, intellectual or physical problems

Music therapy: the use of music to meet a person's health and wellbeing needs

Novice: a beginner

Therapeutic: another term for 'healing'

Creative and therapeutic activities

Creative and therapeutic activities are used in health and social care settings to:

- help people to acquire, improve and practise a range of physical and intellectual skills and abilities
- enable people to explore and express feelings they may not be able to put into words
- provide opportunities for people to socialise and form relationships with others.

Creative and therapeutic activities can be used to meet an individual's physical, intellectual, emotional or social needs.

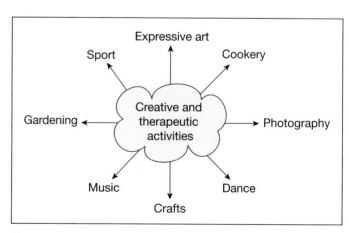

Figure 9.1 Examples of creative and therapeutic activities

Over to you!

Make a list of creative activities which you have taken part in. For each activity, jot down a few words or a phrase to explain the effect or impact that participating in the activity had on you. If you had to choose one of these creative activities as a way of 'de-stressing' yourself, which one would it be?

Art, photography and craft activities

Expressive art, photography and craft activities are widely used in settings such as residential care homes, day centres, pre-school groups, children's and family centres. Painting, pottery, making cards and producing photographs and collages are popular activities with people of all ages. Art, craft and photography are expressive activities that provide people with a way of being creative while using intellectual and physical skills. In some settings, people with mental health problems, learning difficulties or terminal illness use **art therapy** services to explore and express feelings that are too difficult or too painful for them to talk about.

Drama and role-play

Drama, role-play and music are used in a wide variety of health and social care settings including hospitals, specialist units for people with learning disabilities and mental health problems, residential care settings for older people and specialist schools. Performing drama or music can help individuals, couples, families or groups of people to express and explore their thoughts, ideas and relationships.

Drama can involve creating and acting in plays purely for the pleasure of taking part in theatrical activities. However, in care settings **drama therapy** is normally used to help an individual or a group of people to:

▶ solve a problem

▶ find out some inner truths about themselves

▶ explore and correct unhealthy ways of relating or communicating.

Role-play and drama are used to distance the person from the difficult or painful thing they want to deal with, as it allows them to 'act out' their thoughts and feelings towards it in a safe, **therapeutic** way.

Activity

When was the last time you took part in an art or craft activity – on your own or as part of a small group? How did it feel to be 'creative'? Do you find this relaxing, exciting or challenging and daunting? Compare your experiences and thoughts with those of a class colleague.

Case study

Sanjiv works in a day centre for young people with emotional and behavioural problems. Some of the people who use the day centre have been referred by the police or the courts. Sanjiv has found that they often have low self-esteem, find it hard to talk about their feelings and struggle to be tolerant of others. He uses a drama activity called 'The Empty Chair' to help small groups of these people to improve their self-awareness and their ability to relate to others.

Six people, including Sanjiv, sit on chairs in a circle. There is a seventh empty chair to Sanjiv's right. When everyone is seated, Sanjiv tells them that the activity is about describing people. He tells the group that if they think he is describing them they should go and occupy the empty chair. The person on the left of the new empty chair then has to carry on by saying, 'there is an empty chair to my right, please sit with me if

you are _____' (they describe a tangible feature – tall, black, have long hair). After a few rounds, Sanjiv then asks about personal qualities and attributes. For example, 'sit with me if you are a good friend/trusted daughter/kind son'. He then moves on to ask about feelings. For example, 'sit with me if you have been happy/very angry/lonely lately'. He then helps the group to talk about these feelings and try to understand why they have them and how they can cope with them.

1. How might 'The Empty Chair' activity be therapeutic for the young people at the day centre?

2. Which aspects of their PIES needs does the activity address?

3. Explain what makes 'The Empty Chair' a drama or role-play activity.

Music

Music can be used in a variety of different ways in health and social care settings. A care practitioner might encourage and support an individual to play an instrument or listen to their favourite music because it brings them pleasure, is relaxing and enables them to maintain their skills and interests, for example. However, **music therapy** is used for therapeutic purposes in the same way as drama therapy. Music therapy can be used to:

▶ improve learning

▶ reduce stress

▶ build self-esteem

▶ help communication

▶ support exercise.

Music therapists work in settings where people with learning disabilities, mental health problems, sensory impairments and physical disorders receive care.

Activity

Go to the Nordoff-Robbins music therapy website (www.nordoff-robbins.org.uk) and investigate what music therapy involves. Using the Frequently Asked Questions feature, find out:

• how music therapy can help people
• what a typical music therapy session might involve
• what the difference is between 'music therapy' and the other uses of music for therapeutic purposes.

Movement and exercise

Physical activities such as dancing, swimming and keep-fit exercise (e.g. stretching, Pilates, using gym equipment) are used in day care, hospital and community settings. They can be used to help people to:

▶ relax and de-stress

▶ communicate without using words

▶ express difficult emotions

▶ improve or maintain their physical strength, suppleness and skills.

Movement therapy is a specialist use of movement and exercise activity (usually dance) in care settings. It focuses on strengthening the body–mind connection so that a person can achieve better physical and mental wellbeing. It is used to help and support people with learning and physical disabilities, people experiencing mental health problems, people with sensory impairments and children and young people who have behavioural and emotional problems.

Other forms of exercise include walking and cycling, as well as joining in sports such as football, tennis and cricket in a controlled and supported way. These promote physical fitness and a sense of wellbeing, provide opportunities for people to develop relationships and teamwork skills, and can be therapeutic in terms of relieving stress.

Activity

Identify a form of exercise (e.g. sport or keep-fit) or movement (e.g. dancing) that you take part in or have participated in at some time in the past. Make some notes on:

• what you do physically when you take part in this activity

• how you feel during and after taking part in the activity

• how, if at all, this activity has a therapeutic effect on you.

Case study

Dr Collins, a GP, has many patients living on a large housing estate. He has recently started prescribing outdoor exercise for people who have weight problems, mild depression or who feel 'unwell' but have no obvious illness he can diagnose. Dr Collins is working with the health promotion team employed by the primary health care trust to develop the idea of a 'Green Gym'. This consists of a series of regular organised walks and other outdoor activities in the local area. The Green Gym aims to help participants to relax and de-stress, gives them an opportunity to exercise and also to build some social relationships.

1. Which aspects of health and wellbeing can be improved or maintained by joining the Green Gym?

2. How might participating in the Green Gym promote the health and wellbeing of isolated older people?

3. Suggest an outdoor activity that members of the Green Gym could participate in to improve their physical health.

Yoga and massage

Yoga is a combination of breathing exercises, physical postures and meditation. It is used in day care centres, residential homes and other community settings with people who have a wide range of physical conditions and emotional problems. Yoga encourages relaxation and is very helpful for people who are feeling stressed. It involves a range of different physical postures and breathing activities, some of which can be tried and practised immediately by complete **novices**. A trained and experienced yoga teacher would be needed for more difficult, demanding and complex yoga activities.

Massage involves manipulating the soft tissues of the body using gentle movements and pressure. Massage is used to:

▶ promote relaxation and decrease stress

▶ improve physical functioning

▶ promote physical health and wellbeing.

Massage is typically used to help people who have stress-related problems or difficulties with pain.

Horse riding and animals as therapy

Therapeutic horse riding, or adaptive riding, can help people with a range of physical, intellectual, emotional and social problems. Adaptive riding is particularly popular with people who have physical disabilities or learning difficulties. As well as learning to ride a horse, the disabled person can also:

▶ experience companionship

▶ learn leadership and decision-making skills

▶ boost their self-confidence and self-esteem

▶ learn to take and accept responsibility.

Horse riding can be used for leisure and recreation as well as therapy. The skills needed to build a relationship with a horse can be applied to relationships with people, physical fitness can be improved and general enjoyment gained from controlling and working with the horse.

Care settings such as mental health units, nursing homes for older people and early years settings for disabled children may also use animals within their treatment programmes. Animal-assisted therapy aims to improve the functioning and PIES needs of people using care services. Many different types of animals are used to provide comfort, encourage nurturing, reduce loneliness and provide a way of meeting others. People with learning difficulties, such as autism, behavioural problems and mental distress have been shown to benefit from forms of animal-assisted therapy.

Gardening and multi-sensory stimulation

Horticultural therapy uses gardening to promote and improve wellbeing. A horticultural therapist may use all of the phases of gardening, from preparing soil and sewing seeds to watering and cropping plants and vegetables, to promote an individual's health and wellbeing. An individual may enjoy gardening on their own or being part of a group or team of people involved in gardening projects. These activities and projects can be adapted to meet the PIES and care needs of people with a variety of health and development problems.

Snoezelen are controlled multi-sensory environments. Specially designed rooms are used to deliver sensory stimulation to an individual's different senses. Sound, colour, textures and scents can be used to stimulate the person and give them pleasure. Multi-sensory stimulation is used with people of all ages who have brain injuries and older people with dementia. It has been shown to have short-term effects on emotion and behaviour. One of the main advantages of multi-sensory stimulation is that it doesn't rely on verbal communication. This can be very important to people with autism, brain injuries or dementia-related illnesses.

Activity

Go to the Thrive website (www.thrive.org.uk), read 'About Thrive' and obtain a copy of the leaflet called *Using gardening to change lives*. Use the information to explain in a poster or leaflet how gardening can be a therapeutic activity for people with care needs.

Activity

The Dee Hadlow Centre provides a range of services for disabled people. Inside the centre there is a very popular multi-sensory room. This incorporates activities that are passive (emphasising relaxation) and fully interactive (an adult uses switches to make the equipment work). The multi-sensory room offers a safe haven, quiet and free from disruptions, where service users can relax. Soft switches, microphones and contact sensors can be used to make the lights, sounds and equipment in the room work. The room is very popular with deaf-blind people, people with complex physical disabilities and people with learning disabilities. They enjoy the stimulation that the coloured lights, various sounds and sensory equipment give them and also like being able to make things happen in the room.

1. Which client groups tend to benefit from multi-sensory rooms?

2. How are users' senses stimulated in the multi-sensory room?

3. Describe how spending time in a multi-sensory room might have a positive effect on an individual's health and wellbeing.

Writing and quizzes

Writing creative stories, poems or plays or more autobiographical 'life history' accounts can be very therapeutic for some people. Keeping diaries or journals, writing letters that may or may not be sent, and simply putting thoughts down on paper can also be used to help an individual express ideas, thoughts and experiences that haven't been or can't be spoken about.

When writing is used for therapeutic purposes, people are often encouraged and supported to write about deeply personal and sometimes traumatic experiences that they struggle to speak about. Writing can help the person to return to troubling events or distressing issues and allows them to take control of how they express and respond to their emotions. Once the person has written about their experiences, they have a choice about whether to share, keep or destroy their writing.

Taking part in a quiz is a fun, sociable way for people to stimulate and use their intellectual abilities and social skills. Quizzes require people to recall knowledge and solve problems. They are often used as a way of bringing people together in small groups to develop and practise their communication and social skills. Getting questions right and scoring points can boost self-esteem. Sharing ideas and bonding with team members can also promote social skills and social relationships.

Games

Games include a wide variety of different pastimes, from playing cards or board games to watching football, rugby or athletics on the television. People can participate in games in different ways, e.g. as a player or observer. Games can be played individually or in groups. Health and social care settings tend to have a variety of board games available for patients or residents who want some intellectual stimulation and social activity. Games that require people to solve problems, be competitive or use strategies to beat an opponent or another team can be very involving and exciting. Taking part in games can meet an individual's physical, intellectual, emotional and social needs, depending on the game and the way the person participates.

Over to you!

Have you ever kept a personal journal or diary? What kinds of things did you write in it? Did you use it to express and disclose personal feelings or thoughts that you were shy, embarrassed or afraid to discuss with other people? What kind of PIES needs did writing your diary or journal help you to meet?

Activity

Go to the website of the English Federation of Disability Sport (www.efds.co.uk) and investigate one form of sport adapted for disabled people. As well as identifying the range of sports available for disabled people, make a list of the barriers that can prevent disabled people from participating in sport. Produce a poster or summary diagram outlining Opportunities and Barriers.

Cooking

Cooking can be both creative and therapeutic. It involves planning, preparing and cooking food to make something that the person or others will enjoy. Cooking can be used as a therapeutic activity to help someone develop their thinking skills (e.g. about ingredients, cooking methods and temperatures) and physical skills (e.g. chopping, stirring, cleaning and balancing), for example. It can also be a good way of building a person's self-esteem, as they may feel a sense of satisfaction from completing a recipe or making a meal, and may receive praise and thanks from the people who eat it! Cooking is part of the activity programme in many different types of care setting. Appropriate facilities, equipment and supervision are needed to ensure that safety and hygiene rules are observed.

Activity

Imagine that you are given the job of organising the 'What's cooking?' group at a day centre for older people. The women who attend the centre are quite enthusiastic about cooking, but have memory problems and can easily become confused. The men who attend usually have very little, if any, previous experience of preparing food. Debbie, the occupational therapist in charge of the day centre, has asked you to organise and run a cooking session next week. She has suggested that participants could make some kind of cake, but that the cake-making preparation would need to take no more than half an hour to keep everybody interested. She has asked you to complete the planning sheet below with your ideas for the session.

Activity Plan: Cake-making	
Planning questions	**Answers**
Who is the activity aimed at?	
What will the participants do during the session?	
What skills and abilities are needed by participants?	
What equipment and facilities will be needed?	
Are there any health and safety considerations?	

Topic check

1. Identify five different forms of creative or therapeutic activity that can be used in care settings.
2. Why is drama sometimes used as a therapeutic activity in care settings?
3. What is horticultural therapy?
4. Describe the purpose of animal-assisted therapy and give an example.
5. What is a multi-sensory environment and how can it be therapeutic?
6. Describe how writing can be used as a creative and therapeutic activity in care settings.

Benefits of creative and therapeutic activities

This topic will explain how taking part in creative and therapeutic activity can be beneficial for people who use care services. It explains, for example:

■ what the benefit of creative and therapeutic activities are for people with physical, intellectual, emotional and social care needs

■ how individual's with different PIES needs may benefit from taking part in creative and therapeutic activities

■ what factors influence the choice of activities for a particular individual.

 Key terms

Cognitive: related to thinking, reasoning and remembering

Dexterity: the ability to use your hands in a fluid, skilful way

Mobility: the ability to move freely in a coordinated way

Participation: another term for 'taking part'

Stroke: a condition that results from lack of oxygen to the brain when blood vessels become blocked or burst

The benefits of creative and therapeutic activity

Creative and therapeutic activities are used for specific purposes in health and social care settings. **Participation** in creative and therapeutic activity should meet the physical, intellectual, emotional or social needs of an individual. When these activities are used as part of a treatment programme they need to be carefully chosen and organised in ways that are appropriate to an individual's particular needs.

Physical needs and benefits

People who use health and social care services often do so because they have physical health problems and physical care needs. Examples include:

▶ **mobility** problems resulting from painful joints, fractures or conditions that cause physical weakness

▶ **dexterity** problems resulting from stiff or damaged muscles and inflamed tendons

▶ balance and coordination problems resulting from tremors and other involuntary muscle movements

▶ circulatory and respiratory problems that result in fatigue, breathlessness and lack of stamina

- weakness or paralysis of limbs as a result of **strokes**, brain injury or accidents

- loss of a limb, e.g. as a result of an accident, infection or cancer.

People who have physical needs may use creative and therapeutic activities as a way of:

- learning new physical skills

- reducing the symptoms of their physical or mental health problems (e.g. reducing anxiety)

- maintaining, adapting or improving their existing physical skills (e.g. dexterity) or movement abilities

- maintaining or improving their physical and hand–eye coordination

- maintaining or improving physical strength and fitness.

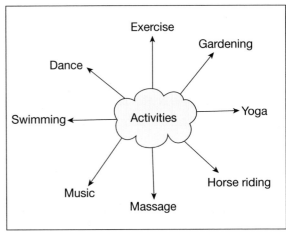

Figure 9.2 Activities with physical benefits

Cooking, movement, exercise, horse riding and team games can all be used to help people to learn new physical skills and promote their physical fitness. People with learning disabilities or mental health problems are sometimes encouraged to take part in team games such as football or outdoor adventure activities, such as long-distance walking, climbing and camping trips to promote both their physical health and their social skills. Exercise and movement programmes using a gym or a suitable outdoor area are increasingly being prescribed as treatment for people who have heart or respiratory problems. Occupational therapists and physiotherapists also use adapted equipment and exercise programmes to help stroke patients practise and relearn basic physical skills such as walking, going to the toilet and holding cutlery.

Intellectual needs and benefits

People who have learning disabilities or brain injuries caused by accidents, drug or alcohol misuse or by conditions such as Alzheimer's disease have **cognitive** problems and intellectual care needs. Examples include:

- problems with confusion and memory loss

- learning difficulties that result from conditions such as Down's syndrome

- mental health problems that can cause distress, problems with decision-making and difficulties with motivation, concentration and communication

- communication and language problems that can result from brain injuries caused by having a stroke, a head injury or by misuse of drugs and alcohol.

People who have intellectual care needs may use creative and therapeutic activities as a way of:

- learning new thinking and problem-solving skills

- regaining lost skills

- becoming more organised and independent

- maintaining, adapting or improving existing thinking and memory skills

- expressing their thoughts and imaginative ideas.

Activity

Using the internet, investigate 'reminiscence therapy'. Find out what this involves, how it is carried out with older people who have cognitive problems and what the benefits are. Produce a leaflet or poster summarising your findings.

Emotional needs and benefits

People who experience physical illness, mental distress or social problems are also likely to have a range of emotional needs. These can be the result of:

- relationship breakdown or the loss of loved ones
- loss of health, skills or abilities as a result of a condition, illness or negative life event
- low self-confidence and poor self-esteem as a result of being unwell or less capable than previously
- mood swings and marked changes in behaviour as a side effect of medication or treatment
- hopelessness, depression or anger in response to the frustration of not getting better.

People who have emotional care needs may use creative and therapeutic activities as a way of:

- learning how to explore, control and express their feelings
- developing or boosting their self-esteem and self-concept
- maintaining, adapting or improving their motivation and coping strategies
- expressing distressing or troubling thoughts and feelings
- developing new interests.

Social needs and benefits

People have social needs when they lack relationships, become isolated or don't have the skills needed to establish and maintain good relationships with others. People who use health and social care services may also have social needs because they:

- feel lonely, isolated and frightened when they are admitted to a care setting where they don't know anyone else
- have a poor relationship or no relationship with members of their family, or lack friends who can provide them with support
- have a mental health problem, learning difficulty or a condition such as Alzheimer's disease that makes trusting and communicating with other people difficult.

Creative and therapeutic activities such as drama, music and dance, as well as taking part in games and craft activities, provide participants with opportunities to:

- meet and interact with others
- develop friendships
- become part of supportive social networks.

Over to you!

Identify a couple of creative or therapeutic activities that you might choose to take part in as a way of boosting your self-confidence or helping you to overcome a personal setback in your life. What would you choose to do that might be emotionally beneficial?

Activity

Analyse the possible benefits for a group of older people who have limited social contact, taking part in a weekly quiz at a local day centre. Identify the PIES benefits that could result from taking part in this type of activity.

Case study

Edward is 3 years of age. He attends the Stepping Stones pre-school nursery for 2½ hours twice a week. Edward's mum was reluctant to enrol him at first, but was persuaded by a neighbour that Edward would benefit from attending. Edward really loves going to the nursery and looks forward to meeting his new friends, playing with a variety of different toys and games and painting. He particularly likes listening to stories read by the nursery teacher or one of the nursery nurses. Since starting at the nursery six months ago, Edward has become more self-confident, talks a lot more and has learnt a lot of different things. When asked what he likes best about the nursery Edward always says, 'my friends who play with me'.

1. Identify two creative or therapeutic activities that Edward takes part in at the nursery.

2. Analyse one of these activities and explain, using PIES, the benefits this could have for Edward.

3. What have been the main social benefits for Edward of attending the nursery?

Assessment activity 9.1 (P1, P2, M1)

Imagine that you are a member of the creative and therapeutic activities team at your local hospital. You have been asked to make a presentation about the use of creative activities in care to a group of young people who are considering a career in the health and social care field.

- Prepare a presentation covering the range of different types of creative and therapeutic activities that exist.

- Outline the benefits of creative and therapeutic activities for people using health or care services.

You should prepare your presentation using appropriate information technology packages. You should also produce a handout summarising the key points of your presentation, which the young people could take away with them.

Topic check

1 Identify four different ways in which an individual may benefit from taking part in creative and therapeutic activity.

2 Describe an example of a creative or therapeutic activity that may help an individual to improve their hand–eye coordination.

3 In what way might taking part in a quiz provide an individual with cognitive benefits?

4 Describe an example of a creative or therapeutic activity that has emotional benefits for participants.

5 Explain how participation in creative activities can have social benefits for people who use care services.

6 Describe an example of a creative or therapeutic activity that could be used to boost the motivation of a person who has become depressed.

Health and safety for creative and therapeutic activity

▶ Getting started

Creative and therapeutic activities have many potential benefits for people who use care services. However, there are also some hazards and risks involved in providing and taking part in these activities. When you have completed this topic, you should:

- know about a range of health and safety legislation and regulations relevant to creative and therapeutic activities
- be able to explain the main points of law affecting the provision of creative and therapeutic activities.

🔑 Key terms

Hazard: anything that can cause harm.

Health and Safety Executive: the government body that enforces health and safety laws

Legislation: written laws, also known as 'statutes' and Acts of Parliament

Regulations: detailed legal rules

Risk: the chance of harm being done by a hazard

Risk assessment: a careful examination of what could cause harm to people

Toxic: poisonous

Health and safety law

Care settings in the UK have to provide services in a way that conforms to health and safety law. A range of health and safety laws exist to protect people who use services and care workers from hazards and harm. People who use creative and therapeutic activities need to understand the main principles of health and safety law and the importance of **risk assessments**.

Making risk assessments

Care organisations are, by law, required to carry out formal risk assessments of their care settings. Risk assessment aims to identify **hazards** and potential **risks** to the health, safety and security of care practitioners, people who use care services and visitors to a care setting. Hazards that might be present in creative and therapeutic activity include:

- ▶ **toxic** and flammable materials such as glue, paint, solvents and detergents
- ▶ equipment such as scissors, knives or other sharp implements
- ▶ electricity, gas or wood fires
- ▶ physical contact (e.g. tackling) when playing sports or other games.

Risk assessment recognises that a range of care activities, equipment and the way a care setting is organised can be hazardous but that steps can be taken to minimise or remove the risk of people being harmed. The law doesn't expect care workers to completely remove all risks but to protect people as far as is reasonably practicable. The ultimate aim of a risk assessment is to ensure that people take part in creative and therapeutic activities without coming to any harm. The **Health and Safety Executive** has identified five stages of a risk assessment (see Figure 9.3).

Figure 9.3 The stages of risk assessment

Stage	Key questions	Purpose
1. Identify the hazards	What are the hazards?	To identify all hazards
2. Decide who might be harmed and how	Who is at risk?	To evaluate the risk of hazards causing harm
3. Evaluate the risk and decide on precautions	What are the risks?	• To evaluate risk control measures • To identify risk control responsibilities
4. Record your findings and implement them	• What needs to be done? • Who needs to do what?	To record all findings and the risk control plan
5. Review the assessment and update if necessary	• Is risk controlled? • Are further controls needed?	To monitor and maintain an accurate and up-to-date risk control system

Care workers who use creative and therapeutic activities sometimes undertake risk assessments on behalf of the care organisation that employs them. A care worker should always think about hazards and risks whenever they plan or participate in activities with people who use services.

The Health and Safety at Work Act 1974

The Health and Safety at Work Act 1974 is the key piece of health and safety **legislation** affecting care settings in the UK. A care organisation is responsible for providing:

▶ a safe and secure work environment

▶ safe equipment

▶ information and training about health and safety.

Care workers have a responsibility to:

▶ work safely within the care setting

▶ monitor their work environment for health and safety problems that may develop

▶ report and respond appropriately to any health and safety risks.

Risk assessments, health and safety training and a range of health and safety equipment must be provided to ensure that creative and therapeutic activities meet the requirements of this law.

Food safety laws

Care workers who use food as part of creative and therapeutic activity must practise good food hygiene in the workplace. For example, food provided for people who use services and for visitors must be safely stored and prepared and must not be 'injurious to health'. The Food Standards Act 1999 established the Food Standards Agency (www.food.gov.uk), which monitors food safety in the UK. The main aim of the Food Standards Agency is to protect public health in relation to food.

There are a range of food safety laws in the UK. The General Food Regulations 2004 are important because they require care practitioners who prepare and serve food to ensure that:

▷ all food is fit for human consumption

▷ food is not injurious to health

▷ food is not falsely described or presented.

Activity

The Food Standards Agency provides comprehensive and up-to-date information and advice on food hygiene through their *Eat Well* website (www.eatwell.gov.uk). You can find out about ways of preventing food poisoning by reading the Germ Watch section of the site.

Health and safety regulations

Many of the detailed laws affecting health and safety in relation to creative and therapeutic activity are known as **regulations**. These are forms of law that put into practice the principles established by earlier legislation, such as the Health and Safety at Work Act 1974.

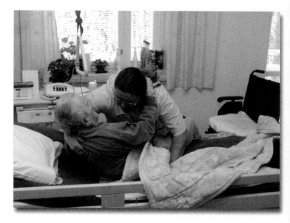

The Manual Handling Operations Regulations 1992

These regulations are designed to protect people from the hazards and risks involved in lifting or moving people or objects in care settings. Many care workers have sustained serious back and neck injuries as a result of lifting and handling accidents. These regulations require care workers to:

▷ avoid hazardous manual handling operations wherever possible – this can be done by redesigning tasks to avoid moving heavy loads or by using lifting equipment, such as a hoist

▷ risk assess any hazardous manual handling operations that cannot be avoided

▷ reduce the risk of injury so far as is reasonably practicable where manual handling cannot be avoided.

 Over to you!

Identify how creative and therapeutic activities might involve moving or handling heavy loads. Compare your list of suggestions with that of a colleague.

Control of Substances Hazardous to Health Regulations 2002

The Control of Substances Hazardous to Health (COSHH) Regulations 2002 state that all hazardous substances must be correctly handled and stored to minimise the risks they present (see Topic 4.2 for more on this).

The Reporting of Injuries, Diseases and Dangerous Occurrences Regulations 1995

The Reporting of Injuries, Diseases and Dangerous Occurrences Regulations (RIDDOR) 1995 identify a range of situations that must, by law, be recorded and reported (see Topic 4.2 for more on this).

Organisational policies and codes of practice

Care organisations place a high priority on health and safety. As a result they generally produce detailed policies, procedures and codes of practice relating to health and safety issues in the care workplace. Care practitioners are expected to be familiar with the health and safety policies and procedures that apply in their own care setting. They are often given specific health and safety training during their induction training and through regular refresher courses. Failure to follow organisational policies can lead to disciplinary action and even dismissal if an individual's care practice is thought to be dangerous to others.

Assessment activity 9.3 (P3, M2, D1)

As part of your work in the creative and therapeutic activities team in your local hospital, you help to provide 'information days' for students interested in this kind of work. Your manager has asked you to produce a handout which:

- identifies the relevant health and safety legislation, guidelines and policies affecting the provision of creative and therapeutic activities in care settings

- gives information on the role of the professional in planning, implementing and supporting creative and therapeutic activities (see Topic 9.4).

Topic check

1 Identify six different hazards that might be present in creative and therapeutic activities.

2 What is a risk assessment and why should it be undertaken when planning to use a creative or therapeutic activity in a care setting?

3 Describe the responsibilities of care organisations (employers) and care workers (employees) imposed by the Health and Safety at Work Act 1974.

4 Explain how food safety laws are relevant to the use of creative and therapeutic activities.

5 How do the Manual Handling Operations Regulations 1992 seek to protect care workers and people who use services during creative or therapeutic activities?

6 What does the abbreviation COSHH stand for and how do these regulations protect people involved in creative and therapeutic activities?

The role of the professional

Creative and therapeutic activities have to be carefully planned and implemented in ways that are safe, empowering and enjoyable for people who use services. When you have completed this topic, you should:

■ be able to identify the principles and values that affect the way creative and therapeutic activities are provided

■ understand the need to promote inclusion in creative and therapeutic activity

■ know how professionals involved in providing creative and therapeutic activities can motivate, support and help participants

Key terms

Inclusion: being part of the group or making sure that others are part of the group

Occupational therapist: a practitioner who helps people to engage as independently as possible in activities (occupations) that enhance their health and wellbeing

Purposeful activity: meaningful activity which enables a person to achieve a goal and which meets one or more of the individual's needs

Treatment plan: a professional's plan for treating a patient

Who uses creative and therapeutic activities?

Creative and therapeutic activities are used as part of treatment plans by care workers from a number of different disciplinary backgrounds. These include:

▷ **occupational therapists** (OTs), technical instructors and occupational therapy assistants who plan and implement **purposeful activities** for individuals

▷ physiotherapists and physiotherapy assistants who use forms of exercise, massage and yoga to help people with mobility and other physical problems

▷ hospital play specialists who use a variety of play activities to promote the learning and development of children and young people who are in hospital

▷ nursery nurses and nannies who use a variety of play activities to promote the development and wellbeing of young children

▷ doctors, nurses and social workers who may suggest that an individual takes part in specific activities as part of a broader **treatment plan** activity assistants (sometimes also called activity coordinators) employed in residential care settings to promote and support social activities among residents.

Care workers such as occupational therapists, hospital play workers and activity assistants focus most of their time and attention on planning and implementing creative and therapeutic activities. Other practitioners, such as doctors, nurses and social workers, may suggest or use creative activities as part of an individual's treatment plan but will not focus most of their time on this.

Over to you!

Use the NHS Careers website (www.nhscareers.nhs.uk) or the College of Occupational Therapy website (www.cot.co.uk) to investigate the role of occupational therapists and the way they use purposeful activities to promote health and wellbeing.

Principles, values and inclusion

Care values are covered in detail in Unit 2. Care practitioners who plan and use creative and therapeutic activities need to ensure that they:

▶ use an anti-discriminatory approach in the way they practise

▶ promote equality of opportunity for each person who uses services

▶ empower individuals through the activities they use

▶ promote independence and self-care skills

▶ maintain confidentiality about individual's needs and personal circumstances

▶ respect diversity by acknowledging cultural differences and personal beliefs.

Good care practice should be inclusive of individuals with diverse needs and backgrounds. Providing a variety of creative activities in a care setting is a good way of ensuring that the needs, abilities and interests of all service users are catered for. Care practitioners who use creative and therapeutic activities in their work can support **inclusion** through:

▶ providing opportunities for the development of friendships via activities that have a strong social focus

▶ promoting and supporting interaction between participants so that people use and develop their communication skills

▶ supporting and encouraging people to try activities that offer them new experiences and opportunities for personal development and expression.

Activity

Identify examples of creative and therapeutic activities that could be used to:

- develop friendships between a group of isolated older people
- enable teenagers with learning disabilities to practise using their communication skills
- provide an adult with physical disabilities with a new experience of physical activity
- encourage a group of toddlers (aged 2–3 years) to express themselves.

Strategies for supporting creative and therapeutic activities

Care practitioners use a number of different strategies to encourage and help people to take part in creative and therapeutic activities. These include:

- motivating people to try new activities, follow their interests and use their skills and abilities as best they can – giving praise, getting people to think positively and setting achievable goals all help to motivate people

- supporting enjoyment and being available to offer support when individuals require it – this helps people to have a positive experience of creative activities

- offering practical help to enable people to access different activities and use the facilities and equipment that are available

- providing resources such as art materials, photography equipment, yoga mats or access to music or computer equipment

- ensuring health, safety and security by risk assessing activities and monitoring the way that people participate – it is vital that people who use creative and therapeutic activities as part of their treatment are able to do so safely.

Activity

Produce a poster titled 'You can do it!' which invites and motivates a group of teenagers or older people to take part in an art and craft or a dance group. Your poster should be positive, encouraging and supportive.

Case study

Jayne Marshall is an occupational therapist working at Edward Watson House, a day centre for older people. Most of the people who use the day centre have a diagnosis of dementia or depression. Jayne and her colleagues use a variety of different creative activities in individual and group sessions with the people who attend Edward Watson House. The activities currently on offer include painting and drawing, pottery, knitting and making soft toys. Many of the people who attend also like to take part in cookery sessions, making cakes and lunchtime meals. Jayne also supervises a walk around the local park once a week. The people who come on the walk use this as an opportunity to take exercise, take photographs of trees, birds and park scenes and sometimes have a picnic if the weather is good. Jayne tries to encourage conversation and

friendships between the people in all of the groups she runs. She has noticed that this has a positive effect on some people's confidence and can lift their mood if they are feeling down.

1. Identify an example of the PIES benefits associated with three of the creative activities that are on offer at Edward Watson House.

2. Describe two important care values that Jayne should use when undertaking creative and therapeutic activities with the people who use Edward Watson House.

3. Explain how Jayne tries to support inclusion when she uses creative activities with people at Edward Watson House.

Topic check

1 Identify four care values that should be used when undertaking creative and therapeutic activities.

2 Describe the role of an occupational therapist.

3 Suggest how a creative and therapeutic activity could be used to promote independence.

4 Describe how one example of creative activity could be used to develop the communication skills of participants.

5 Identify and describe two strategies a care practitioner could use to support people who would benefit from taking part in creative and therapeutic activities.

6 What role does a care practitioner have in relation to health, safety and security when using creative activities with patients?

Implementing creative and therapeutic activities

Getting started

This topic focuses on planning and implementing creative and therapeutic activities. When you have completed this topic, you should:

- know about a range of factors that affect choice of creative and therapeutic activities
- be able to plan a creative and therapeutic activity for an individual using health and social care services.

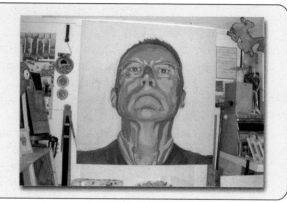

Assessing activity needs

Care practitioners who use creative and therapeutic activities in health and social care settings have to plan their work carefully. Using a care planning cycle, this might involve:

- assessment of the care needs of an individual and their suitability for different types of creative activity
- planning of a suitable activity programme in collaboration with the individual
- implementation of the creative activities
- an evaluation and review of how well the activities met the individual's needs.

In addition to assessing the care needs of an individual, a care practitioner should consider a range of factors that are likely to have an impact on the individual's preferences, and suitability, for different types of creative activity.

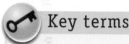
Key terms

Analyse: consider in detail
Consent: agreement
Stereotype: an over-generalised and over-simplified view of an individual or group of people

Choosing activities

When choosing creative and therapeutic activities that may benefit an individual, care workers need to take several factors into account. These include:

- the potential benefits and therapeutic effect of the activities
- the person's age, gender, social and cultural background
- the person's preferences for and motivation to take part in particular activities.

Care workers should always assess an individual's care needs before they suggest or prescribe any treatment. Activities that meet an individual's needs, which help them to learn, maintain or regain skills or which improve their relationships or self-esteem, are likely to be beneficial and therapeutic for the person. Care practitioners need to consider a range of factors that may affect the choice of activities for an individual (see Figure 9.4).

Potential benefits

Topic 9.2 described how creative and therapeutic activities can have physical, intellectual, emotional and social benefits for an individual. A care practitioner should **analyse** both the individual's needs and the potential benefits of an activity before they suggest or select it as part of a treatment programme. There will be a clear benefit to the individual if the activity enables them to develop, improve or regain any physical, intellectual, emotional or social skills or abilities.

Choice of activities should take into account:

▶ the physical needs of the individual, including their stage of physical growth and development, physical fitness, any mobility, balance or other physical problems and any requirements they have for physical assistance and support

▶ the sensory needs of the individual, including any hearing or visual impairment, speech or communication problems and any requirements the person has for assistance, support or specialist equipment

▶ any developmental needs the individual has, as these may affect their physical and communication skills and their intellectual abilities (see Unit 8).

▶ the individual's communication needs, especially if they have speech or hearing problems or if their first language is not English. Some people may require additional support to enable them to communicate effectively.

▶ whether the person is socially isolated. An individual may be less able or less willing to participate in some creative activities if they have few existing social contacts or sources of support.

▶ an individual's learning disability as this will affect their ability to make decisions, establish relationships, communicate and be independent.

Creative and therapeutic activities can be used to help people to develop their skills and abilities in many of these areas. However, a person's existing capabilities and level of functioning will also affect the extent to which they are able to access and benefit from different forms of creative and therapeutic activity.

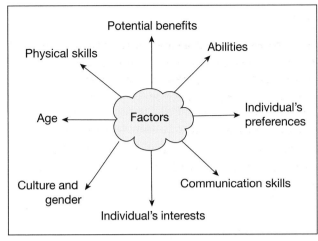

Figure 9.4 Factors affecting choice of activities

 Over to you!

Imagine that you had to recommend some creative or therapeutic activities for your mum or dad to participate in while they were in hospital recovering from an operation. Identify three factors you would take into account before suggesting something.

Interests and preferences

An individual's interests and preferences for taking part in particular activities are probably the most important factors affecting choice. It is bad practice to choose activities for an individual without consulting them. Ignoring what the individual would like to do in favour of your own preferences is also likely to be counter-productive as they may not wish to participate in or be motivated by your choice of activities. The person has to be motivated for the activity to have any therapeutic benefit for them. This means that they:

▷ have to want to do it

▷ can see the benefits for them

▷ are likely to enjoy it and are capable of taking part.

Care workers often have to provide information and sometimes offer encouragement and support before people have enough confidence to take part in creative and therapeutic activities.

Age

An individual's age may affect their interests, skills and abilities. Younger children and older adults who have dexterity or mobility problems may find certain activities – such as yoga, cookery or horse riding – difficult. However, they may be more interested in other activities because they match their age and stage of development better. Many activities, such as music, cookery and art, can be adapted and presented in age-specific ways so that they match an individual's age-related level of ability, knowledge and interest.

Ability

An individual's physical and intellectual abilities may affect their opportunities and motivation to take part in some creative and therapeutic activities. For some people, this occurs because they have not yet developed the abilities needed to read, play music or use computers, for example. However, other people who have physical disabilities or learning difficulties may find it difficult to participate in creative activities because of their specific physical or intellectual needs. In these circumstances, activities and equipment may need to be adapted to enable an individual to participate. Occupational therapists are often asked to assess the activity needs of disabled people and to find ways of adapting activities and equipment to enable individuals to participate. A careful analysis of an individual's abilities should be carried out before any creative or therapeutic activities are suggested or used as part of their treatment plan.

Communication skills

Communication skills are essential to establish good relationships and enable interaction between people. An individual's age, intellectual ability, sensory impairment

Over to you!

How could an activity like painting be adapted to meet the needs, skills and abilities of a young child (3–4), an adolescent (14–15) and an older person (65)?

Activity

Most sports can be adapted to enable disabled people to participate. Investigate the website of the English Federation of Disability Sport (www.efds.co.uk) and find out how disabled people participate in a range of sports activities.

or cultural background could affect their ability to communicate with others. For example, children and people with learning disabilities tend to have less well-developed communication skills than adults. A person whose first language is not English may also require some communication support in order to participate fully in some creative activities that rely on speech and the use of language.

Culture and gender

A person's cultural background affects their values, lifestyle and beliefs. A person's gender can affect how they think about and manage physical contact with other people. Culture and gender may influence, for example, the way a person uses or reveals their body and their expectations about touch and proximity. Mixed sex massage, swimming or exercise classes may be unsuitable for men and women who hold certain religious beliefs, for example. Similarly, cooking may be a therapeutic activity if it enables an individual to prepare, cook and eat food that expresses their cultural identity. It is always important to assess whether an activity, or the way it is presented and run, could offend and individual because of their gender or cultural background.

Gender may also influence in other ways the types of activities that people are interested in and feel motivated to take part in. It is important not to **stereotype** men and women, but it is likely that males are more likely to want to participate in football than flower arranging, for example. Similarly, many girls and women may be drawn to art, cooking and yoga in a way that many (but not all) men are not. It is important to get to know an individual's needs and preferences for different types of activities because it is possible that they may not conform to expected gender patterns. Nevertheless, the way an activity is presented or carried out should take into account gender differences so that one gender isn't put off or excluded from taking part.

 Case study

Northway Swimming and Leisure Centre produces a detailed programme of activities, events and session times for members of the public. Abigail Evans, a community occupational therapist, has obtained a copy of the latest programme. She is trying to organise some leisure and swimming activities for the people she supports as part of her mental health caseload. Abigail works with a socially and culturally mixed group of people. Many of the people she sees are socially isolated and would benefit from joining in with group activities. However, they would all prefer them to be held away from the hospital and near to their own homes. Northway Swimming and Leisure Centre seems like the ideal venue.

After looking through the latest programme, Abigail has identified 'mixed adult swimming', the fitness gym and a Pilates class as possible sessions that six of her clients could join in together.

1. Are any of the activities chosen by Abigail likely to be unsuitable for a culturally mixed group of people?

2. Do you think that the gender of Abigail's clients might affect their enthusiasm for any of the activities she has chosen?

3. What kind of exercise or fitness activity would you suggest for a culturally mixed group of men and women?

Planning and implementing creative and therapeutic activities

The process of planning and implementing creative and therapeutic activities is best learnt by doing it yourself. This final section of Unit 9 is based on a sequence of activities that requires you to:

▶ assess an individual's needs and identify one or more suitable creative activities to meet these needs

▶ plan and explain how you would carry out the creative activity in a health or social care environment

▶ evaluate the effectiveness of your planned activity in terms of how well it meets the holistic needs of the individual.

Over to you!

List the advantages and disadvantages of planning and providing gender-specific activity groups, such as 'Cooking for Men' or 'Women-only swimming' sessions. Are there circumstances where a gender-specific group could be more beneficial to the participants than a mixed group?

Assessment activity 9.4 (P5, M3, D2)

Part 1 – Identifying the individual and the activity

Identify a creative or therapeutic activity for an individual using health or social care services. You should:

- Identify an individual who could benefit from taking part in creative and therapeutic activities, explaining why you chose the individual.
- Identify a form of creative or therapeutic activity the individual would benefit from.
- Describe the needs of the individual.
- Describe how the person could benefit from participating in the suggested activity.

Part 2 – Planning the activity

Outline a plan for carrying out your proposed activity in a health or social care environment. Your plan should:

- Provide a step-by-step guide to the way you intend to carry out the activity.
- Describe the care setting where you plan to carry out the activity.
- Identify the materials and other resources that you will need.
- Indicate when (and for how long) you will carry out the activity.

- Identify any health and safety issues associated with the activity and ways of minimising risk.
- Describe how you intend to use care values in the way that you organise and carry out the planned creative or therapeutic activity.

Part 3 – Carrying out the activity

You should ensure that you obtain the **consent** of your tutor, workplace supervisor and the individual for whom you are planning the activity before you carry out the activity in a care setting. You should then use your plan to carry out the creative or therapeutic activity with the chosen individual.

Part 4 – Evaluating the activity

Evaluate the effectiveness of your creative or therapeutic activity. You should:

- Describe what went well and what went badly during your activity session.
- Explain the extent to which the planned activity met the holistic needs of the individual.
- Describe how you would change or improve your activity if you were to do it again.

Creative and Therapeutic Activity Planning Sheet	
Questions	**Responses**
1. Who might be a suitable person to take part in a creative or therapeutic activity? Explain why in your response.	
2. What form of creative or therapeutic activity would this person benefit from?	
3. What needs does the person have that could be met through participation in this activity?	
4. When, where and how would you carry out the creative or therapeutic activity?	
5. What kinds of equipment or materials would be needed for your activity session?	
6. Are there any health and safety issues associated with your planned activity that you would have to consider?	

Topic check

1 Identify three different factors that should be taken into account when planning creative and therapeutic activities in a care setting.

2 Explain why an individual's interests and preferences should be taken into account when planning creative and therapeutic activities.

3 What impact might a person's culture have on their preference for particular creative or therapeutic activities?

4 How could the care planning cycle be used when planning creative and therapeutic activities?

Assessment summary

The overall grade you achieve for this unit depends on how well you meet the grading criteria set out at the start of the chapter (see page 213). You must complete:

- all of the P criteria to achieve a **pass** grade
- all of the P and the M criteria to achieve a **merit** grade
- all of the P, M and D criteria to achieve a **distinction** grade.

Your tutor will assess the assessment activities that you complete for this unit. The work you produce should provide evidence which demonstrates that you have achieved each of the assessment criteria. The table below identifies what you need to demonstrate to meet each of the pass, merit and distinction criteria for this unit. You should always check and self-assess your work before you submit your assignments for marking.

Remember that you MUST provide evidence for all of the P criteria to pass the unit.

Grading criteria	You need to demonstrate that you can:	Have you got the evidence?
P1	Identify creative and therapeutic activities for people using health and social care services	
P2	Identify the benefits of creative and therapeutic activities for individuals using health and social care services	
M1	Outline the benefits of creative and therapeutic activities for individuals using health and social care services	
P3	Identify legislation, guidelines and policies relevant to the implementation of creative and therapeutic activities	
M2	Outline legislation, guidelines and policies relevant to the implementation of creative and therapeutic activities	
D1	Describe the importance of relevant legislation, guidelines and policies relevant to the implementation of creative and therapeutic activities	
P4	Explain the role of the professional when planning creative and therapeutic activities in a health and social care environment	
P5	Plan a creative or therapeutic activity for an individual using health or social care services	
M3	Carry out a planned creative or therapeutic activity in a health or social care environment	
D2	Present an evaluation of the effectiveness of your planned activity to meet the holistic needs of an individual	

Always ask your tutor to explain any assignment tasks or assessment criteria that you don't understand fully. Being clear about the task before you begin gives you the best chance of succeeding. Good luck with your Unit 9 assessment work!

10 Health and social care services

Unit outline

This unit introduces you to:

▶ the way health and social care services are provided
▶ the difficulties that some individuals face in accessing health and social care services
▶ how and why care organisations and practitioners work in partnership
▶ a range of work roles in the health and social care sectors.

People working in the health and social care sector should have a good understanding of how services are provided. Knowledge and understanding of the range of health and social care organisations and services available helps practitioners to deliver high-quality care provision.

Learning outcomes

1 **Know key elements of health and social care services.**
2 **Know barriers to accessing health and social care services.**
3 **Understand the principles of partnership in health and social care.**
4 **Understand the requirements of job roles in health and social care.**

Grading guide

To achieve a **pass**, your evidence must show you are able to:	To achieve a **merit**, your evidence must show you are able to:	To achieve a **distinction**, your evidence must show you are able to :
P1 Identify the key elements of health and social care services		
P2 Identify the main barriers to accessing health and social care	**M1** Describe how the barriers to accessing health and social care may be overcome	
P3 Explain the benefits of interagency partnerships	**M2** Discuss the ways in which the agencies work together to benefit individuals	**D1** Assess the factors that could prevent these organisations working together
P4 Explain the skills required for two different job roles in health and social care	**M3** Compare the skill requirements of the two different job roles in health and social care	**D2** Assess potential workforce development activities for the two job roles

Provision of health and social care services

Getting started

This topic is about types of health and social care services and the way they are organised in the UK. When you have completed this topic, you should:

■ know about the different types of care service in the UK

■ be able to explain the characteristics of each type of care service.

Key terms

Informal sector: consists of people who provide physical or emotional support for members of their own family, friends or neighbours

Multi-agency working: involves care workers from different care organisations or agencies working together

Private sector: consists of care businesses and practitioners who charge for their services

Statutory sector: consists of NHS and local authority organisations that are funded and run by the government

Voluntary sector: consists of registered charities and not-for-profit organisations

Types of care services

Health and social care services in the UK are delivered by **statutory sector**, **voluntary sector**, **private sector** and **informal sector** care providers.

The statutory sector

By law the government has to provide some types of care services. These laws are called 'statutes' – this is where the term 'statutory' comes from. Examples of statutory care organisations include the National Health Service (NHS) and local authorities (local councils). The NHS provides health care services for people of all ages throughout the UK. Local authorities provide social care and some early years services to people in their area.

The voluntary sector

The voluntary care sector consists of a large number of charities, local support groups and not-for-profit organisations. Voluntary sector organisations:

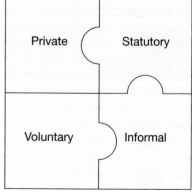

Figure 10.1 Four care sectors

- provide care services because they see a need for them
- are independent of government
- don't have a legal (or 'statutory') duty to provide care services
- don't try to make a profit and often don't charge for their services
- often recruit workers who are unpaid volunteers.

MENCAP is an example of a voluntary sector organisation that recruits volunteers to work with people who have learning disabilities.

The private sector

The private care sector is made up of care businesses and self-employed care practitioners. Examples of care businesses include private hospitals and care homes. Examples of self-employed practitioners include dentists, counsellors and osteopaths. Private sector care providers usually charge people a fee for the services they provide, and work to make a profit.

 Over to you!

Do you know of any private practitioners or care businesses providing care services in your local area? Make a list of your local private sector providers and identify the kinds of services each offers.

The informal sector

The informal sector consists of the very large number of unpaid people who look after their partners, children, relatives, friends or neighbours who have care needs. Because they are not trained, employed or paid to provide care, these people are known as informal carers.

Care providers in each of the four sectors make an important contribution to the overall delivery of care services in the UK. A care provider will usually focus on providing either health care, social care or early years services. However, in practice care providers from different sectors (or from different parts of the same sector) often work together to help clients with complex needs. This is called **multi-agency working**.

 Over to you!

Do you know where you nearest NHS hospital is? What is the name of your local authority?

 Over to you!

Can you think of three voluntary organisations that provide care services in your local area?

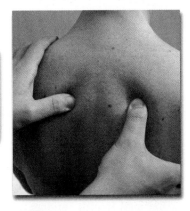

 Over to you!

Do you know of anyone who is an informal carer? What kinds of care, assistance or support do they provide?

 Topic check

1. Name the four main care sectors.
2. Which care sector is funded and run by the government?
3. What is distinctive about the voluntary sector?
4. Describe two examples of private sector care services.
5. Who provides care in the informal sector?
6. What does multi-agency working involve?

Health care provision

Getting started

This topic is about the provision of health care services in the UK. When you have completed this topic, you should:

- know about different types of health care provider
- be able to describe the roles of key health care organisations
- be able to describe the types of health care services available in the UK.

Key terms

Children's trusts: specialist organisations that bring together all statutory services for children and young people in a local area

Chronic: another term for 'ongoing' or 'long term'

Health promotion: activities and services that help people to live healthier lives

Mental health trusts: specialist statutory sector providers of secondary and tertiary care services for people with mental health problems

National Health Service: the main government-controlled provider of health care services in the UK

NHS Trusts: statutory organisations that provide health care services to the public through hospitals and community health services

Primary care trusts: NHS organisations that assess local health needs, fund community health services and monitor local NHS providers

Primary health care: first contact assessment, diagnosis and treatment services provided in the community

Secondary health care: emergency and specialist health care services provided in hospitals or specialist clinics

Strategic Health Authorities: organisations that plan and monitor the regional provision of statutory health care services in the UK

Tertiary health care: specialised care, such as hospice-based end-of-life care services

The National Health Service (NHS)

The **National Health Service** (NHS) is the main provider of health care services in the UK. The NHS was launched in 1948 to tackle widespread problems of ill health and to provide free health services for everyone living in the UK. Before this, health services were not available to many people. Some voluntary services existed but most people had to pay a doctor privately or join an insurance scheme if they wanted health care services. This meant that most people didn't receive good health care because they couldn't afford to pay.

The NHS is a large and complex organisation with three main levels. These are the:

▶ national level – where the Department of Health plans and makes decisions about the NHS as a whole

▶ regional level – where regional bodies, such as **Strategic Health Authorities**, put the government's plans into practice for their region or part of the country

▶ local level – where local organisations, such as **Primary Care Trusts**, commission local services, and **NHS Trust** providers actually deliver health care services to the public.

Figure 10.2 shows how the various parts of the NHS are organised into these different levels.

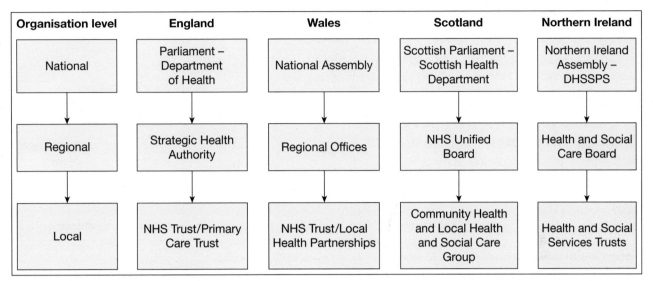

Organisation level	England	Wales	Scotland	Northern Ireland
National	Parliament – Department of Health	National Assembly	Scottish Parliament – Scottish Health Department	Northern Ireland Assembly – DHSSPS
Regional	Strategic Health Authority	Regional Offices	NHS Unified Board	Health and Social Care Board
Local	NHS Trust/Primary Care Trust	NHS Trust/Local Health Partnerships	Community Health and Local Health and Social Care Group	Health and Social Services Trusts

Figure 10.2 Structure of the NHS

Mental health trusts are specialised local-level providers of mental health services. They provide psychological therapies and other specialist forms of care for people suffering from significant mental health problems. In a similar way, **Children's trusts** are specialised local providers of health, social care and early years services for children and young people. They aim to bring together and coordinate services aimed at meeting the diverse and sometimes complex needs of children in a particular area.

Activity

Is there a Mental Health Trust or a Children's Trust in your local area? Carry out some research and identify the location and the range of services offered by either a Mental Health Trust or a Children's Trust near to where you live.

Types of NHS services

Statutory health services are usually provided by NHS Trust organisations. These organisations provide **primary health care**, **secondary health care** or **tertiary health care** services.

Primary health care is provided in community settings, such as health centres, clinics and people's homes by GPs, practice nurses, pharmacists, opticians and dentists, for example. Primary health care providers assess and treat general health problems and also provide **health promotion** and illness prevention services. Some people use primary health care services regularly because they have a **chronic** health problem or a disability. However, most people use primary health care services on an occasional basis for minor illnesses.

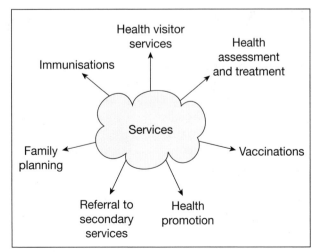

Figure 10.3 Examples of primary health care services for client groups

The specialist types of care and treatment that are provided in a hospital or a specialist clinic are known as secondary health care services. Secondary care focuses on very specific, and often complex, health problems rather than on general, everyday problems. For example, large general hospitals usually have an accident and emergency (A&E) department that deals with life-threatening as well as minor injuries, a theatre or surgical department that deals with operations and a maternity unit that deals with childbirth. All of these departments provide secondary health care services.

Tertiary health care services are specialised services such as end-of-life care provided in hospices, or the very specialised services provided by the Hospital for Sick Children at Great Ormond Street in London. Tertiary care providers are specialists in their field and often centres of excellence. People are referred to these services when they need care that is not available at their local NHS Trust hospital.

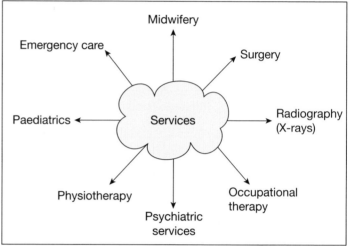

Figure 10.4 Examples of secondary health care services for client groups

Private sector health care services

Private sector health care services are provided by care businesses, such as BUPA and Nuffield Hospitals, and by private practitioners. Private sector providers offer some specialist services, such as cosmetic surgery or dentistry, that are not available from the NHS. However, they also offer alternatives to NHS services that some people are willing to pay for. Many dentists, physiotherapists and counsellors work as private practitioners

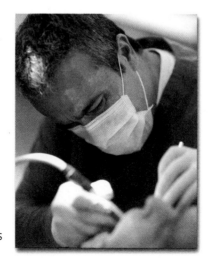

and many people use private hospitals to ensure that they receive treatment quickly. People who use private sector health care services have to pay for their care through health insurance or by paying the costs directly from their own finances.

Informal health care provision

Informal carers sometimes provide physical care and basic health care services for relatives, friends and neighbours. They may, for example, give non-prescription medicines, like cough mixture or paracetamol, for minor ailments or treat small cuts and bruises. Informal carers sometimes receive training in more complex health care techniques. This can include training to give insulin injections or to change dressings so they can support their relatives at home.

Over to you!

Make a list of informal care that you have a) provided for others and b) received from others in the last couple of years. If you became unwell, who would be your main informal carer now?

Case study

Ashok is 9 years old. Last Christmas he was admitted to an NHS children's hospital when he fell over on his new rollerblades. Ashok broke his ankle and banged his head hard against the pavement. He stayed in the children's hospital for 3 days while tests were done and his ankle was put in plaster. Ashok felt frightened and lonely in hospital, even though the nursing and medical staff were friendly and helpful. Ashok's GP took over responsibility for his care and treatment when Ashok was discharged from hospital a few days after Christmas.

1. What kind of health care services did Ashok need as a result of his accident?
2. Was the children's hospital Ashok stayed in part of the statutory or the private sector?
3. Ashok's GP is a primary care practitioner. What does primary health care involve?
4. What kind of informal health care would you expect Ashok's parents to provide for him?

Topic check

1. When did the NHS first start providing free health care services?
2. What roles do the Department of Health and Strategic Health Authorities play in the NHS?
3. Describe two examples of primary health care services.
4. Describe two examples of secondary health care services.
5. Explain what tertiary health care involves.
6. What role do informal carers play in providing health care services?

Social care and children's services

▶ Getting started

This topic is about the kinds of non-medical social care services that are provided for children, adults and older people throughout the UK. When you have completed this topic, you should:

- know about different types of social care provider
- be able to describe the roles of key social care organisations
- be able to describe the types of social care services available in the UK.

🔑 Key terms

Domiciliary support: social care services provided in a person's home, also known as home care services

Eligibility criteria: the rules that local authorities use to decide who can receive services

Local authority: the local government (council) body with responsibility for social care services in a local area

MIND: a national mental health organisation

NSPCC: the National Society for the Prevention of Cruelty to Children

Residential home care: care homes that provide supported accommodation for people unable to live in their own homes

Secretary of State for Health: the government minister (politician) responsible for NHS and social care delivery

Social care: non-medical support and assistance for children and adults who have personal, emotional or financial problems

Sure Start: a government programme designed to bring together early education, childcare, health and family support services

Statutory social care

Social care organisations provide forms of support or assistance to people who are unable to meet their own personal and social needs independently. The **Secretary of State for Health** has overall responsibility for statutory social care and children's services. The Department of Health is the part of government that plans and manages statutory social care services at a national level.

Providers of social care services

Local authorities are the main local providers of social care for people of all ages. A local authority will usually have separate

departments that provide statutory social care services for adults and services for children. These departments buy some care services from private and voluntary sector providers but also provide some of the services themselves. Services for adults include social work, day centres and residential home care. Services for children and young people include child protection, adoption and fostering and youth work. The Children Act 1989 makes local authorities legally responsible for the welfare of children in need.

Activity

Foster care is a form of social care that is provided for children and adolescents. Use the internet to find out more about what foster care involves. You could start with the Fostering Network site (www.fostering.net/) or go to your local authority's website to search for information.

Services for children

Children's trusts are a new form of statutory care organisation that bring together health, social care and early years services in order to meet the needs of vulnerable children and families. Many statutory social care services for children and families are provided through **Sure Start** children's centres, extended schools, youth clubs and health care clinics. A local Sure Start centre will typically:

▶ be the first point of contact for all care-related enquiries from children, families and professionals

▶ receive and make referrals for services for children

▶ identify, refer and monitor vulnerable children.

The care practitioners who are employed by a children's trust:

▶ assess children's needs

▶ give information and advice

▶ receive and make referrals for emergency and preventive services

▶ complete and manage information about a child and their family.

Integrating children's services through children's trusts is seen as a way of protecting vulnerable children and of improving the opportunities and life experiences of the poorest and most disadvantaged children.

Activity

Identify the location of your nearest Sure Start children's centre and find out:
• what the aims of the centre are
• what services they provide
• who the services are aimed at
• which professionals work at the centre.

Voluntary social care services

The voluntary sector is a major provider of social care services in the UK. Voluntary sector social care organisations first began in the UK as a way of tackling major social problems such as poverty, unemployment and poor housing during the 19th century. A wide range of voluntary social care services is now provided in the UK for people of all ages. Some large organisations, like the **NSPCC** and **MIND**, provide services throughout the country. Other smaller organisations focus on specific local social care issues. The social care services that are provided by voluntary organisations often fill the gaps left by the statutory sector and play a vital part in supporting vulnerable people of all ages.

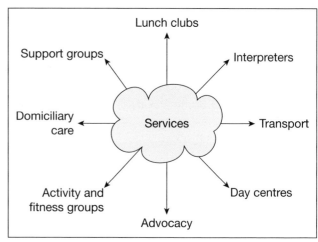

Figure 10.5 Examples of voluntary social care services for client groups

Activity

Which voluntary organisations provide social care services for people in your local area? Try to identify at least one organisation that works on behalf of children, disabled people and older people. Add a brief summary of your findings to those of your class colleagues to make a directory of services provided by local voluntary organisations.

Private social care services

There are relatively few social care organisations in the private sector. Private social care organisations tend to provide specialised **residential home care** for older people or disabled people, or **domiciliary support**. People who use private sector social care services either have to pay for the cost of the services themselves or, if they meet the **eligibility criteria**, they may have some or all of their fees paid by their local authority.

Activity

Find out about the range of private social care services available to people in your local area. Try to identify at least one service each for children, adults and older people.

Informal social care provision

Many people who need social care and support are not catered for by the statutory or voluntary sectors and cannot afford to buy services from the private sector either. These people rely on informal social care and support from relatives, friends and neighbours. Basic services such as housing, financial assistance and emotional support are often provided this way.

Informal social care is also provided through the thousands of small local support groups that exist throughout the UK. These groups are usually run by informal carers and by people who have social care needs themselves. They provide practical and emotional support to both informal carers and the people they care for.

Case study

Mrs Bell is 79 years old and lives alone. She has some memory impairment and forgets what time of the day it is, whether she has eaten, and also the names of all but her closest relatives and her neighbour, Mrs Scott. Mrs Bell is unable to walk far due to her arthritis, very rarely goes out alone, and feels frightened of using her bath as she has difficulty getting in and out.

1. What forms of informal social care would Mrs Bell benefit from?
2. Who might be able to provide each form of informal care for Mrs Bell?
3. If you were a relative or neighbour of Mrs Bell's, how would you feel about giving up some of your time to offer Mrs Bell informal care and support?

Over to you!

Do you provide informal care for anyone at present? How might this change later in your life?

Activity

What kinds of informal support groups exist in your local area? Find out by looking for posters and leaflets in places like the local library, sports centre, church halls, mosques or synagogues and in local day centres.

Assessment activity 10.1 (P1)

Imagine that you are on a placement at a large local health centre. This health centre is linked to the local university and provides support and placements for health workers from abroad visiting your country. Your manager has asked you to contribute to a training session for a new group of visiting health workers.

- Specifically, she has asked you to produce a chart that identifies the health and social care provision which may be accessed in your country.
- You should produce your chart using appropriate information technology packages. It should identify the main forms of care provision and the settings in which these types of care are provided.

Topic check

1 Identify two examples of social care services.
2 Give two reasons why some people may need social care services.
3 Which government department is responsible for planning statutory social care services?
4 Who are the main providers of statutory social care services?
5 What part does the voluntary sector play in providing social care services in the UK?
6 Give an example of a social care service available in the private sector.
7 Explain what domiciliary care involves.
8 What is an informal support group?

Partnership and multi-agency working

▶ Getting started

This topic focuses on the different ways in which care organisations work in partnership with each other and with service users in the health and social care sector. When you have completed this topic, you should:

- ■ know about different forms of partnership working in the health and social care sector

- ■ be able to explain the purposes of partnership working in the health and social care sector.

🔑 Key terms

Holistic: an approach that takes into account the 'whole' person

Inter-agency working: collaboration between different care organisations

Multidisciplinary team: a care team consisting of practitioners from different care professions

Integrated workforce: a group of care practitioners with different but complementary care skills

Partnership working: ways of working together with practitioners from other care professions or other care organisations to provide a joint service

Service user forums: opportunities for people who use care services to have a say about their experiences and concerns and to influence service developments

Working in partnership

Topic 10.1 identified the four different types of service provider in the UK care system. Topics 10.2 and 10.3 described the range of services that are provided by local health and social care organisations. This may have given you the impression that different types of care organisations work separately from each other. In reality there is an increasing emphasis on **partnership working** within the health and social care sector.

Partnership working involves different types of care providers working together. It is likely that care practitioners with different professional backgrounds, and care organisations from different care sectors, are working together to provide services for people in your local area. A care organisation might become involved in partnership working through:

- ▶ inter-agency working
- ▶ working with **service user forums**
- ▶ liaising with organisations in another care sector
- ▶ developing an integrated multidisciplinary workforce.

Purposes of partnership working

The main aim of partnership working is to improve the quality and efficiency of service provision. This can be achieved by:

▶ adopting an **holistic** approach to the assessment and care delivery

▶ identifying and working towards achieving common aims

▶ integrating care practitioners into **multidisciplinary teams** to maximise expertise

▶ reducing the duplication of service provision

▶ ensuring that a consistent approach is taken within an area of care practice

▶ pooling and sharing resources.

Some of the benefits of partnership working include:

▶ better and quicker access to care services and care practitioner expertise

▶ earlier identification of and response to an individual's health, social care and developmental problems

▶ better links between service providers

▶ more cost-effective services saving money that can be spent on other services

▶ more efficient and effective local care services.

 Activity

Sure Start children's centres are an example of partnership working in action. Using the internet and local resources, investigate how 'partnerships' are a feature of the work of your local Sure Start centre. Try to find out which agencies and practitioners are involved, what they do and what they are aiming to achieve. Produce a summary diagram or a brief report to illustrate your findings.

Inter-agency working

Health and social care organisations, or agencies as they are sometimes called, work together in different ways:

▶ Services are integrated by setting up multidisciplinary teams in which a range of separate services merge together and work in a collaborative way to meet the needs of a particular client group. Community mental health care, child protection and drug and alcohol services usually involve inter-agency working.

▶ Multi-agency panels are set up so that practitioners employed by a variety of different care organisations can meet regularly as a panel or network. They discuss individuals with complex needs who would benefit from inter-agency input. Child protection panels are an example of this type of multi-agency service.

Service user forums

The people who use care services should be the main focus of the provision a care organisation offers. Service users often have important things to say about how care services ought to be developed. Service user forums are a way of providing the people who use services with opportunities to express their ideas, concerns and experiences of local care services. Examples of service user forums that work in partnership with local authorities and NHS Trusts include Older Person's Forums, Children and Families Services Forums and Mental Health Forums.

Activity

Do you know of any users of services forums in your local area? Investigate the websites of your local NHS Trust and your local authority to find examples of this kind of partnership working.

 Case study

Pauline had her first episode of mental health problems when she was 19 years old. She was admitted to hospital and given a diagnosis of schizophrenia after she started hearing 'voices' telling her that she was 'useless', 'stupid' and 'ugly'. Pauline found the voices very distressing. Hospital treatment helped Pauline to cope with the voices and she gradually became less distressed and returned to live at home. Despite this, Pauline was readmitted to hospital on several occasions during her twenties and early thirties. She is now 36 years old.

Pauline says that there are good and bad sides to being admitted to hospital. It does help her at times, but she is also critical of the way she is sometimes treated and would like to change some aspects of her service provision. Because she

spoke out about her experiences and has demanded changes to admission and treatment procedures in the past, Pauline was invited to become a member of the Mental Health Service User's Forum run by her local NHS Trust. She now attends monthly meetings where she gives her views on trust policies and practices relating to mental health services, and tries to make sure that patients' views are heard.

1. What kinds of issue are discussed at the Service User Forum that Pauline attends?

2. What kind of expertise does Pauline have that makes her a good person to invite to the service user forum?

3. How might a service user forum such as the one described help to improve services for patients?

Voluntary and statutory sector liaison

Statutory health care, early years and social care organisations often work closely with voluntary organisations in their area to:

▶ identify and assess care needs in the population

▶ fund and make referrals to voluntary sector services

▶ obtain information about the experiences of service users and their carers in the local area.

Local authorities frequently provide grants to voluntary sector organisations in order to fund services such as community transport, home care for older people and Citizen's Advice provision.

Workforce integration

The development of integrated care organisations such as Sure Start children's centres, mental health trusts and children's trusts depends on workforce integration. This involves bringing together people from different care professions to create a workforce that is expert at caring for a particular client group. For example, Sure Start children's centres are based on a workforce of social workers, health visitors and nursery nurses (among others) who have specialist skills and experience in supporting children and families. Workforce integration is a way of ensuring that care practitioners work in partnership for the benefit of service users.

Case study

Peter is 64 years of age. He has mental health problems, diabetes and had a serious heart attack a year ago. Peter tries to be as active as he can. He attends a MIND day centre three days each week, goes to an exercise group at his GP practice for people recovering from heart problems and enjoys socialising with other residents in the small private sector care home where he lives. Peter has a social worker who coordinates the care he receives. The people who work with Peter meet a couple of times each year to discuss his needs and what they can do as a team to help him.

1. Identify the different forms of care Peter receives.

2. In which care sectors are the organisations and practitioners involved with Peter based?

3. How might Peter benefit from a partnership approach to his care?

Assessment activity 10.2 (P3, M2, D1)

Imagine that you have begun work as a child support worker at a local children's centre. Your supervisor has told you about multi-agency working and the importance of this in work with children and young people.

To assess your understanding of this approach to practice, you have been asked to produce a report on how multi-agency support could be provided for a child who has several health, developmental and social care needs.

Your report should:

- discuss how different agencies work together to benefit children
- explain what the benefits of multi-agency partnerships are
- consider reasons that could prevent organisations working together in an effective way.

Topic check

1 Identify three different forms of partnership working in the health and social care sector.

2 Explain the purpose of partnership working.

3 Outline three of the benefits of partnership working.

4 Describe what inter-agency working involves.

5 What is a service user forum?

6 What does workforce integration involve?

Getting started

This topic is about ways of accessing (or obtaining) health and social care services and the barriers that prevent some people from being able to obtain the care services they need. When you have completed this topic, you should:

- know about different ways of gaining access to health and social care services

- be able to describe a range of barriers that can prevent people from accessing health and social care.

Key terms

Domiciliary support: forms of support and assistance provided in a person's home

Eligibility criteria: the rules that are used to decide whether a person can receive a care service

Means test: an assessment of a person's financial means (savings and income)

Postcode lottery: this refers to the unequal availability of care services in different parts of the UK

Referral: a method of directing someone to a care service

Ultrasound scan: a specialist scanning method (like an X-ray) used to check the developing baby

Access to care services

A person may need to access health and social care services because they require:

- care

- practical or developmental support

- diagnosis, advice or guidance

- treatment or therapy.

The referral system

People access health and social care services through one of the following types of **referral**:

- Self-referral is where the person applies for a care service themselves (e.g. when a person makes an appointment to see their GP).

- Professional referral is where a care worker puts the person in touch with another care professional (e.g. when a GP refers a pregnant woman to hospital for an **ultrasound scan**).

▶ Third-party referral is where a person who is not a care professional applies for a care service on behalf of someone else (e.g. when a person phones the local social services department to request **domiciliary support** for her elderly mother).

Referral to health care services

Most people use either self-referrals or third-party referrals when they want to access primary health care services. Secondary and tertiary health care services, which are generally hospital-based, usually require a professional referral from a person's GP or a hospital consultant. However, some secondary care, such as accident and emergency (A&E) services and private sector health care services, can also be accessed by self-referral.

Referral to social care and children's services

Access to social care can be by self-, third-party or professional referral. Referrals to statutory organisations, like adult or children's social care departments, will usually be dealt with by a duty social worker. It is the social worker's job to find out what exactly the situation is and what is needed. An individual will receive social care services if a need is identified and they also meet the **eligibility criteria** to obtain services. If the referral concerns a child, a special assessment is carried out to see if the child is 'at risk' and in need of child protection services. If this isn't the case, an assessment will be carried out to see whether the child is 'in need'. Appropriate services and support will then be provided.

A lot of domiciliary, day and residential care is available directly from voluntary and private social care organisations. A self- or third-party referral can be used to gain access to these services. People can usually access the services they need if they meet eligibility requirements for voluntary services or if they have the ability to pay and the organisation have the staff to supply the service for private sector services.

 Activity

Identify the type(s) of referral involved in each of the following situations:

1. Mrs Arkwright is 78 years old and is frail. Her home carer noticed that she has a bad cough and rang Mrs Arkwright's GP, asking him to make a home visit.

2. Rosie Abdi, a social worker, has received a phone call about a 3-year-old child who is being left alone during the day. Rosie has asked the family's GP to accompany her on a visit to the child's home.

3. Mr Ghupta, aged 35, has a long-term mental health problem. He takes himself to his local health centre or to the local hospital's accident and emergency department when he feels unwell and needs treatment.

4. Ellisha, aged 29, is 5 months pregnant. Her GP has made an appointment for her to have an ultrasound scan at the local hospital.

5. Jim has had a bad back for 3 days. His wife has made him an appointment with a private sector osteopath.

6. Yolanda, aged 18, spoke to the college nurse today about the severe period pain she has been experiencing over the last few months. The nurse offered to refer her to the local hospital's Women's Centre, but Yolanda declined.

7. Greg, aged 32, has found out that one of his work colleagues has chickenpox. Greg phoned his mum to find out whether he had ever had chickenpox and what he should do about his concerns.

Barriers to accessing services

There are occasions where people have a need for a care service, but they are unable to get it. Some of the most common 'barriers' to obtaining health and social care services are set out in Figure 10.6.

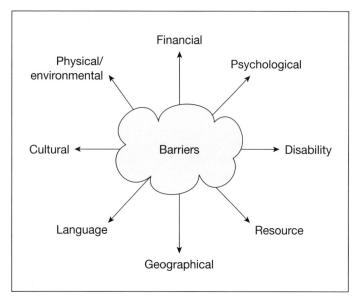

Figure 10.6 Barriers to access

Financial barriers

A financial barrier to accessing care occurs when a person can't afford to purchase services which an organisation charges for. For example, unless you fall into an exempt group you will have to pay for NHS prescriptions, eye tests and dental services. Private sector care companies and self-employed care practitioners also require people to pay for the services they provide. Many social care services are **means tested**. These services can only be accessed if the person who requires them contributes to the cost of the service.

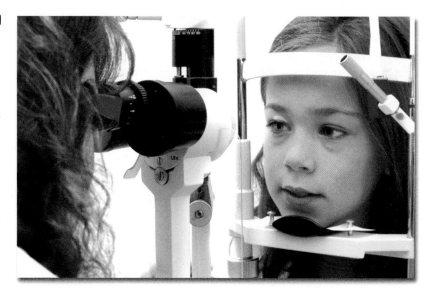

Some people pay into insurance schemes or are given health insurance by their employers to cover their health and social care costs. People who don't have insurance to pay for their care and have limited savings face financial barriers that prevent them from obtaining some forms of health and social care services which they could benefit from.

Geographical barriers

Health and social care services may be difficult to access if they are located several miles away from where a person lives. This is a particular problem for people who live in rural (countryside) areas. Some people have to travel very long distances to obtain specialist health care treatment that isn't available in their area. People who rely on public transport are even less likely to use services that are difficult for them to get to. As a result, the geographical location of services may act as a barrier to people getting the care they need.

Disability

People sometimes also face problems accessing care services because their physical or sensory disabilities mean they can't get into the places where the services are provided. Other people may be unable to leave their own homes to go to the places where care is available because they are physically frail, are mentally unwell or have mobility problems. Physical 'barriers' within buildings that cause access problems for disabled people include outside steps, narrow doorways and corridors, internal stairs and a lack of lifts. Wheelchair users and parents with prams may also be put off or prevented from using services where these barriers are present.

Activity

How well would you cope at school or college if you had a visual impairment or became a wheelchair user because of an accident, injury or illness? Are there physical barriers in your school or college that would prevent you from accessing some of the facilities or areas of the buildings you are now able to use? In this activity you are required to conduct an access survey of your school or college buildings. You should:

1. Obtain a map of the school or college buildings and, after assessing the internal and external environment, mark on it any 'barriers to access' that exist for people who have the following disabilities:

   • visual impairments

   • mobility problems (e.g. wheelchair users)

   • hearing impairments

   • learning disabilities.

   If you are unable to obtain a map, create a table identifying those areas in which there are 'barriers to access' for disabled people.

2. Describe the nature of each barrier – why does it prevent access to disabled people?

3. Suggest ways in which each of the barriers to access that you identify could be overcome to enable a disabled person to use the facilities in your school or college in the same way as a non-disabled person.

Cultural and language barriers

The UK is a multicultural country in which people speak a variety of languages. In areas where there are large numbers of people from minority ethnic communities, health and social care providers try to ensure that language barriers are overcome by providing multilingual signs, interpreters and bilingual staff. However, information about health and social care services is not always translated from English or provided in the formats needed by people who have eyesight or hearing problems. People from minority groups, different cultures or with hearing or visual impairments can therefore struggle to find and use care services because of their cultural, language and communication needs.

 Case study

Charles Joyce, aged 55, has multiple myeloma, a cancer of the blood cells. His doctors have told him he will not survive the winter unless he receives the cancer drug Revlimid. Mr Joyce has been denied the drug, which costs £4000 a month, by his Primary Care Trust, even though his doctors say it could prolong his life by up to 3 years. If Mr Joyce lived a mile and half away from his current home, his case would be dealt with by a different Primary Care Trust. This Trust does fund treatment for patients who require Revlimid. Mr Joyce believes he is the victim of a 'postcode lottery' and intends to take his Primary Care Trust to the High Court in the hope of having their decision overturned.

1. Do you think Mr Joyce is the victim of the 'postcode lottery'?

2. What are the barriers to Mr Joyce accessing the care he needs in this situation?

3. Are there any ways in which Mr Joyce could overcome the barriers to care he faces?

Resource barriers

Service users sometimes find that health and social care organisations have staff shortages or don't have enough money to provide the care services they need when they need them. As a result, lack of human or financial resources can mean service users have to go on a waiting list for treatment. The area where a service user lives can also affect their ability to access care services. If a person lives in an area that has staffing shortages or a lack of funding for care services, they may have to wait longer or may even find that a particular service isn't available to them. By contrast, another person living nearby but in a different health or local authority area may get the treatment or services they require. This situation is known as the **postcode lottery**.

Psychological barriers

Fear and embarrassment sometimes prevent people from seeking or using the health and social care services they need. For example, the rate of testicular cancer is higher than it should be partly because men are often reluctant to conduct self-examinations or seek help early if they find anything unusual. You may also know someone who is too scared to go to their doctor or dentist. People who have problems with alcoholism, drug misuse, eating disorders, obesity, sexually transmitted diseases and mental illness are also sometimes too embarrassed, frightened or ashamed to seek help when they need it.

Over to you!

Why do you think there is a stigma attached to receiving help or support from local authority social services departments?

Assessment activity 10.3 (P2, M1)

A local voluntary organisation Care4U is campaigning to raise awareness of how people can gain access to the range of care services in your local area. They believe that everyone training to work in the health and social care field should know about the barriers that prevent some people from accessing the care services they need. You have been asked to produce a set of information sheets which:

- identify the main barriers to accessing health and social care
- describe how the barriers to access may be overcome.

The information sheets should be suitable for students training to work in health and social care settings.

Topic check

1　Identify three different kinds of referral used in the health and social care sector.
2　What kind of referral is most often used to obtain primary health care services?
3　What is a professional referral?
4　Explain how language barriers can prevent some people from gaining the care services they need.
5　Describe three examples of physical barriers that might prevent a wheelchair user from accessing care services.
6　How do psychological barriers prevent some people from accessing health and social care services?
7　Describe two ways in which a person living in a rural area may face geographical barriers when they require health care services.

Working in the health care sector

▶ Getting started

This topic is about the range of job roles that exist within the health care sector and the skills, personal requirements and qualifications needed for these job roles. When you have completed this topic, you should:

- know about a range of job roles in the health care sector
- be able to describe the care skills required to work in the health care sector
- know about the personal attributes and qualifications required for health care job roles.

🔑 Key terms

Antenatal care: pre-birth care for a pregnant woman

Mental health nurse: a registered nurse who works with people with mental health problems

Multidisciplinary team: a group of health care practitioners who work together but have different job roles

NVQ: National Vocational Qualification

Postnatal care: care provided for a woman and baby following the baby's birth

Registered nurse: a qualified nurse who is registered with the Nursing and Midwifery Council (NMC)

Working in health care

There is a wide range of job roles in the health sector. These can be divided into direct and indirect roles:

▶ In direct care roles the health care worker provides care directly to people who use health care services. Examples include doctors, nurses, midwives, health visitors, dentists, opticians, pharmacists, paramedics, occupational therapists and physiotherapists.

▶ In indirect care roles the health care worker supports the provision of health care services provided by others. Examples include medical receptionists, medical laboratory technicians, porters and cleaners.

Health care providers in the statutory and private sectors employ a large number of people in both direct and indirect care job roles. For example, the NHS employs more people than any other organisation in Europe.

People employed in health care roles usually deal with individuals who have physical, medical-related problems such as a disease, injury or acute illness. However, some people who use health care services have a combination of health, social care or developmental problems that mean a health care worker has to provide more than one type of care for that person. For example, a **mental health nurse** might need to offer their clients both health and social care.

Health care skills

Health care workers are expected to develop and use a range of skills and knowledge in their daily work. These include:

▶ knowledge of care values (see Unit 1) that set out the principles of good care practice

▶ the knowledge and skills required to identify and meet an individual's basic care needs, including eating, drinking, using the toilet and maintaining mobility

▶ maintaining health, safety and personal hygiene in order to minimise accidents and cross-infection (see Unit 4)

▶ providing active support for service users in a way that assists them to meet their needs without reducing their independence

▶ effective communication and interpersonal skills that enable them to make supportive relationships with colleagues and people who use care services (see Unit 1).

Areas of health care work

Jobs roles in the health care sector can be grouped into a number of different areas of work (see Figure 10.7). There are many specialist roles in each of these areas of health care work. Health care workers tend to become more specialist as their careers progress. For example, a nurse may begin her career working on a general medical ward to gain experience and then do further training to become a clinical nurse specialist in wound care.

Figure 10.7 Areas of health care work

Areas of health care work	Job roles	Qualifications
Medicine	• Hospital doctor or GP (general practitioner/family doctor) • Paramedic • Operating department practitioner • Medical laboratory technician	• Medical degree • Foundation degree and in-service training in paramedic science • GCSEs and further in-service training • GCSEs and further in-service training
Midwifery	Hospital or community midwife	Degree in midwifery/registered midwife award
Nursing	• Hospital or community-based nurse • Nursing assistant	• Degree or Diploma in Nursing/Registered Nurse award • **NVQ** HSC 2
Professions allied to medicine	• Occupational Therapy • Physiotherapist • Dietician	Degree in Occupational Therapy, Physiotherapy or Dietetics and registered practitioner award
Specialist health care practice	• Optician • Dentist • Pharmacist • Hospital play worker	• Degree in ophthalmology, dentistry or pharmacology and registration with the relevant professional body • GCSEs and an NVQ3 in Childcare or Play Specialist award
Managerial and administrative work	• Medical receptionist • Hospital manager	Dependent on job role, ranging from GCSEs to degree and specialist professional qualifications (e.g. accountancy)

Medicine

People who work in medicine usually have a direct care role treating patients who are physically or mentally unwell and in need of diagnosis and treatment. Doctors are the most well-known group of medical workers. All doctors of medicine have at least one degree in medicine. Many doctors obtain further qualifications to enable them to work in specialist areas of medicine, such as anaesthetics (pain control), cardiology (heart-related), paediatrics (children's medicine) or psychiatry (mental health). Doctors work in both the NHS and in the private sector. In general, doctors:

▶ assess and diagnose physical and mental health problems

▶ carry out physical and psychological investigations and examinations

▶ prescribe medication and other forms of treatment for health problems

▶ monitor and support patients who are receiving treatment for health problems.

Doctors who are General Practitioners (GPs) work as part of a primary health care team, while hospital doctors work as part of **multidisciplinary teams** alongside other health care practitioners such as nurses and physiotherapists.

Operating department practitioners

Operating department practitioners (ODPs) work with surgeons, anaesthetists and theatre nurses to ensure that operations are carried out in a safe and effective way. ODPs need good management and communication skills as well as detailed knowledge of operating theatre procedures. An ODP may be involved in the anaesthetic phase, the surgical phase or the recovery phase of an operation. ODPs require a minimum of GCSE level qualifications but go on to receive in-service training and usually obtain a Diploma in Operating Department Practice.

Medical laboratory technicians

Medical laboratory technicians work behind the scenes in hospitals. They may use computers to analyse laboratory test data, be responsible for sorting and labelling body tissues for analysis, or may have a specialist role in taking and testing blood samples, for example. The work they do helps doctors and other practitioners to diagnose patients' health problems.

Specialist health care practitioners

There is a wide variety of specialist roles within the health care sector. People who train to work as dentists, opticians or pharmacists require similar entry qualifications to people who train as doctors. Each of these areas of specialist health care practice requires several years of education and training. Dentists, opticians and pharmacists have to be registered with their professional body in order to practise. People working in these areas of health care may become self-employed private practitioners or may work in NHS services.

 Activity

Using the NHS Careers website (www. nhscareers.nhs.uk), investigate and produce brief profiles of the work roles and qualifications of dentists, optician and pharmacists.

A hospital play worker works as a specialist member of a health care team. The role of a play worker is to organise and support play activities for babies, children and young people who are receiving care in hospital. Play workers need to have good organisational and communication skills and must understand the learning and support needs of children and young people. Hospital play specialists usually have a nursery nursing or NVQ3 childcare qualification, though many also obtain a play specialist qualification as part of their in-service training.

Nursing

There are approximately 345,000 qualified nurses working in adult (also called general) nursing, children's nursing, learning disability nursing or mental health nursing. There are important differences in the type of training and work that these different groups of nurses do. Nurses are employed to work in in-patient (hospitals, nursing homes, clinics) or in community settings (GP surgeries, patient's homes, schools).

When qualified, a **registered nurse** generally works as a staff nurse to gain experience and improve their practical skills. The day-to-day work that nurses do depends on the specialist area of care they work in. For example, a mental health nurse spends a lot of time talking with mentally distressed people and providing emotional support. A general nurse working in accident and emergency will spend more time treating people's wounds and injuries.

Nurses spend a lot of time in very close contact with patients, providing a wide range of direct care and support. Nursing is often a physically and emotionally tiring job. Caring for people who are sick and dependent can also involve carrying out tasks that may be unpleasant or physically demanding, such as changing soiled beds or cleaning infected wounds. As well as carrying out their direct care role, nurses also have to complete administrative work relating to patients, often have a role in training student nurses and have a lot of contact with the relatives of those they provide care for.

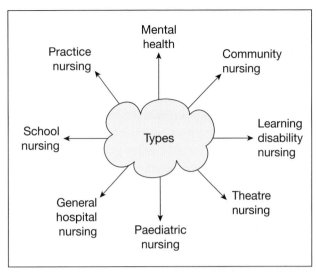

Figure 10.8 Different types of nursing

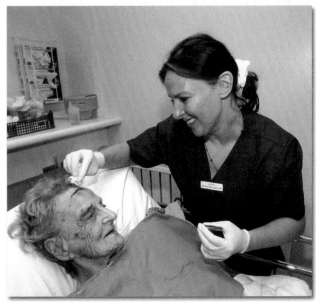

Activity

Find out about the real day-to-day work that nurses do by carrying out an interview with somebody who works as a nurse. You could invite the school or college nurse to talk to your class or arrange to meet and talk with a nurse who works in a local care organisation. Remember to prepare plenty of questions before your interview.

Midwifery

Midwives work with women in all stages of pregnancy, during labour and shortly after they have delivered their baby. Many midwives work in hospital services, especially the delivery suite where babies are born. An increasing number of midwives are now also working in the community, visiting women at home, at GP practices and at children's centres. Midwives now have to obtain a degree to become a registered, practising midwife. However, it is also possible to qualify as a midwife by taking a shorter course in midwifery after obtaining a degree and some experience in nursing. Once qualified, midwives develop their practical skills, knowledge and experience by working in hospital and community settings, providing **antenatal care** and **postnatal care**, support and education and delivering babies.

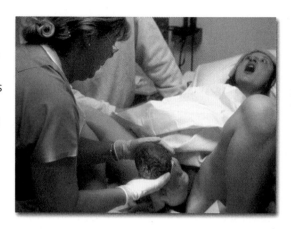

Health visiting

Health visitors work with families, particularly mothers and young children, at home and in community settings. The role of the health visitor is to monitor and promote the health and development of young children. A health visitor will usually visit a mother and newborn baby at home a few days after the birth. Health visitors can provide advice on topics such as feeding, sleep, health and illness, physical and emotional development and other general childcare matters. People who work as health visitors are usually also qualified nurses or midwives (and often both).

Nursing assistant

People who are interested in direct health care work often begin their careers by gaining some vocational training and experience as a nursing assistant. Nursing assistants frequently take an NVQ (National Vocational Qualification) course and are employed in all areas of health care. They usually have a lot of direct patient contact, assisting registered nurses and other staff in providing care. The role of a nursing assistant is different from that of a registered nurse in a number of important ways:

- ▶ Nursing assistants carry out most of the domestic tasks in a care setting, such as making beds.
- ▶ The physical care that nursing assistants provide relates to routine procedures such as lifting, bathing and dressing patients.
- ▶ Nursing assistants carry out care planned by registered nurses.

Like nurses, nursing assistants work day and night shifts and may also work at weekends. There is no minimum age requirement for nursing assistants, but personal maturity is one of the key factors that employers take into account when recruiting people to these posts.

 Over to you!

Which organisations employ nursing assistants in your local area?

 Activity

Find out more about the work of nursing assistants by arranging to talk to a member of staff at a local hospital or nursing home. You might also be able to find information by looking at careers websites or by obtaining a job description when a vacancy for this kind of role is advertised in your local newspaper.

Professions allied to medicine

Physiotherapists and occupational therapists are examples of professions allied to medicine. Both focus on particular aspects of health care, though each has its own specialist training and set of professional skills.

Physiotherapists diagnose and treat movement and other physical health problems using specialist physiotherapy techniques, massage and therapeutic exercises. They also provide a lot of health promotion and illness prevention guidance. Physiotherapists are employed in the NHS, in private sector organisations and as private practitioners. They can be found in a variety of health care areas, including out-patient departments, intensive care units, women's health (especially labour) units, stroke rehabilitation units, children's services and in a variety of specialist services for people with mental health problems, learning or physical disabilities. Qualified physiotherapists have a degree in physiotherapy and then gain plenty of 'hands-on' experience to improve their knowledge and practical skills. They tend to work in multidisciplinary teams with other health care workers in both community and hospital settings.

Occupational therapists (OTs) work in hospital, community or specialist educational or care home settings with people of all ages who have physical or mental health problems or learning disabilities. OTs usually work with other practitioners such as doctors, nurses, physiotherapists and social workers as part of a multidisciplinary team. Occupational therapists assess people who are having difficulties with some aspect of daily living. They then develop treatment plans that involve the person taking part in forms of purposeful activity that will prevent their problems becoming worse and which will enable them to live as independently as they would like. At the end of a course of occupational therapy the individual and the OT will evaluate how effective the treatment has been.

Case study

Annette Harley, aged 35, is a paediatric physiotherapist. She works with children and young people who have physical development and movement problems. Annette works at a large District General Hospital, in the paediatric outpatients department. She sees babies, children and young people who have been referred by a GP or hospital consultant for assessment or treatment of growth or movement problems. Annette begins her assessment of a child's needs by looking at X-rays of the affected parts of their body (e.g. hips, limbs or joints). She then carries out a physical examination of the child or young person and asks them and their parents questions about what they can and can't do and what they see as the problem. Annette then has to diagnose what is wrong and work out a treatment plan. This might involve more

referrals to see specialist doctors, or surgeons if an operation is necessary. Her treatment plans are more likely to involve a series of exercises or the prescription of specialist equipment to help correct growth or movement problems. Annette enjoys the practical nature of her job and says that the fact she is helping to improve children's lives is the factor that motivates her when the job gets tiring and stressful.

1. Which client group does a paediatric physiotherapist like Annette work with?

2. What qualifications are needed to work as a physiotherapist?

3. Describe two aspects of Annette's role as a physiotherapist.

Management, administration and ancillary services

Health care organisations employ a wide range of people to carry out the support, administrative, management and ancillary jobs that are essential both for the organisation to function and for the direct care workers to work efficiently. People who work in administrative roles include medical receptionists, ward clerks and medical secretaries. Health care organisations also employ people in managerial roles to ensure that functions such as finance, catering and maintenance are managed and run effectively. Managers have more authority and responsibility than administrative staff and are often responsible for a group of staff and a department. People who are employed in specialist managerial or administrative roles, such as finance or secretarial work, may have vocational qualifications in appropriate areas such as accountancy, typing or business practice.

Ancillary and maintenance workers are the people who keep a care organisation running smoothly. Porters, who move patients around hospitals, electricians and domestic assistants who clean in-patient areas and change beds are examples of ancillary workers employed in hospitals. People employed in ancillary roles may have vocational qualifications appropriate to the area in which they work, such as catering or electrical work. Many obtain their jobs because of their previous experience and the practical skills they have.

Workforce development

Skills for Health is the sector skills council for health care in the UK. It represents the interests of employers and workers in these areas of the care sector. Its main role is to develop training standards, identify workforce development needs and fund training for staff working in health care settings throughout the UK. Skills for Health aims to:

▶ develop and manage workforce competences in health care
▶ establish a profile of the UK health care workforce

 Case study

Manish Gupta is the facilities manager at St Joseph's hospital. He is responsible for the safe and efficient running of the catering, laundry, portering and gardening services that operate behind the scenes at St Joseph's. Manish works with the staff in each of the areas mentioned, holding daily meetings to discuss staffing and operational issues. He also liaises with other managers responsible for the direct care and financial aspects of running the hospital. Manish's job is mainly 9–5, but he can be contacted to sort out problems that occur outside of office hours.

Manish has a very busy working day involving a lot of meetings. He uses a range of business and management skills in his work, but says that being a good communicator and problem-solver are the key skills needed for his role.

1. What type of work role does Manish Gupta have at St Joseph's hospital?

2. Describe two key aspects of Manish's role.

3. What kind of qualifications and skills would be needed to obtain a post like the one Manish has?

▶ improve skills in the health care workforce

▶ influence education and training supply.

The purpose of Skills for Health is to develop a flexible and skilled health care workforce in order to improve health and health care in the UK. They do this by establishing standards of care and training and approving the qualifications needed to work in health care.

Over to you!

Find out more about the role of Skills for Health by visiting their website at www.skillsforhealth.org.uk.

Case study

Anthea Johnson works as a domestic services assistant in an outpatient clinic attached to St Joseph's hospital. She works 5 days a week, 5 a.m. to 8 a.m. She is responsible for cleaning the floors, desks and other surfaces, and generally tidies the department each morning before other people arrive. Anthea is currently taking an NVQ level 2 in Cleaning. She says her job is very physical and requires physical

fitness and attention to detail. She is well organised and can work on her own, but currently works as part of a domestic services team.

1. What are the main work tasks of a domestic services assistant like Anthea?

2. What kinds of skills and qualities are needed to work as a domestic services assistant?

Activity

What kinds of care work are you most interested in? Do you know what qualifications and experience are needed for this kind of work?

Research the care profession or job role that you are most interested in and produce a profile of the role.

Your profile should identify: entry routes and qualifications needed; training; what the work really involves; and ways of developing a career in this area.

Topic check

1 Name four different areas of health care work.

2 Give two examples of direct care roles and two examples of indirect care roles in health care.

3 What qualifications are needed to work as a doctor?

4 Describe the care role of a health visitor.

5 Which health care professional specialises in the use of purposeful activity?

6 Explain why care organisations need to employ a range of ancillary workers.

Working in the social care sector

▶ Getting started

This topic is about the range of job roles that exist within the social care and early years sectors and the skills, personal requirements and qualifications needed for these job roles. When you have completed this topic, you should:

- know about a range of job roles in the social care and early years sectors
- be able to describe the care skills required to work in the social care and early years sectors
- know about the personal attributes and qualifications required for social care and early years job roles.

 Key terms

Care packages: care services selected and provided to meet an individual's particular needs

Early years roles: jobs working with young children, usually under the age of 8

Empathy: the ability to understand another person's feelings and put yourself in their position

Social care: forms of non-medical care provided for vulnerable people

Working in social care

Social care involves providing various forms of non-medical support and assistance to people who are vulnerable and who have social, emotional or financial difficulties. People working in **early years roles** are usually employed in childcare and early education services for children under the age of 8. Social care provision includes forms of direct care, such as counselling, as well as indirect care, such as arranging housing or access to other support services. Social care services are provided by care practitioners who have a variety of different jobs titles, including social workers, youth workers and social care support workers.

Skills for social care and early years work

In a similar way to health care workers, social care workers need to use a variety of skills and knowledge in their daily work. These include:

- knowledge of care values (see Unit 1) that set out the principles of good care practice
- the knowledge and skills required to identify and meet an individual's basic care needs

▶ maintaining health, safety and personal hygiene in order to minimise accidents and cross-infection (see Unit 4)

▶ providing active support for service users in a way that assists them to meet their needs without reducing their independence

▶ effective communication and interpersonal skills that enable them to make supportive relationships with colleagues and people who use care services (see Unit 1).

Areas of social care work

Job roles in the social care sector can be grouped into a number of different areas of work (see Figure 10.9). Social care workers tend to specialise in working in a particular setting (e.g. residential or community) and with particular age groups (e.g. children, adults or older people).

Figure 10.9 Areas of social care work

Area of social care work	Job roles	Qualifications
Social work	Social worker	Degree in social work and registration with the General Social Care Council
Community work	Community worker	No specific qualifications needed – NVQ, degree and other qualifications as well as experience are relevant
Residential social care	• Residential social worker • Care assistant	• NVQ or social work qualification, depending on job role and responsibilities • GCSEs or NVQ qualifications
Family support	Family support worker	No specific qualifications needed – NVQ or other in-service training is often undertaken
Managerial and administrative work	Care manager	Various – from NVQ and specialist qualifications (e.g. accountancy) to degrees
Childcare	Childminder	NVQ2 or 3 in Childcare
Early education	Nursery nurse	NNEB or BTEC Nursery Nursing qualifications

Social work

Social workers usually have a degree or diploma in social work and must be registered with the General Social Care Council (GSCC) to work as a social worker. Many of the people who require social work assistance are socially excluded, experiencing some form of life crisis, or are 'at risk' because they are vulnerable in some way. Social workers work with members of all age groups in a variety of community, hospital, residential home, education and day care settings.

Most qualified social workers have a caseload of people they work with in community and residential settings. Some social workers specialise in working with members of particular client groups, such as 'at risk' children, vulnerable older people or adults with mental health problems. However, other social workers work as care coordinators or care managers and specialise in assessing clients' needs and purchasing **care packages** for them.

Activity

Find out more about the role of a social worker by looking at the social work careers website www.socialworkcareers.co.uk. You might also be able to get information by looking at other careers websites, or by obtaining a job description when a vacancy for a social worker is advertised in your local paper.

Over to you!

Make a list of reasons why social work is sometimes a difficult and stressful job.

Residential home manager

A residential home manager is responsible for the day-to-day running of a residential care home. As well as ensuring that staff are delivering high-quality care, a residential home manager will also be responsible for:

▶ recruiting, training and developing members of staff

▶ managing the care home's budget

▶ ensuring the home has good connections with other local services

▶ dealing with any problems or complaints that arise.

Some residential home managers are qualified nurses or social workers and play a part in providing care within the home. In addition to their care qualification and experience, many residential home managers have management experience and qualifications and may have gained a specialist NVQ qualification in residential home management.

Care assistant

Care assistants working in social care settings provide the practical help people need in their everyday lives. This can range from assistance with washing and dressing to providing help with cooking, cleaning and housework. The forms of assistance offered by a care assistant depend on the needs and disabilities of the person they are working with. Some care assistants work in an individual's home while others work in day centre or residential care settings. No specific qualifications are needed for care assistant work. However, many care assistants do have GCSEs and go on the gain NVQ qualifications and undertake in-service training courses.

Family support worker

Family support workers are employed by local authorities and voluntary organisations to provide emotional and practical support, help and advice to families who are experiencing difficulties. These difficulties may be the result of a parent experiencing ill health, drug or alcohol problems, financial difficulties, disability or mental health problems, for example. The purpose of family support is usually to keep the family together when there is some risk one or more of the children may be taken into care.

Family support workers are often managed by social workers who plan and monitor the kind of support the family requires. This could involve, for example, demonstrating parenting skills, helping parents to understand and respond to their children's

Case study

Bhupinder Mann is employed as a family support worker by a local authority. She works with one family at a time, often working a shift system that can include days, nights and weekend work. She has taken an NVQ Level 2 course in Children's Care, Learning and Development, and has also completed food hygiene and counselling courses. Bhupinder works with children and families in their own homes. She has recently helped a family where the parents are physically disabled and needed help washing, dressing and feeding their baby. Bhupinder showed both parents how to do this and helped them reorganise their home to make childcare easier. Bhupinder enjoys the practical side of her job and feels that it is important to be well organised and understanding to do the job efficiently.

'My job is quite tiring, but I think it's important to help people. I enjoy the practical work and think of my clients as friends as well.'

behavioural difficulties or showing them how to promote learning through play. No specific qualifications are needed to become a family support worker. However, maturity and experience of working with children and families in statutory or voluntary services are usually required.

Youth worker

Youth workers help young people aged between 13 and 19 years to learn, grow and develop. Their day-to-day work can involve:

- organising sports, art or drama activities
- supporting young people to develop ideas and make changes in their lives
- organising outings and breaks to places like outward bound and activity centres
- supporting young people in organising their own activities and projects
- raising awareness about issues such as health and politics
- supporting young people in developing skills such as literacy and numeracy
- working with specific groups such as young people who are homeless.

Youth workers are usually members of youth justice or social care teams and work closely with other professionals. They work in youth clubs, schools, community centres, faith centres (church, mosque, synagogue etc.) or in Connexions centres. The skills and qualities needed for youth work include:

- the ability to develop and lead programmes of informal learning
- the ability to relate to young people from a wide range of backgrounds
- excellent communication and listening skills
- a positive approach to working with young people.

Counsellor

Counsellors provide people with opportunities and the support needed to discuss feelings and problems they are experiencing. A counsellor may specialise in a particular type of problem – such as bereavement, marital or drug problems – or may work with a particular age or client group. Counsellors need to have very good listening and communication skills. **Empathy** is a key part of a counsellor's work, but it is also important that the counsellor remains detached and objective about the person's problems. A range of different counselling qualifications exists. Organisations that employ counsellors usually require potential applicants to have a Diploma in Counselling and some experience.

Working in early years

There is a wide range of care roles and career opportunities in the childcare and early years field (see Figure 10.10). Childcare and early years work involves lots of busy, hands-on activities with children. Care workers in this area are also responsible for the safety and development of the children they care for and work with.

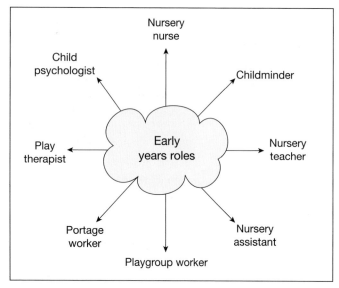

Figure 10.10 Examples of early years roles

Childminder

Childminders usually work at home providing childcare services for babies and pre-school children. Some childminders also provide care and learning activities for older children before and after school. The childminder's role is to provide a safe, stimulating environment for the children they care for. This might also involve providing some practical care such as nappy changing, bathing and feeding infants and younger children, or accompanying older children on after-school trips to the playground or cinema or on other activities.

Nursery nurse

A qualified nursery nurse has achieved a Level 3 qualification such as an NNEB, CACHE or BTEC Diploma in Nursery Nursing. Most nursery nurses are employed in private and local authority nurseries, usually providing direct care and education for healthy children under the age of 5, though some nursery nurses have specialist roles in hospitals and special education units for sick and disabled children. The main care role of a nursery nurse involves:

▶ supporting and encouraging children's physical, intellectual, emotional and social development through play

▶ providing basic physical care for children in the form of feeding, washing and cleaning

▶ observing children's participation in play, monitoring their progress, identifying any problems and reporting back on this to colleagues and parents

▶ managing the health and safety of children in the nursery environment.

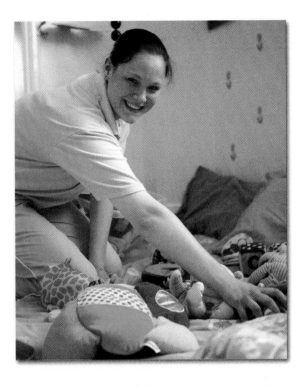

Nanny

The job role of a nanny involves working in a family home looking after the family's children on a full- or part-time basis. Some nannies live with the family full time. As well as providing practical help and safeguarding the family's children, a nanny may also help the children with school work, organise and attend nursery or after-school activities and have a range of housekeeping responsibilities (washing and ironing clothes, making beds, cleaning etc.).

Over to you!

Make a list of the personal qualities that a person who works closely with children, such as a nursery nurse or a nanny, would require.

Over to you!

What kinds of skills and qualities do you think nannies need to perform their role? Make a list of these and think how the items on your list relate to the work that a nanny does.

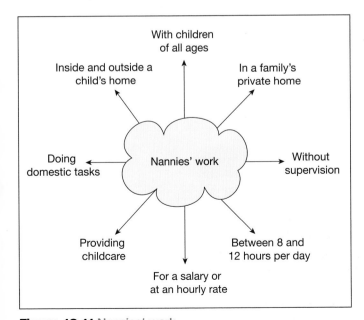

Figure 10.11 Nannies' work

Foster parent

Fostering is a way of providing a family life for children who cannot live with their own parents. All children in foster care are legally looked after by a local authority. However, they are placed with foster parents whose role it is to provide high-quality care. Foster parents work in partnership with the local authority to do this. Foster parents may also work with other professionals such as therapists, teachers or doctors to help the child deal with emotional traumas or physical or learning disabilities.

Foster parents need to have enough maturity to work with the complex problems that fostered children may have, need to be physically fit and be able to relate well to children and young people. Local authorities assess all potential foster parents in detail before they place children with them, though they try to recruit people from all kinds of backgrounds.

Over to you!

Further Education colleges provide a lot of childcare and early years courses for full- and part-time students. Find out what's available at your local FE college by looking at their website or by obtaining a prospectus of courses.

Workforce development

Skills for Care and Development is the sector skills council for social care, children, early years and young people's workforces in the UK. It represents the interests of employers and workers in these areas of the care sector. Its main role is to develop training standards, identify development needs and fund training for staff working in social care and early years settings. Skills for Care and Development carries out its workforce development role through the following organisations:

▶ Care Council for Wales (www.ccwales.org.uk)

▶ Children's Workforce Development Council (www.cwdcouncil.org.uk)

▶ General Social Care Council (www.gscc.org.uk)

▶ Northern Ireland Social Care Council (www.niscc.info)

▶ Scottish Social Services Council (www.sssc.uk.com)

▶ Skills for Care (www.skillsforcare.org).

These organisations work with social care and early years providers throughout the UK. They establish standards of care and training and approve the qualifications needed to work in social care and with children.

Activity

Using the internet, investigate the workforce development role of one or more of the bodies that work with Skills for Care and Development. Identify their aims and the ways they are trying to develop the skills and standards of workers in their part of the health and social care sector.

Case study

Skills for Care (www.skillsforcare.org.uk) is the main body responsible for establishing the training standards and development needs of nearly 1 million social care staff in England. It is known as a sector skills council. *Skills for Care* provide over £25 million in funding to support improved training and qualifications for managers and staff in the social care sector. As a sector skills council, *Skills for Care* work with social care employers and training providers throughout the United Kingdom to establish social care standards

and qualifications that are designed to ensure that social care workers have the skills needed to deliver high-quality care for service users.

1. Using the information provided, describe the role of a sector skills council.

2. How does *Skills for Care* try to promote workforce development?

3. Explain how the work of *Skills for Care* affects the quality of care provision in social care settings.

Assessment activity 10.4 (P4, M3, D2)

Your local careers service is updating the information it has on careers in health and social care. It has asked local health and social care students to use their knowledge and understanding to produce a profile of:

- a health care occupation – covering the job role, skills requirements and continuing professional development opportunities

- a social care occupation – covering the job role, skills requirements and continuing professional development opportunities.

Identify and research two different occupations within the health and social care field. Your profiles should provide concise and accurate information that would be useful to older adolescents and young adults considering a career in health and social care.

Topic check

1 What qualifications are needed to train as a social worker?
2 What kinds of care services do domiciliary care workers provide?
3 Name two client groups that domiciliary care workers are most likely to work with.
4 What qualifications do nursery nurses usually have?
5 What skills do you think are needed to work with children under the age of 8?
6 Describe how the work of a nursery nurse is different from that of an early years teacher.

Assessment summary

The overall grade you achieve for this unit depends on how well you meet the grading criteria set out at the start of the chapter (see page 241). You must complete:

■ all of the P criteria to achieve a **pass** grade
■ all of the P and the M criteria to achieve a **merit** grade
■ all of the P, M and D criteria to achieve a **distinction** grade.

Your tutor will assess the assessment activities that you complete for this unit. The work you produce should provide evidence which demonstrates that you have achieved each of the assessment criteria. The table below identifies what you need to demonstrate to meet each of the pass, merit and distinction criteria for this unit. You should always check and self-assess your work before you submit your assignments for marking.

Remember that you MUST provide evidence for all of the P criteria to pass the unit.

Grading criteria	You need to demonstrate that you can:	Have you got the evidence?
P1	Identify the key elements of health and social care services	
P2	Identify the main barriers to accessing health and social care	
M1	Describe how the barriers to accessing health and social care may be overcome	
P3	Explain the benefits of interagency partnerships	
M2	Discuss the ways in which the agencies work together to benefit individuals	
D1	Assess the factors that could prevent these organisations working together	
P4	Explain the skills required for two different job roles in health and social care	
M3	Compare the skill requirements of two different job roles in health and social care	
D2	Assess potential workforce development activities for the two job roles	

Always ask your tutor to explain any assignment tasks or assessment criteria that you don't understand fully. Being clear about the task before you begin gives you the best chance of succeeding. Good luck with your Unit 10 assessment work!

11 The impact of diet on health

Unit outline

This unit introduces you to the dietary needs of people who use care services and to the components of a balanced diet. It also considers the effects of an unbalanced diet. You will investigate and examine the dietary needs of people who use care services and produce some diet plans to meet these needs. You will also study food safety issues and the principles of good food hygiene.

Learning outcomes

1. **Know dietary needs of individuals at different life stages.**
2. **Understand effects of unbalanced diets on the health of individuals.**
3. **Know specific dietary needs of service users.**
4. **Understand principles of food safety and hygiene.**

Grading guide

To achieve a **pass**, your evidence must show you are able to:	To achieve a **merit**, your evidence must show you are able to:	To achieve a **distinction**, your evidence must show you are able to:
P1 Identify the components of a balanced diet	**M1** Discuss how the components of a balanced diet contribute to an individual's health at different life stages	
P2 Identify the different dietary needs at each life stage		
P3 Explain two medical conditions related to unbalanced diets		
P4 Identify two service users with specific dietary needs	**M2** Outline a two-day diet plan for two service users with specific dietary needs	**D1** Justify how the two day diet plan meets the dietary needs of the two service users
P5 Outline relevant legislation relating to preparing, cooking and serving food	**M3** Discuss the effects of unsafe practices when preparing, cooking and serving food in a health or social care setting	**D2** Assess the effectiveness of safe practices when preparing, cooking and serving food at a health or social care setting
P6 Explain safe practices necessary in preparing, cooking and serving food in a health or social care setting		

What is a balanced diet?

Getting started

This topic focuses on the way a balanced diet provides the basis for good health and development. When you have completed this topic, you should:

- know what a balanced diet consists of
- be able to identify food sources of the five main nutrients
- understand the relative proportions of the five food groups in a balanced diet.

Key terms

Balanced diet: a diet that contains adequate amounts of all the nutrients needed for growth and activity

Deficiency: a lack of something

Dietary Reference Values: statistics produced by the Department of Health which recommend nutritional intake for different sections of the UK population

Macronutrients: nutrients required in relatively large amounts to enable the body to function

Malnutrition: inadequate nutrition caused by over- or under-eating or a diet that lacks nutrients

Micronutrients: nutrients required by the human body in small amounts only

Nutrients: naturally occurring chemical substances found in the food we eat

Obese: extremely overweight

Food for health, growth and development

Food is essential for life and plays a very important role in an individual's physical health, growth and development. The food we eat should be nutritious if it is going to be beneficial to our physical health. This means it should contain a variety of **nutrients**. There are five basic nutrients, which help the body in different ways:

▶ *Carbohydrates* and *fats* provide the body with energy.

▶ *Proteins* provide the chemical substances needed to build and repair body cells and tissues.

▶ *Vitamins* help to regulate the chemical reactions that continuously take place in our bodies.

▶ *Minerals* are needed for control of body function and to build and repair certain tissues.

Carbohydrates, proteins and fats are referred to as **macronutrients** because the human body requires a lot of them to function. Vitamins and minerals are referred to as **micronutrients** as they are needed in much smaller amounts.

As well as eating food that contains a balance of these five nutrients, people also need fibre and water in their diet. Although these are not counted as nutrients they are vital for physical health. Figure 11.1 provides more information on the sources and functions of nutrients.

Over to you!

Can you identify at least two sources of each nutrient in the food that you have eaten over the last 2 days? Are any of these nutrients missing from your diet?

Figure 11.1 Sources of nutrients

Nutrients	Food sources	Function
Carbohydrates – the three types of carbohydrates are simple (sugars), complex (starch) and non-starch polysaccharides (fibre).	Sugar sources: milk, fruit and fruit juice and sugar-based products (e.g. biscuits, cakes, chocolate) Starch sources: potatoes, yams, cereals Fibre sources: fruit and vegetables and food made from bran	Sugars and starch are good energy sources. Fibre helps gut function and prevents constipation.
Fats and oils – saturated fats found in animal and dairy products are less healthy fats and can cause heart disease. Unsaturated fats are found in olive oil and have a beneficial effect on the heart. Polyunsaturated fats are found in fish and soya oil and also have health benefits.	Animal and dairy sources: meat, butter, cheese Plant sources: vegetable and nut oils Fish sources: mackerel, tuna and other oily fish	Fats and oils are a source of energy and warmth for the body.
Proteins are the only source of essential amino acids for human beings. Essential amino acids play a vital role in many of the chemical processes that occur in the body.	Animal protein sources: meat, fish, milk, cheese and eggs Plant protein sources: peas, beans, cereals and seeds	Proteins are essential for the growth and repair of body tissues and are a source of energy. They also supply essential amino acids.
Vitamins – A, B, C, D, E and K	Fruit and vegetables	Vitamins are needed to maintain various body functions, including eyesight, healthy skin and gums, bone strength and blood clotting.
Minerals – calcium, sodium, iron and potassium	Minerals can be obtained from vegetables, meat, dairy products and salt.	Like vitamins, minerals are needed to support various body functions.

Activity

Using the internet, find out the names of vitamins A, C, B1, B2, B3, B6, B12 and vitamin E. Identify a source of food containing each of these vitamins and find out what role the vitamin plays in the body. Present your findings in a table.

Balancing your diet

A healthy intake of food contains suitable amounts of each of the five basic nutrients. This is a **balanced diet**. A person who consumes a balanced diet will obtain sufficient nourishment to enable their body to grow and function properly. Consuming a balanced diet will reduce the risk of diet-related conditions, such as heart disease, strokes and diabetes, and **malnutrition**. A balanced diet will also provide sufficient energy for the person to meet their activity needs. The amount and types of foods that are healthy for a person to eat varies for each individual and changes over the course of their life.

The balance of good health

The food pyramid in Figure 11.2 shows the five main food groups, and the proportion of each food type, that make up a balanced diet.

You will see from the food pyramid that a balanced diet is based on starchy, carbohydrate foods. These are the main source of energy in an individual's diet. Fruit and vegetables make up the next step of the pyramid. They are a main source of vitamins and minerals as well as fibre in the diet. Protein foods can come from animal or vegetable sources but should be eaten only in moderate amounts. Sugars and fats are at the top of the food pyramid because they should be eaten least often and should form only a very small part of a person's diet. Sugary and fatty foods provide calories (energy) but tend to have very little additional nutritional value.

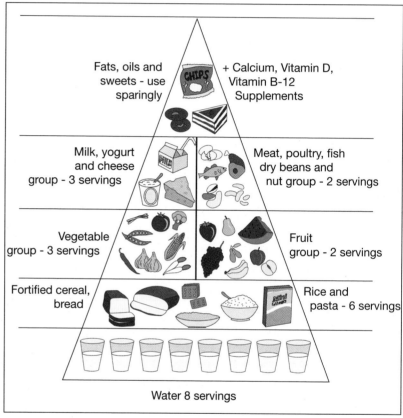

Figure 11.2 The balance of good health

How to eat a balanced, healthy diet

1. Eat a variety of different foods.
2. Eat the right amount to be a healthy weight.
3. Eat plenty of foods rich in starch and fibre, such as bread, cereals and potatoes.
4. Eat plenty of fruit and vegetables.
5. Eat moderate amounts of meat and fish.
6. Consume moderate amounts of milk and dairy products.
7. Consume small amounts of fatty and sugary foods.
8. Drink plenty of water.

Dietary reference values

One way of working out how much an individual needs to eat to have a balanced, healthy diet is to refer to **Dietary Reference Values** (DRVs). The Department of Health produces a table of DRVs that provides guidance on the amount of energy or the amount of an individual nutrient that different age groups need for good health. There are three different values for each nutrient:

▶ Reference Nutrient Intake (RNI) – the amount of a nutrient that is sufficient for almost every member of a defined group of people. The RNI is higher than most people's needs.

▶ Estimated Average Requirement (EAR) – this is an estimate of the average need for food energy or a nutrient for a defined group of people. Some members of the group will need more than this average while others will need less.

▶ Lower Reference Nutrient Intake (LRNI) – the amount of a nutrient that is sufficient for a small number of individuals in a group of people. These people will have the lowest nutritional needs.

DRVs provide some guidance on the daily intake of each nutrient and can be used as the basis for the recommendations and diet-related treatment plans of dieticians, doctors and other practitioners who are promoting healthy eating and a balanced diet.

Figure 11.3 Estimated Average Requirement (EARs) for energy

Age	EARs in MJ/d (kcal/d)	
	Males	Females
0–3 months	2.28 (545)	2.16 (515)
4–6 months	2.89 (690)	2.69 (645)
7–9 months	3.44 (825)	3.20 (765)
10–12 months	3.85 (920)	3.61 (865)
1–3 years	5.15 (1230)	4.86 (1165)
4–6 years	7.16 (1715)	6.46 (1545)
7–10 years	8.24 (1970)	7.28 (1740)
11–14 years	9.27 (2220)	7.72 (1845)
15–18 years	11.51 (2755)	8.83 (2110)
19–50 years	10.60 (2550)	8.10 (1940)
51–59 years	10.60 (2550)	8.00 (1900)
60–64 years	9.93 (2380)	7.99 (1900)
65–74 years	9.71 (2330)	7.96 (1900)
75+ years	8.77 (2100)	7.61 (1810)
Pregnancy		+0.80 (200)
Source: Committee on Medical Aspects of Food and Nutrition Policy (COMA), 2002		

Energy balance

An individual's diet needs to contain an energy balance. Some foods provide large amounts of energy per gram of the food while others do not. An individual who balances the types of food they consume should be able to achieve a good energy balance from their diet.

Nutrient deficiencies and malnutrition

A diet that contains a sufficient amount and variety of food lays the foundations for good health. In general terms, no food is unhealthy in itself. However, unbalanced and insufficient diets can be the cause of health problems.

People who eat too much (over-nutrition) or too little food (under-nutrition), or who consume a diet that does not provide them with enough nutrients or energy to meet their needs, will become malnourished and may become **obese**. Eating too much food is linked to obesity, heart disease and dental health problems and is associated with developed, Western societies. Eating too little food deprives the body of essential nutrients and can lead to health problems like kwashiorkor, iron **deficiency** and ultimately to starvation (see topic 11.4). Under-nutrition is rare in the UK but is more common in less developed countries where there are significant food shortages.

Activity

How much do you know about your food intake and the nutritional quality of your diet? Many people like to think that they 'eat a healthy diet', but don't really know what the nutritional strengths and weaknesses of their diet are. For this activity, you must keep a food diary for 5 consecutive days, recording all of the food and drink you consume on a copy of the food diary sheet below. You should then write a brief profile of your dietary intake, answering the questions below.

Food Diary			
Date	Food and drink consumed	Portion size (S, M, L)	Nutrients consumed

1. Describe the range of food that makes up your diet.
2. Are you over-consuming, or lacking any particular nutrients in your diet?
3. Do you need to think about adjusting the range or amount of foods in your diet to make it healthier?

Case study

Marina is a 21-year-old student teacher. She has been overweight since her early teens. Marina is reluctant to talk about her size but admits that she is 'too heavy'. Marina doesn't cook for herself, eats a lot of take-away food and ready meals and consumes cans of fizzy drink throughout the day. Though she doesn't drink alcohol every night, Marina consumes almost twice the recommended number of units of alcohol for a woman in a week. Marina's knowledge of nutrition is poor. She doesn't really know or understand anything about her nutritional needs or the nutrients in her food. Marina says she just enjoys eating and chooses food that she knows she will enjoy.

Marina is now 5 stone overweight and is aware that she is developing some health problems as a result of this. Her feet are always cold and often 'blue' in colour. She becomes breathless if she has to walk any distance, tires quickly if she has to lift things and says she often has aches and pains in her ankles, knees and shoulders.

1. What is wrong with Marina's dietary intake at the moment?

2. What does Marina need to do in order to eat a balanced diet?

3. How will eating a balanced diet help Marina to improve her health?

Topic check

1 Identify the five main nutrients that are part of a balanced diet.
2 Identify two sources of carbohydrate and describe the function of this nutrient in the body.
3 What kinds of nutrients are contained in fruit and vegetables and how do they contribute to the functioning of the body?
4 What are dietary reference values?
5 Explain why 'balance' should be a feature of a healthy diet.
6 Explain the term 'malnutrition' and describe two causes of it.

Getting started

This topic focuses on the dietary needs of people in different life stages. As people grow and develop, their dietary needs change. When you have completed this topic, you should:

■ know about the dietary needs of individuals in each human life stage

■ be able to explain the reasons for differences in diet during each life stage.

Key terms

Colostrum: thick, yellow breast milk that is rich in protein, minerals and antibodies

Kilocalories: the energy value in food equal to 1000 calories

Lactate: to produce milk

Sedentary: lacking in physical activity

Dietary needs at different life stages

An individual's dietary needs change as they grow and develop and move through different life stages. An infant's food needs are very different from those of an adolescent or an older person, for example.

The type, amount and range of foods that a person eats should vary according to their life stage, the kind of environment they live in and the lifestyle they lead. Figure 11.4 sets out the recommended daily amounts of food, expressed in **kilocalories**, that males and females need as they age.

Figure 11.4 Recommended daily amounts (kilocalories) throughout the lifespan

Age range	Males Kilocalories	Females Kilocalories
0–3 months (formula fed)	545	515
4–6 months	690	645
7–9 months	825	765
10–12 months	920	865
1–3 years	1230	1165
4–6 years	1715	1545
7–10 years	1970	1740
11–14 years	2220	1845
15–18 years	2755	2110
19–59 years	2550	1940
60–64 years	2380	1900
65–74 years	2330	1900
75+ years	2100	1810
Pregnant		+200*
Lactating:		
1 month		+450
2 months		+530
3 months		+570
4–6 months		+480
6+ months		+240

* last trimester only
Source: DEFRA (1995) Manual of Nutrition, 10th edition

Infancy (0–3 years)

Nutrition is very important in the early years of life. Babies and infants need the right types of food to help them grow and develop normally, and to prevent them from developing certain illnesses. Breast milk contains all the nutrients that a young baby needs. The first milk from a mother's breast is **colostrum**. This is a protein-rich liquid which contains antibodies that protect the baby against infection. Colostrum is produced for 2 or 3 days, after which time the breast starts to **lactate** (produce milk).

Formula milk is an alternative to breast milk. It is produced as liquid and powdered milk. Formula milk is different from cows' milk, which doesn't contain the right balance of nutrients for a baby. Different formula milks are available to suit an infant's stage of feeding. Infants gradually move to mixed feeding, changing from milk to solid foods, from about 6 months old.

Childhood (4–10 years)

Children need the right types of food to promote their physical growth and to provide 'fuel' or energy for their high level of physical activity. High-energy and growth foods like bread, potatoes, milk, cheese, meat, fish, fruit and vegetables can support growth and development during this life stage. Sugar-rich sweets and high-fat snacks appeal to many children but are best avoided, as they don't provide nutrients and can cause weight and other health problems.

Over to you!

Look at Figure 11.4 and identify the recommended daily kilocalories for:

- a 7–10-year-old boy
- a 25-year-old woman
- a 40-year-old man.

Activity

Weaning foods can be prepared at home by sieving, liquidising or mashing a variety of fruits, vegetables or dairy products. Identify three examples of each of these types of food that are suitable for weaning a baby on to solid food.

Case study

Lewis is an active, healthy 8-year-old boy. His favourite foods are ice cream, chips and chicken. Lewis always asks for one of these every day and would really like to eat them all most of the time. Lewis's mum tries to give him a varied diet but is struggling to get Lewis to eat fresh fruit and vegetables. Lewis says he doesn't like vegetables and that his friends all eat crisps at break times, not fruit. Lewis often complains that he is feeling hungry and seems to want to eat most of the time. Despite this, his mum has recently discovered that Lewis throws away the fruit she gives him to take to school as a snack. Lewis's mum has told him that his health will suffer if he doesn't eat fresh fruit and vegetables and that eating a lot of crisps and sweets is bad for him. This doesn't seem to have made any difference to the way he thinks about food.

1. Why do you think Lewis might often feel hungry?

2. What would you say or do to explain to Lewis the importance of eating fruit and vegetables?

3. What might be the health consequences of eating too many sweets and crisps during childhood?

Over to you!

What kinds of foods would you include in a lunch box for an active, growing child? Your choice should support growth and development and meet the child's high energy needs.

Adolescence (11–18 years)

Adolescents experience a growth spurt during puberty. As a result they have very high energy needs, which result in big appetites. It is important for adolescents to choose healthy, nutritious foods to meet their growth and energy needs. However, because many adolescents have a lot of choice over their dietary intake, food and drinks that are high in fat and sugar can become a significant feature of some teenagers' diets. High-fat and sugar-laden snacks can add a significant number of calories to a person's diet while providing very few nutrients. Diet-related obesity, diabetes and problems related to nutritional deficiency can result from a poor diet during this life stage. Eating a balanced diet throughout adolescence is much better for health and development than bouts of dieting to overcome weight gain.

Adulthood (19–65 years)

A healthy diet for an adult should include plenty of complex carbohydrates (bread, potatoes, pasta, rice), moderate amounts of meat or fish and plenty of fruit and vegetables. The amount of food an adult needs is likely to vary and is affected by:

▶ gender

▶ body size

▶ height

▶ weight

▶ the environment (e.g. whether an individual lives in a cold or a warm country)

▶ the amount of physical activity an individual does in their daily life.

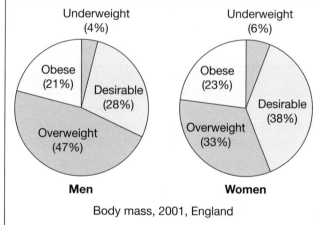

Figure 11.5 Statistics on obesity

An adult who is very active will burn more energy (calories) than a person who lives a **sedentary** life. Obesity that is the result of over-eating is an increasing problem in the UK adult population. Heart disease, strokes and some cancers are all linked to consuming too much food, particularly foods that are high in saturated fat, salt and sugar. People who consume a lot of processed food, especially takeaway and ready meals, increase their risk of developing diet-related health problems. Consuming alcohol, particularly more than the recommended limits, will also add calories to a person's diet and often contributes to weight gain during adulthood.

Women who are pregnant or breastfeeding need to ensure that their diet is very nutritious in order to provide nourishment for themselves and their growing baby.

A woman who is pregnant or breastfeeding should consume a diet that contains sufficient energy, protein, iron, calcium, folate and vitamins C and D. It is also important to avoid certain foods that may contain substances that can adversely affect the development of the baby.

Over to you!

How can a woman adjust her diet when she is pregnant?

Old age (65 years+)

An individual's nutritional needs generally decline during old age. This is because physical changes, such as weight loss and reduced activity levels, mean older people use less energy. However, eating less can also lead to nutritional deficiencies if a person's diet becomes too basic or they don't eat enough. Older people can become malnourished if their diet becomes deficient in any of the main nutrients. A lack of iron and vitamins and minerals, and eating convenience foods that are high in salt, fat or sugar can cause health problems or make existing health problems worse.

 Case study

Lunchtime at Greenvale House residential home is a highlight of the day. The residents sit together in a small dining room to eat lunch. This is prepared in the kitchen of Greenvale House by the two full-time kitchen staff. The support workers at Greenvale House all join in with lunch and try to make it a social occasion, while also paying attention to the nutritional intake of residents. Most of the residents are able to make healthy choices and eat a balanced diet. They tend to eat less than the support workers, though they are also less physically active. The catering staff plan a weekly menu that gives each resident the opportunity to choose from a range of meals available each day. All of the menus include hot and cold options and are designed to keep each individual's intake of fat, sugar and salt within acceptable limits.

1. Why would you expect a resident of Greenvale House to consume less food than a younger support worker?

2. Which five nutrients should be included in the dietary intake of residents at Greenvale House?

3. Explain why it is important to keep the consumption of fat, sugar and salt within acceptable limits.

Topic check

1 Why are women recommended to breast feed their babies?
2 Describe the nutritional difference between formula milk specially prepared for babies and ordinary cows' milk.
3 Identify three different foods that help to meet the high energy needs of children.
4 Explain why it is important for adolescents to eat a balanced diet.
5 What effect does an adult's level of activity have on their dietary needs?
6 Explain how the recommended daily amounts of kilocalories for males and females vary according to a person's life stage.

What factors influence an individual's diet?

This topic focuses on the broad range of factors that influence a person's diet. When you have completed this topic, you should:

- be able to identify a range of factors that affect an individual's diet

- know how different factors can influence a person's dietary intake.

🔑 Key terms

Culture: the shared beliefs, values, language, customs and traditions (way of life) of a group of people

Developed country: a relatively wealthy, technologically advanced country such as the UK

Food desert: an area or place where people experience problems in obtaining healthy food

Less developed country: a relatively poor country with few resources and little non-agricultural industry

The media: methods of communication (television, radio, internet, newspapers) used to reach a mass audience

Peer group: a group of people of about the same age and status

Sacred: believed to be holy or having a special religious significance

Social class: a group of people with the same economic, social and educational status and resources

Influences on diet

Who decides what your diet consists of? Many adolescents would say that they have a lot of individual choice and can make their own decisions about the food and drink they consume. However, parents and other care providers often play a very significant part in choosing the diet of infants, children and adolescents. Adults and older people are typically seen as being able to make their own, entirely free choices. A closer look at people's dietary choices suggests that they are influenced and guided by a range of different factors including religion and **culture**, **social class** background and, increasingly, **the media**.

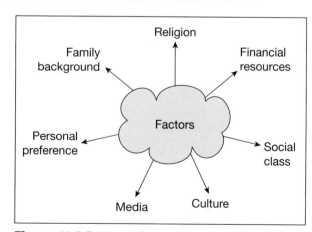

Figure 11.6 Factors influencing the diet of individuals

Culture

Food has a big significance for many people who see it as being more than 'fuel' for their energy needs. The food that people choose to eat often gives them a sense of identity and provides a link to their culture. People from the same cultural background tend to eat the same types of food. They also share ideas about what tastes good

and how food should be prepared and cooked. Many national and cultural celebrations are marked by people preparing special feasts or meals or eating food that has a special cultural significance for people.

Over to you!

What kind of choices do you make about your own dietary intake? What kinds of factors are you aware of that influence your diet?

Vegetarians and vegans

Some people choose to avoid certain foods, such as meat and fish, because of non-religious but ethically based beliefs and values. This includes, for example, vegetarians and vegans. People who have a vegetarian diet don't eat meat or fish, though most will eat eggs and dairy products. Vegetarians can still get all the nutrients they need from a varied vegetarian diet. This should include sources of plant protein such as cereals, beans, eggs and cheese. Vegans, who eat no animal products at all, can get all of their essential nutrients provided that their dietary intake is varied. For example, they can get protein from nuts and pulses and can avoid vitamin and mineral deficiencies by using supplements from non-animal sources, such as yeast extract for vitamin B_{12}.

Activity

Investigate the food practices and festivals of Islam or Judaism. Produce a leaflet or poster that could be used to inform health, social care or early years workers about the food preferences, restrictions and 'rules' of followers of the religion you choose.

Social class

A social class consists of people who have generally similar economic, social and educational status. In general terms people often make a distinction between working-class, middle-class and upper-class groups. The attitudes and values people have, their income and lifestyle choices (about issues such as diet), are sometimes seen an indicator of their social class status. Knowledge of food, understanding of dietary issues and simply being able to afford some types of food but not others are all linked to social class. Evidence from research studies such as the National Food Survey (ONS, 2008) indicates that people in the higher, more well-off social classes tend to eat healthier food while poorer people in the lower social classes are more likely to eat food that has a higher fat and sugar content.

Religion

Some religions set out dietary restrictions for their followers. These usually prevent people from consuming certain foods because they are thought to be 'unclean' or are from a **sacred** source. Many religious beliefs about food also have an important health and safety function. For example, in the past food preparation and preservation techniques were more basic. The lack of basic mechanisms to refrigerate or preserve foods led to the development of rituals by religious leaders, such as draining the blood from slaughtered animals and avoiding foods that spoil easily (eggs, meat, dairy products).

Activity

Using the internet, library sources and people you know, carry out an investigation into the types of food and kind of diet that people from a different cultural background from you consume. You could focus on Indian, Turkish, Caribbean, Chinese, Bengali or Mediterranean diets, for example.

Avoidance of over-eating (gluttony) and stimulants (especially alcohol), and eating a vegetarian diet were also incorporated into some religious beliefs as ways of promoting healthier, 'purer' lives for followers. In a similar way, fasting is seen as a way to purify or improve the body and attract the approval of God, Allah or Buddha. Pregnant or nursing mothers, people who have chronic illnesses or who are acutely unwell and those who are frail or disabled are not usually expected to fast.

Figure 11.7 Religious beliefs and food

Religion	Restrictions	Rationale	Feasting and fasting
Buddhism	Refrain from eating meat – most Buddhists eat a vegetarian diet, although some eat fish No beef products	Natural foods of the earth are considered most pure	Feasting on the anniversary of the birth, enlightenment and death of Buddha
Hinduism	Most Hindus eat a vegetarian diet, but some eat restricted amounts of meat and fish Cows are sacred, so no beef is eaten, but milk, yoghurt and butter are seen as 'pure'	Cows are sacred and can't be eaten Fasting promotes spiritual growth	Feasting on major Hindu holidays and days that have personal meaning
Islam	Food must be *Halal* (permitted) No pork or birds of prey (these are *Haram* – forbidden) Avoid overindulgence and stimulants (especially alcohol)	Failure to eat properly minimises spiritual awareness Fasting cleanses evil elements	Regular fasting but especially during Ramadan (ninth month of the Islamic year), when Muslims fast from sunrise until sunset
Judaism	Food must be *Kosher* (correct) No pork or shellfish Meat and dairy products must be prepared and eaten separately	Land animals without cloven hooves are seen as unclean Kosher process is based on the *Torah* (religious scripture)	Fasting is practised during Yom Kippur and other festivals
Roman Catholicism (Christianity)	Meat restricted on certain days	Restrictions mark religious festivals in a symbolic way	Feasting at Easter and Christmas Fasting during Lent
Protestantism (Christianity)	Few restrictions on food choices and little fasting observed	Gluttony and drunkenness are 'sins' to be controlled	Feasting at Easter and Christmas

The media

The media is a term given to several different sources of information. These include newspapers, magazines, television, radio and the internet. Information about diet, from recipes and cookery programmes to news stories about food scares and diet-related health problems such as obesity, appear frequently in the media. The media can have a huge impact on an individual's knowledge about food, diet and health as well as their attitudes towards their own diet. People may choose certain foods because they are being strongly advertised and seem popular in the media. Alternatively, news stories about diet-related research or food scares can cause people to change their diets to avoid certain foods. Though we might like to think that we are making free and well-informed choices about what we eat and drink, the media play a very important role in persuading us that it would be good, or better, to eat or drink specific food products.

Activity

In a small group, carry out a survey of print (newspaper and magazine) and television media to identify examples of food-related articles, programmes or advertisements. Try to identify:

- who the food-related information is targeted at
- what kinds of food-related 'messages' are being communicated
- whether food is being discussed in a positive, healthy way or in a more negative, unhealthy way
- what you think the impact of the media might be on people who see or read the material you find.

Peer pressure

Peer pressure is the term given to the way an individual can be influenced by their **peer group** to change their attitudes, values or behaviour in order to be an accepted part of the group. It is a factor that can influence the dietary choices of people in all life stages but is perhaps strongest during childhood, adolescence and early adulthood. During these life stages individuals often want to find ways of 'fitting in' and making friends, and are wary of being too different from others. One consequence can be that peer pressure leads to unhealthy dietary choices. Adolescents, for example, may show a preference for and eat less healthy takeaway-style fast food rather than a healthy balanced diet, so that they don't look 'uncool' or too different from their friends.

Family and personal preferences

Everybody learns something about food and the food 'rules' and preferences of their family as part of their primary socialisation during infancy and childhood. Many of our food preferences and attitudes towards what and how we should eat are established in early childhood. Personal preferences do have a big effect on what food we choose to buy and consume in every life stage. Personal preferences about diet may be modified by the beliefs a person goes on to develop about issues such as killing animals and eating meat, or by health concerns related to diet.

Geographic location

The place where a person lives can have a significant effect on their diet. This may sound odd in an age of national supermarket chains and in a country such as the UK where there is an abundance of food. In **less developed countries**, people from the same part of the country tend to eat the same foods, harvest and pick the same produce and cook the same kinds of meals. In the UK, most people go to the shops to buy their food rather than grow it themselves. However, not everyone has the same access to high-quality, fresh food or even to a good range of shops. Minority communities and low-income groups living in socially deprived parts of UK towns and cities are more likely to live in '**food deserts**' where they have little or no opportunity to buy fresh food because local shops don't sell it. For practical and financial reasons, people living in areas like this make use of the fast-food outlets and convenience, processed foods that are available to them.

Over to you!

Can you think of any instances where you have experienced peer pressure to choose or try particular foods? Were you under pressure to eat healthier or less healthy food?

Availability of food

The vast majority of the UK population has access to sufficient food. This is both a positive thing because it means under-nutrition and starvation are very rare in the UK, but it is also a problem for those people who over-consume. In less developed countries where there is insufficient food to feed the whole population, people may have diets that provide them with too few nutrients. This can lead to conditions and illnesses such as kwashiorkor and marasmus (see Topic 11.4) and in severe case to starvation. The abundance of food in **developed countries** such as the UK plays a significant part in the growing obesity problem within the population. Knowing how much to eat and when to stop eating can become a problem when there seems to be a limitless supply of food.

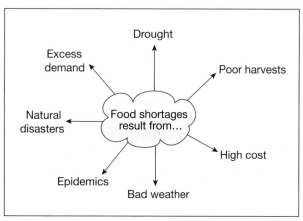

Figure 11.8 Food shortages result from...

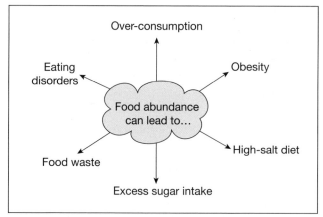

Figure 11.9 Food abundance can lead to...

Activity

Read through the following food-related facts and then answer the questions below.

- Wasting food costs the average family with children £680 per year.
- People mainly throw away food because they prepare or cook too much or don't use it in time before it goes off.
- If people in the UK stopped wasting food that could be eaten, this would have the same environmental impact as taking one in very four cars off the road.
- In England the proportion of men classed as obese increased from 13.2% in 1993 to 23.1% in 2005.
- In England the proportion of women classed as obese increased from 16.4% to 24.8% in 2005.
- In 2002, the direct cost of treating obesity was estimated at between £45.8 and £49.0 million, and between £945 million and £1075 million for treating the consequences of obesity.
- Obese women are almost 13 times more likely to develop Type 2 diabetes than non-obese women, while obese men are nearly five times more likely to develop the illness.
- Among boys and girls aged 2 to 15, the proportion who were obese increased from 10.9% in 1995 to 18% in 2005 among boys, and from 12% to 18.1% among girls.
- In the UK, total energy intake fell by approximately 20% between 1974 and 2004.

1. Why are people throwing away food in the UK?
2. What impact is the availability of food having on the weight (and health) of people in the UK?
3. What impact could buying and consuming less food have on the health of the UK population?

Financial resources

An individual's ability to buy a sufficient amount of good-quality food that will give them a balanced diet is linked to factors such as social class and geographical location, which you have already learnt about. People who are in the higher social classes and who live in affluent areas with plenty of local facilities tend to have more money and better access to healthy food. People who live on low incomes in more deprived areas are less likely to be able to afford and have access to the healthier foods that will provide them with a balanced, nutritious diet.

Over to you!

Go to the Love Food Hate Waste website (www.lovefoodhatewaste.com) and find out how much food (in tonnes) is wasted in the UK each year.

Case study

Leila is 35 years of age. She is the mother of two children, aged 5 and 10. They all moved to the Seaborn Estate 2 years ago when they were re-housed by the local council. Leila now regrets moving from her small flat in a busy, inner-city area. Her biggest complaint is that there are few facilities and no 'proper shops' on the estate where she lives. The nearest shop selling fresh fruit and vegetables is a bus ride or 2-mile walk away. Leila has got into the habit of doing much of her shopping at a small local convenience store on the estate. This sells tins, ready meals and processed foods in packets, but no fresh food. She is also a regular customer at the local take away as her children love pizzas and burger and chips. Leila is now frustrated with the problems she has obtaining healthy food. She is convinced that the diet her family consumes has worsened since they moved house.

1. What factor(s) have the greatest influence on the type of diet Leila and her children consume?

2. How does the concept of a 'food desert' help to explain Leila's food choices?

3. Suggest two things Leila could do to improve the quality of her family's diet.

Topic check

1. Identify five different factors that can influence an individual's dietary intake.

2. Describe, using an example of a particular faith, how religious beliefs can affect the food a person eats.

3. How can a person's social class background affect their diet?

4. Explain how peer pressure can affect a person's food choices, particularly during childhood and adolescence.

5. What is a 'food desert' and how can living in an area like this affect a person's diet?

6. Describe, using examples, the link between an individual's financial resources and their diet.

The health effects of an unbalanced diet

Getting started

This topic focuses on the impact that an unbalanced diet can have on an individual's health. When you have completed this topic, you should:

- be able to identify a range of medical conditions related to unbalanced diets
- know about different forms of malnutrition
- be able to describe examples of medical conditions resulting from over- and under-nutrition.

Key terms

Atheroma plaques: abnormal fatty deposits that develop within the walls of the arteries

Cholesterol: a fat-like substance that is made by the body and carried in the blood but which also occurs in meat, dairy products and some fish

Insulin: a hormone secreted by the pancreas that is needed to convert sugar, starch and other food into glucose

Obesity: a medical condition in which there is an excess of body fat and a body mass index (BMI) of 30+

Oedema: swelling caused by fluid building up in the body

Prevalence: something is prevalent when it is widespread

Rod function: the way the light sensitive cells in the eye work for night and low-light vision

Saturated fats: types of fat that raise cholesterol levels, found mainly in dairy products and meat

Diet and ill health

The links between an unbalanced diet and ill health are widely known. Diets that are high in sugar, **saturated fats** and salt can lead to long-term health problems. Malnutrition is the term given to an inadequate or unbalanced diet. This covers both over-nutrition and under-nutrition.

Over-nutrition

Over-nutrition occurs where a person consumes too much food. A person who overeats may also be consuming a diet that contains an inappropriate balance of nutrients. This is likely to be the case where the individual consumes a diet that is high in saturated fats, salt and sugar. A range of health problems can occur as a result of over-nutrition. These include:

- **Obesity** occurs when excess food that can't be used as energy is converted into body fat.

- Coronary heart disease can occur when excess saturated fat in the diet increases **cholesterol** levels, which can lead to **atheroma plaques** clogging up the arteries. Narrowing of the arteries leads to heart disease and blockage leads to a heart attack.

- Type 2 diabetes is a condition where excess glucose (sugar) is present in the blood because the person's body can't produce enough **insulin** to convert it into energy. High levels of blood glucose damage blood vessels, nerves and organs. This form of diabetes is closely linked to obesity.

Over to you!

Why do you think that over-nutrition has become a growing health problem in developed Western countries over the last 30 years? Make a list of reasons to explain the increasing **prevalence** of over-nutrition and the health problems that result from it.

Under-nutrition

Under-nutrition is caused by not eating enough food or by eating a diet that contains too few or an inappropriate balance of essential nutrients. Under-nutrition is much more common in less developed countries, where food is scarce, than in more developed countries such as the UK. However, babies, older people and those with medical conditions that affect their ability to absorb nutrients or who starve themselves (anorexia nervosa) may be undernourished.

Kwashiorkor and marasmus are health problems that result from under-nutrition. They are usually experienced by children in less developed countries. Marasmus results from a diet that contains insufficient energy and protein to meet the child's needs. It leads to loss of muscle and body fat, infection, dehydration and circulatory disorders. Kwashiorkor is a similar condition – it also results from a diet that contains insufficient protein. The effects of this are slow growth, tiredness, **oedema**, diarrhoea and a swollen stomach.

Activity

How can Kwashiorkor be treated? Using books or the internet, investigate how different types of food need to be given in a controlled way to children suffering from kwashiorkor.

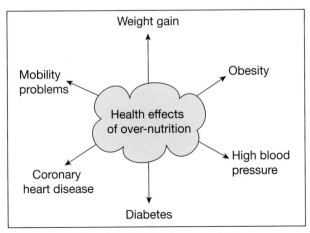

Figure 11.10 Health effects of over-nutrition

Nutrient deficiencies

Nutrient deficiencies are a form of under-nutrition. They occur where a person's long-term diet lacks some important nutrients. For example, people who don't eat fruit or vegetables may develop health problems because of the lack of vitamins and minerals in their diet. Figure 11.11 identifies examples of conditions that result from specific nutrient deficiencies.

Figure 11.11 The effect on health of nutritional deficiencies

Condition	Deficiency	Effect on health
Anaemia	Iron	Lack of iron limits the ability of the blood to carry oxygen and other nutrients around the body. Anaemia results in tiredness, weakness and breathlessness.
Rickets	Calcium and vitamin D	Rickets is a disease of infancy and childhood that affects the skeletal system. A lack of calcium and vitamin D results in a softening of the bones leading to fractures and deformity and muscle weakness.
Night blindness	Vitamin A	This condition prevents sufferers from seeing in dim light or when it is dark. Lack of vitamin A (found in carrots and other fruit and vegetables) affects **rod function** in the eye.
Beriberi	Thiamine (vitamin B1)	Beriberi is a disease of the nervous system caused by a lack of thiamine in the diet. Thiamine is found in unrefined cereals, fresh fruit, fresh meat and fresh vegetables. Thiamine is needed to break down energy molecules such as glucose and is also present in nerve cells. Symptoms of beriberi include weight loss, severe tiredness, pain in the limbs, irregular heart rate and oedema.
Scurvy	Vitamin C	Vitamin C is found in fruit and vegetables and is needed for healthy skin and gums and wound healing. The symptoms of scurvy include spongy, bleeding gums (and loose teeth), bleeding under the skin and general weakness.

Tooth decay doesn't result directly from a nutrient deficiency. It is caused by acid that dissolves the enamel surface of the teeth exposing the inner dentine which then decays. The acid is produced by bacteria that feeds on sugar in the mouth.

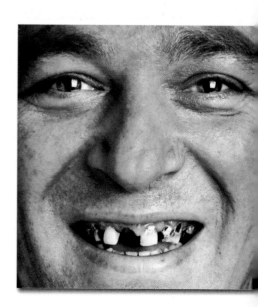

Case study

Andre is 15 years of age. He is already 5 stone overweight for a boy of his height. Andre's doctor is concerned about the effects of Andre's weight on his health. He has warned Andre that he must lose weight and exercise more in order to reduce the risk of him developing Type 2 diabetes and heart disease. Andre doesn't take these warnings seriously. He's never heard of anyone getting diabetes from eating pizza and chips! He also thinks that heart disease is something that older people get because they haven't looked after themselves properly.

1. Produce a leaflet that identifies the links between diet, obesity and Type 2 diabetes. It should be aimed at 15-year-old boys like Andre.

2. How would you explain the causes of heart disease to a 15-year-old boy like Andre? Suggest how you would go about this.

3. Plan a healthy lunch for Andre that is low in fat, salt and sugar but which you think he would enjoy eating.

Assessment activity 11.1 (P1, P2, P3, M1)

A local primary school is trying to become a 'healthy eating' school. They have invited you to share your knowledge of diet and health by contributing to a staff training day. You have been asked to:

- Produce a poster display that identifies the components of a balanced diet.

- Write a leaflet that identifies and discusses the different dietary needs people have during each life stage.

- Produce a handout that describes two medical conditions that can result from unbalanced diets.

Topic check

1 Identify two forms of malnutrition.
2 Explain how a person who eats too much food can be malnourished.
3 How can an unbalanced diet lead to Type 2 diabetes?
4 What are the main causes and symptoms of kwashiorkor?
5 Describe the effects on health of a diet that is deficient in vitamin C.
6 Explain why it is important for infants and children to have sufficient calcium and vitamin D in their diet.

The dietary needs of service users

▶ Getting started

This topic focuses on the links between diet and the health problems users of health and social care services experience. When you have completed this topic, you should:

- be able to identify a range of conditions associated with specific dietary needs
- know how people with health problems can use diet to manage their condition.

🔑 Key terms

Biopsy: a medical test in which living tissue is removed from a patient for diagnostic purposes

Body mass index (BMI): a measure of a person's weight in relation to their height

Diagnosis: the process of identifying a medical condition

Fortified: having something added

Lactose: a type of sugar found in milk and milk products

Immunological reaction: a reaction of the body's immune system

Diet and health

Most people know that the food they eat will have an effect on their health. Eating a balanced, nutritious diet provides the basis of good health. However, where an individual has developed, or is at risk of developing, a medical condition they may have to take extra care with their diet. Some foods may have to be avoided and some foods, or combinations of foods, may be recommended as a way of coping with or avoiding certain conditions.

Coronary heart disease

Coronary heart disease (CHD) is the most common form of heart disease and cause of premature death in the UK. One in every four men and one in every six women die from CHD. It is usually caused by blockage of the arteries that supply the heart with blood. A person who is diagnosed with CHD – often after they have had a heart attack – will be given dietary advice by a health care practitioner to help them to manage their condition and prevent further heart attacks. Typically a person will be advised to:

▶ lose weight

▶ reduce their cholesterol level

▶ lower their blood pressure.

A healthy, balanced diet plays a vital part in achieving these goals and would include:

▶ eating five portions of fruit and vegetables a day

▶ limiting the amount of fat in their diet, especially from meat and dairy products

▶ eating two or three portions of oily fish (mackerel, sardines, tuna, salmon) a week

▶ reducing salt intake

▶ consuming only a moderate amount of alcohol.

A person with coronary heart disease who doesn't make healthy changes to their diet runs a high risk of damaging their heart further and increases their chances of becoming one of the victims of this diet-related disease.

Obesity

Obesity is a medical condition defined as having a **body mass index (BMI)** of more than 30. Obesity is a growing problem in the UK and other developed, Western countries. It can lead to a range of health problems, including heart disease, diabetes, stroke and arthritis. A person who becomes obese should modify their diet so that they:

▶ don't eat too much food or drink excessive amounts of alcohol

▶ have a diet that is low in fat and sugar

▶ eat plenty of fruit, vegetables and starchy (complex carbohydrate) foods.

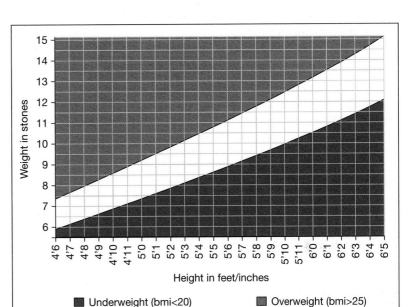

Figure 11.12 What your BMI means

Type 2 diabetes

Diabetes is a condition in which the amount of glucose in the blood is too high. Dietary factors play a part in the development of diabetes and are also important in controlling it. Eating a healthy, balanced diet and maintaining at a healthy weight are important strategies for delaying the onset of or controlling Type 2 diabetes. People with diabetes should eat a diet that is:

▶ low in saturated fat

▶ low in salt

▶ high in fresh fruit and vegetables

▶ high in starchy (complex carbohydrate) foods such as bread, rice and pasta.

> ### Activity
>
> Go to the NHS Choices website (http://www.nhs.uk/conditions) and search for coronary heart disease. Watch the video clip to find out what happens to the body when a person has a heart attack because of CHD.

> ### Over to you!
>
> What kind of foods and drinks do people with Type 2 diabetes have to avoid or limit in their dietary intake?

Lactose intolerance

Lactose is a sugar found in milk and milk products. Some people are unable to digest lactose and suffer digestive symptoms such as:

- flatulence (wind)
- bloating
- diarrhoea
- abdominal pain (cramps).

These symptoms are caused by undigested lactose passing into the colon. Lactose intolerance can be inherited or can result from gastroenteritis or other conditions affecting the digestive system. People who have severe lactose intolerance require a diet without milk or milk-based products. Those with mild lactose intolerance can usually tolerate milk taken with (or in) meals and have fewer symptoms if they consume fermented rather than fresh dairy products. Most people with lactose intolerance can eat yoghurt and cheese because the lactose has either been modified or is virtually non-existent in these products. Because milk and milk products are important sources of essential nutrients, such as calcium and riboflavin, avoiding dairy products is not advisable without good reason and without making other changes to diet to compensate for this.

 Case study

Alice is 1 year old. Her mum, Claire, initially breast-fed her and then gave Alice some formula milk for a few months. Alice often brings her milk back up and doesn't seem to like drinking it. Claire is now concerned that Alice might have a 'milk allergy', as she calls it.

1. Why is milk an important part of a child's diet?

2. What is the correct term for the 'milk allergy' which Claire is referring to?

3. If Alice does have a problem tolerating milk, what other foods could she be given to ensure that she obtains the nutrients she needs?

Gluten/wheat intolerance

Gluten is made when liquid meets non-soluble protein in flour. It is the rubbery, chewing gum-like stuff that gives kneaded dough its elasticity and which enables bread made from wheat flours to rise. Wheat plays a very important part in a nutritious diet for most people. It is found in bread, cakes, pasta, breakfast cereals and as an additive in a wide range of other products including soups, sauces and sausages. Wheat is also **fortified** in the UK with iron, niacin and thiamine. However, some people avoid gluten/wheat products because they have a **diagnosis** of coeliac disease or wheat allergy, or because they believe themselves to be allergic to wheat.

Coeliac disease is the main form of wheat intolerance. Gluten in the diet triggers symptoms of the disease such as general tiredness, diarrhoea, weight loss, constipation, stomach bloating and wind. People with coeliac disease must follow a gluten-free diet. Fresh meat, fish, cheese, eggs, milk, fruit and vegetables are all gluten free. However, because wheat is so widespread in food products, people with coeliac disease are likely to need the advice of a dietician to ensure that their diet avoids gluten while also including sufficient nutrients.

Food allergies

A food allergy is a type of intolerance to food where there is evidence of an **immunological reaction**. The number of people in the population with a diagnosed food allergy is very low. However, many more people have psychological aversions to different foods which are not true allergies but which are reported as such. Examples of food allergies include:

▶ wheat/gluten intolerance (coeliac disease)

▶ lactose intolerance

▶ peanut allergy.

Food allergies can be diagnosed by skin tests using an extract of the food containing the alleged allergen. However, skin tests often report 'false positive' results and many more people believe themselves to have food allergies than actually do. Where a person does have a food allergy the usual treatment is to exclude the food from the person's diet. It is important to ensure that this does not lead to the loss of important sources of nutrients from the diet.

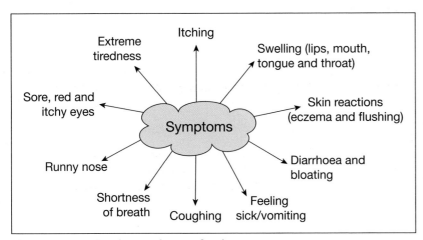

Figure 11.13 Allergic reactions to food

 Case study

Gillian, aged 35, gets painful stomach cramps, bloating and constipation every few months. Her symptoms are making her feel quite unwell, tired and unhappy. Gillian has tried, on and off, to reduce the amount of wheat in her diet and rarely eats bread now as she thinks this has something to do with her problems. Her GP has referred her to a local hospital for a **biopsy**. He also told her that he thinks she may have coeliac disease. Gillian is quite upset about this as the doctor said this is incurable and that she would have to make big changes to her diet.

1. What kind of 'big changes' would you expect Gillian to make to her diet if she does have coeliac disease?

2. Describe how a biopsy is carried out to diagnose coeliac disease.

3. Plan an appetising and nutritious gluten-free lunch and evening meal for Gillian.

Genetic disorders

Individual who have certain genetic disorders can use their diet to relieve some of the symptoms they experience or to prevent their condition from worsening. For example, cystic fibrosis sufferers are often given pancreatic enzymes in powdered form to sprinkle on to their food. This is because their own pancreatic enzymes are prevented from doing their job (digesting food) by the thick, sticky mucous that coats their pancreatic duct.

People who have inherited phenylketonuria (PKU) are unable to break down phenylalanine (an amino acid) into tyrosine. The build up of phenylalanine can lead to problems with brain development, including learning difficulties, seizures and brain damage. People who have PKU are treated with a low-phenylalanine diet that is low in protein. The person's diet then has to be supplemented with artificial protein that does not contain phenylalanine.

Activity

Using the internet, investigate the inherited condition phenylketonuria. Identify how it is diagnosed, the main symptoms, what causes it, the consequences if left untreated and the kinds of food that have to be avoided in a low-phenylalanine diet. Present a summary of your findings in the form of a poster or leaflet.

Case study

Julian was 2½ years old when he was diagnosed with cystic fibrosis. His mum took him to the doctor because he had constant colds, skinny arms and legs and was having trouble sleeping. When she rubbed his back this seemed to make him feel better. Julian's GP referred him to a consultant at the local hospital. She carried out a sweat test, which revealed that Julian's sodium levels were very high. This is a good indicator of cystic fibrosis.

Once the diagnosis was confirmed, Julian began receiving treatment and very close health monitoring. He now receives drugs to help his breathing and digestion, as people with cystic fibrosis have problems with their lung function and struggle to digest food properly. Most people with cystic fibrosis are thin, underweight and lack physical strength as a result. Julian also does exercises every day to keep his lungs clear and to strengthen his body and respiratory system; he knows that these exercises are crucial to his health.

Julian has cystic fibrosis because he inherited a faulty gene from his parents. His life expectancy is lower than other people of his age, but ongoing developments in genetic medicine may benefit him and extend his life.

1. What were the main symptoms of Julian's cystic fibrosis?

2. What impact does cystic fibrosis have on an individual's health and development?

3. What kinds of treatment can be given to help people who have cystic fibrosis?

Assessment activity 11.2 (P4, M2, D1)

People who use health and social care services may have health problems that are the result of an unbalanced diet, or may need to modify their diet because they develop a specific health problem.

- Identify two service users with specific dietary needs. These can be real people who have agreed to talk to you about their dietary needs. Alternatively, you could choose to focus on two of the people described in the case studies in this unit (e.g. Gillian, Andre or Marina). You should say why you think each person has special dietary needs and briefly describe what these needs are.

- Outline a 2-day diet plan for the people you have chosen.

- Justify how your diet plans meet their special dietary needs and provide them with a healthy, balanced diet.

You should present your work in the form of two case studies.

Topic check

1   What kind of diet should a person with coronary heart disease consume?
2   What might be the consequences for a person with coronary heart disease of a diet high in fat and cholesterol?
3   Identify two forms of food allergy.
4   How can people with coeliac disease manage their symptoms through their diet?
5   Describe the symptoms of lactose intolerance and the changes to diet that can relieve them.
6   Explain what phenylketonuria is and the role that diet plays in avoiding the serious health and developmental problems associated with it.

The principles of food safety and hygiene

Providing good, nourishing food that is safe to eat requires a basic knowledge and understanding of the principles of food safety and hygiene. When you have completed this topic, you should:

- be able to describe safe practices in food preparation, cooking and service

- understand the importance of hygiene, temperature and pest control.

Food hygiene and safe practices

 Key terms

Contaminated: made impure or spoilt in some way

Food poisoning: an illness caused by eating food contaminated by harmful substances

Toxins: poisonous substances produced by living cells or organisms

In health and social care settings, the health of vulnerable people, their visitors and care workers may be put at risk if standards of food safety and hygiene are poor. Severe cases of **food poisoning** can even be fatal where people are already very sick or frail. Good food hygiene results from people taking care to ensure that food is stored, handled and cooked safely. The three main elements of good food hygiene are hygiene control, temperature control and pest control. Safe practices in each of these areas are needed to prevent food from becoming **contaminated**.

Hygiene control

Hygiene control involves following food preparation, handling and storage practices that prevent food becoming contaminated by bacteria. The main sources of food contamination are:

- food-to-food contamination, such as bacteria being transferred from raw to cooked meat

- equipment to food contamination, such as bacteria growing on and being transferred from unclean surfaces, utensils or cloths

- food-handler-to-food contamination, such as using unclean hands or fingers to taste food or having poor personal hygiene

- contamination by pests, pets or microbes when food is left to stand at room temperature.

The risk of food contamination is reduced by:

- washing hands thoroughly with soap and water before handling food

- washing hands after using the toilet, touching a client, coughing or sneezing or handling any kind of food or other waste

- wearing protective clothing, particularly an apron, when preparing or serving food

▶ keeping nails short and hair clean and tied back

▶ covering all cuts or wounds with a blue waterproof dressing

▶ covering and storing raw and cooked foods (especially meat) in different fridges or in different areas if there is only one fridge available – raw food should always be kept in a lower part of fridge if kept with cooked food

▶ using separate chopping boards for raw and cooked meat and for non-meat foodstuffs

▶ checking packaging to ensure that food products are only used and consumed within their 'use by' dates – this is particularly important for meat and dairy products.

Figure 11.14 Sources of food poisoning

Source	Symptoms
Salmonella A bacterium found in faeces of infected people and in poultry, eggs, meat and water.	• Abdominal pain, watery and bloody diarrhoea • Headaches • Nausea and vomiting
Campylobacter A bacterium usually found in undercooked meat (especially poultry), unpasteurised milk and untreated water.	• Severe diarrhoea and abdominal pain • Blood in faeces
Bacillus cereus The bacterium found in rice dishes and sometimes in pasta, meat and vegetable dishes, dairy products, soups and sauces.	• Diarrhoea and abdominal pain • Nausea and vomiting
Clostridium perfringens The bacterium that occurs naturally in the intestines of people and animals.	• Diarrhoea and abdominal pain
Escherichia coli (E coli) A bacterium that occurs naturally in the intestines of people and animals. Most types of E coli don't cause illness – some release **toxins** that contaminate food and water.	• Stomach cramps and diarrhoea • Vomiting • Blood in faeces
Staphylococcus aureus A bacterium that is found in the nose and throat. It can produce toxins that contaminate food.	• Diarrhoea and abdominal pain • Severe vomiting

Case study

Erica Jordan is 18 years of age. She has just got a summer job working in the catering department of her local hospital. Erica's job is to plate up the food that patients order so that it can be put into heated trolleys and delivered to them on the wards. Erica is looking forward to getting paid for the work but isn't really taking the job seriously. In the first couple of days her supervisor told her off for not wearing a hat and gloves when working, and for not washing her hands after handling raw meat. Today one of Erica's colleagues saw her using the same spoon to serve rice, then lamb curry and then sponge pudding. Erica put the serving spoon in her mouth between serving each dish.

1. How might Erica's behaviour lead to food contamination?

2. Identify two symptoms of food poisoning that can result from poor food hygiene practices.

3. What should Erica do differently to minimise the risk of food contamination occurring?

Temperature control

The bacteria that cause food poisoning need food, warmth, moisture and time to grow. Maintaining the correct food temperature is therefore an effective way of preventing food poisoning bacteria from growing. Bacteria do not grow below 5 °C or above 63 °C. Bacteria can grow and thrive in the temperature danger zone between these points. As a result, basic temperature control rules are:

▶ Keep hot food hot.

▶ Keep cold food cold.

▶ Keep prepared food out of the temperature danger zone.

Pest control

If food is badly stored or food preparation areas become infested with pests such as rats, mice or cockroaches, the risks of contamination and food poisoning rise considerably. Pests eat, spoil and transfer bacteria to food. They should be kept away from food through safe storage and regular cleaning of food preparation areas. Unsafe and careless disposal of food waste attracts pests and creates additional infection risks.

Hazard Analysis Critical Control Point (HACCP)

Organisations involved in providing food often use the HACCP system to identify the likely risks to food hygiene and safety in their storage, preparation and cooking processes. The HACCP system identifies 'critical points' that could lead to food safety problems if something goes wrong. Once these possible hazards are identified, procedures can be put in place to prevent these problems from occurring.

Legislation and food safety

A number of different laws have been passed to try and promote good food hygiene. Some of these laws, such as the Health and Safety at Work Act 1974, place general duties and responsibilities on employers and employees that should result in the provision of safe and clean food preparation environments and good standards of food hygiene practice. The Reporting of Injuries, Diseases and Dangerous Occurrences Regulations (RIDDOR) 1995 are also designed to have a broad impact on the care workplace. Laws that are specifically designed to promote food safety include:

▶ The Food Safety Act 1990 – this states that people working with food must practise good food hygiene in the workplace. Food provided for people who use services and for visitors must be safely stored and prepared and must not be 'injurious to health'. Local authority environmental health officers enforce this law.

▶ The Food Safety (General Food Hygiene) Regulations 1995, 2005 and 2006 – these regulations refer to the need to identify possible risks surrounding food hygiene and to put controls in place to ensure that any risk is reduced. These regulations also specify how premises that provide food should be equipped and organised.

▶ The Food Safety (Temperature Control) Regulations 1995 – under these regulations businesses that provide food are required to keep food at a safe temperature so that bacteria or other toxins don't develop in it.

 Activity

The Food Standards Agency provides comprehensive and up-to-date information and advice on food hygiene through their eat well website (www.eatwell.gov.uk). You can find out about ways of preventing food poisoning by reading the Germ Watch section of the site.

Assessment activity 11.3 (P5, P6, M3, D2)

The staff who attended your training session on healthy eating and balanced diet (see Assessment activity 11.1) think that one way to become a 'Healthy School' is to prepare more healthy snacks and lunch at the school itself. They have no catering experience or training and are concerned about getting food safety and hygiene issues right. They have asked you to produce a food safety and hygiene booklet that:

- explains safe food preparation, cooking and serving practices

- outlines legislation that affects food preparation, cooking and serving
- discusses the effects of unsafe food preparation, cooking and serving practices
- outlines and assesses the effectiveness of 'Five Top Tips' when preparing, cooking or serving food in a health or social care setting.

Topic check

1 Why should care workers have an understanding of food hygiene principles?
2 Describe three methods of food contamination.
3 Explain how care workers who prepare food can reduce the risk of food contamination.
4 Describe the sources and symptoms of two forms of food poisoning.
5 What are the temperature control rules that care workers should be aware of?
6 Why is pest control vital in food preparation and serving areas of a care setting?

Assessment summary

The overall grade you achieve for this unit depends on how well you meet the grading criteria set out at the start of the chapter (see page 279). You must complete:

- all of the P criteria to achieve a **pass** grade
- all of the P and the M criteria to achieve a **merit** grade
- all of the P, M and D criteria to achieve a **distinction** grade.

Your tutor will assess the assessment activities that you complete for this unit. The work you produce should provide evidence which demonstrates that you have achieved each of the assessment criteria. The table below identifies what you need to demonstrate to meet each of the pass, merit and distinction criteria for this unit. You should always check and self-assess your work before you submit your assignments for marking.

Remember that you MUST provide evidence for all of the P criteria to pass the unit.

Grading criteria	You need to demonstrate that you can:	Have you got the evidence?
P1	Identify the components of a balanced diet	
P2	Identify the different dietary needs at each life stage	
M1	Discuss how the components of a balanced diet contribute to an individual's health at different life stages	
P3	Explain two medical conditions related to unbalanced diets	
P4	Identify two service users with specific dietary needs	
M2	Outline a two-day diet plan for two service users with specific dietary needs	
D1	Justify how the two-day diet plan meets the dietary needs of the two service users	
P5	Outline relevant legislation relating to preparing, cooking and serving food	
P6	Explain safe practices necessary in preparing, cooking and serving food	
M3	Discuss the effects of unsafe practices when preparing, cooking and serving food	
D2	Review the effectiveness of safe practices when preparing, cooking and serving food in a health or social care setting	

Always ask your tutor to explain any assignment tasks or assessment criteria that you don't understand fully. Being clear about the task before you begin gives you the best chance of succeeding. Good luck with your Unit 11 assessment work!